Romans

Contents

One

*

Therefore thou art inexcusable, O man, whosoever thou art that judgest: for wherein thou judgest another, thou condemnest thyself; for thou that judgest doest the same things.

Romans 2 : 1

As we turn to a consideration of Romans chapter two, it may seem to some who worked through the first chapter with us that we took a long time in doing so – twenty studies in all.[1] But when you consider the nature and the character of that chapter, that, indeed, is not at all surprising. There, as we have seen, the Apostle introduces all his major themes. Having done that, he begins to expound them, and I think you will find that we shall be able to proceed at a much more rapid rate now, than we did in the first chapter. The argument is much looser; it is not so closely knit. In saying that, I refer particularly to the second chapter. When we come to parts of the third chapter, we shall find again that every word has tremendous significance, but even so, on the whole, I think we shall be moving a little more rapidly.

And so as we now come to the second chapter and the first verse, clearly the first thing we must do is understand the setting. I should like to underline here the way in which we should approach a passage of Scripture, the method which applies, not only to this, but to any other passage whatsoever. The way to approach Scripture is always the same. First of all, we take the whole passage, and read it right through before we start with any particulars; then we try to discover what it is about in general, what the big theme is, and what the writer is

[1] *Romans, Exposition of Chapter 1: The Gospel of God* (The Banner of Truth Trust, 1985).

[1]

setting out to do. So we must do that with this chapter, and fortunately for us the Apostle provides us with the key in the very first word – 'Therefore'. This tells us that he is continuing something that he has already been saying, or at least that what he is going to say comes out of that, and has a direct relationship to it. We cannot, therefore, proceed to consider this second chapter of the Epistle without again reminding ourselves, and being perfectly clear in our minds, about what he has been saying in the first chapter.

Now, in verse 16 of chapter one the Apostle introduces the great theme of this entire Epistle – this gospel, this message from God which is 'the power of God unto salvation to every one that believeth; to the Jew first, and also to the Greek'. It is a righteousness from God. It is the answer to the great question: How can a man get right with God? The gospel is a great proclamation to the effect that God has provided a righteousness for man, a righteousness by faith, not a righteousness that man works out, but something given by God: 'Therein is the righteousness of God revealed from faith to faith: as it is written, The just shall live by faith'. And he tells us in verse 18 why this is necessary: 'For the wrath of God is revealed from heaven against all ungodliness and unrighteousness of men, who hold [down] the truth in unrighteousness' – a universal statement. So that is his great theme – the righteousness from God which is the only way of righteousness, therefore, in the light of the other doctrine of the wrath of God.

And then, in the remainder of the chapter, the Apostle proceeds to work out this truth as far as the Gentiles in particular are concerned, and he leads us through that terrible description of their condition. God, he says, has manifested His wrath against all ungodliness and unrighteousness in the case of the Gentiles, in that He has abandoned them; He has given them up; He has given them over to a 'reprobate mind'; He has given them over to working these terrible things with each other. That, as we have seen, is an absolute proof of the wrath of God against ungodliness and sin, with particular reference to the Gentiles.

So Paul has said all that, and now he seems, as it were, to hear somebody shouting out, 'Amen! Quite right. I am in absolute agreement'.

[2]

Wait a minute, says the Apostle: 'Therefore thou art inexcusable, O man, whosoever thou art that judgest . . .'.
There is our setting. In other words, the great question that arises at this moment for every one of us is: What is our understanding of what Paul has been saying from chapter one, verse 16, to the end of that chapter? This is the very question that the Apostle himself has been raising. He has said tremendous things, yes; but the whole point is whether we have understood what he has said. Have we really got his meaning? Are we really in agreement with what the Apostle is saying, and not with something that we think he is saying? For the Apostle here raises before us the image of a man who has misunderstood, a man who says, 'I am in entire agreement with what you have said, Paul', and the Apostle has to say to him, 'You are not, you know. You think you are, but you are not, and I am going to prove it to you. You say, "Amen! Hallelujah!" because you think you know what I have said, but you have not understood my meaning'. So he has to take up the case of this man.

This is obviously important for us, because the Apostle is here saying quite frankly that it is possible for all of us to misunderstand what he has just been saying. What I should like to have done before we ever came to deal with this second chapter is to have given everyone this bit of homework: 'State what it is that Paul is saying in Romans chapter one, verse 16 to the end of the chapter'. Then we would all have known exactly whether we had understood or not! But now, here is Paul addressing a man who thinks that he is in entire agreement, while the Apostle is going to show him that he is not.

The question at this point is, who is this 'man'? 'Therefore thou art inexcusable, O man, whosoever thou art that judgest . . .'. You will find that the commentators throughout the centuries have divided themselves into two main schools. One school has said that the Apostle here is, obviously, still thinking of the Gentiles, but is considering people among the Gentiles who were not guilty of the particularly terrible sins that he has just been portraying. He is thinking of certain moral pagans, certain good pagans, because, they say, all pagans do not live that sort of life, all pagans are not guilty of those horrible perversions and other terrible sins. There is, after all, they argue, such a thing as a good pagan, the moral pagan, and there is the

[3]

intellectual pagan, interested in philosophy. There were many great pagan philosophers who exhorted men to live a good life, and so on. Now, they say, surely Paul is dealing with them, with these pagans who might hear his teaching and say, 'We are in entire agreement with what you are saying, Paul, we have been denouncing these sins ourselves'. This first school maintains that Paul is dealing with such people and showing them their error.

The other school says that the Apostle here is taking up the case of the Jew, and is dealing immediately with Jews. Incidentally, the other people, the first group, say that Paul does not start dealing with the Jews until verse 17 of this second chapter, where he addresses the Jew directly – 'Behold, thou art called a Jew, and restest in the law, and makest thy boast of God . . .'. The second school, however, maintains that he starts with the Jews in the first verse of the second chapter.

I suppose, in a sense, that there is no final way of settling this problem; you can agree with either one or the other. But it seems quite clear to me that this is indeed a reference to the Jews, or at any rate, primarily to the Jews. I think perhaps that the two schools have pressed their point a little too far. I am not trying to work a compromise between them, that is not my habit, but I think there is a danger here of over-emphasizing either the one or the other. I would prefer to say that he is dealing primarily with the Jew, but also incidentally with the Gentile and anybody else who may happen to hold this particular position. I say that for this reason: his great emphasis here is on '*thou that judgest*': '. . . whosoever thou art that judgest . . .'. His emphasis is on this judgment, this condemnation, and that, it seems to me, is surely enough to settle the whole question, because that was the great – not to say the greatest – characteristic of the Jew at that particular time.

There are other things that make me say that this verse is dealing with the Jews. You will notice that in chapter two, verse 9 he brings in the Jew: 'Tribulation and anguish, upon every soul of man that doeth evil, of the Jew first, and also of the Gentile'. As he had begun to speak about the Jew and the Gentile in chapter one, verse 16, and in verse 18 had used this great word '*all*': 'all ungodliness and unrighteousness', I suggest that he is dealing with them all along. It is there quite

The Righteous Judgment of God

Contents

[vii]

*To the faithful and enthusiastic Friday-nighters at
Westminster Chapel to whom
the sermons in this volume were preached
from October 5th 1956 to February 8th 1957*

THE BANNER OF TRUTH TRUST
3 Murrayfield Road, Edinburgh EH12 6EL

*

© Mrs D. M. Lloyd-Jones 1989
First published 1989
Reprinted 2005
ISBN 0 85151 545 2

*

Typeset in 10 on 12 pt Trump Medieval
at The Spartan Press Ltd
Lymington, Hants
and printed in the U.S.A. by
Versa Press, Inc., East Peoria, Il

Romans

An Exposition of Chapters 2 : 1–3 : 20
The Righteous Judgment of God

D. M. Lloyd-Jones

THE BANNER OF TRUTH TRUST

specifically in chapter one, and he repeats it again in chapter two, verse 9, and then clinches it in verse 11: 'For there is no respect of persons with God'. Now it was the central fallacy of the Jew to think that there was this kind of respect of persons with God. The Jews at that time divided the whole world into two groups only: the Jews, and those who were not Jews. On one side, the Jews, the chosen people of God; on the other, the dogs, the outsiders, those people without the law. And the Jews' attitude towards them was one of utter condemnation.

There are abundant passages in the Scripture which prove that; there is no need for me to remind you of them. You find this dealt with in the Gospels, you see it in the Acts of the Apostles, and you can also see it in various epistles. Indeed, one of the greatest problems of the early evangelists was how to deal with that particular situation. The Jew, you see, felt that he did not need salvation because he was one of the chosen people of God; and as for the Gentiles, well it was impossible in their case, such people could never have salvation, for they had nothing at all to do with God. So they objected to the gospel for two reasons – one, that the Christian preacher said that the Jew needed salvation, and, two, that he said it was possible for the Gentile to be saved also; and they hated both views. You read the Gospels and you see the Pharisees arguing with our Lord, quarrelling and debating and trying to trip Him and to trap Him – why? There is only one explanation: His preaching made them feel that even they were sinners, and they hated Him for it. But it was an essential part of His message – 'There is none righteous, no, not one . . . All have sinned, and come short of the glory of God'.

So I suggest to you that this argument here is primarily an argument about the Jew. Paul is taking up the case of the Jew who condemns the Gentile, and who, therefore, when he hears Paul condemning the Gentile says, 'Amen. I am in entire agreement'. But, I repeat, we must not confine it only to the Jew, because it is equally true of all who take the same kind of position and attitude as the Jews with respect both to themselves and to others.

Let me try, then, to give you the setting. The Apostle has shown how the wrath of God has been revealed against all ungodliness and unrighteousness of men in the case of the Gentiles, and immediately he hears the Jews saying,

'Absolutely right, Paul; here you are striking the nail on its head. That is what we have always said about those Gentiles; there is nothing too bad to be said about them. Look at them, look at the way they are living; they are dogs, they are to be condemned'.

'But wait a minute', says Paul. 'You are not in agreement with me, and you only think you are because you have misunderstood two things. You are shouting your amen for two wrong reasons'.

In the first place, the Jews thought that Paul was condemning the Gentiles simply because they were Gentiles. The Jews would not listen to any arguments about the Gentiles. A Gentile was a Gentile, that was enough; he was condemned. And they thought that Paul was saying that, but he was not. In the second place, they also thought that Paul's statement was not true of them, simply because they were Jews. It was true of the Gentiles, because they were Gentiles. It was not true of the Jew – why? Well, because he was a Jew and not a Gentile, because he was such a special man.

So you see there was a double error. But I must add something to that: the Jews thought that the Apostle was showing God's wrath upon the Gentiles just because they were Gentiles, and not at all because of the way in which they lived. And in the same way exactly, they thought that all this did not apply to them simply because they were Jews, irrespective of how they might live or might not live. They were excluding actions, behaviour and conduct altogether, and they were determining the whole thing in terms of the question, 'Are you a Jew or are you not a Jew?' But the Apostle is now going on to prove that if you understand that great section in this way, you are missing the whole point. The Jews thought that because they were Jews, and simply because of that fact, they were already saved, whatever they might do, whatever they might be. And in saying that, they believed that the Gentiles were utterly condemned and lost, irrespective of anything they did, simply because they were Gentiles. They were denying the very essence of the gospel, they were contradicting the foundation of the gospel and of Christian salvation; and as a result of doing that, they were leading themselves to certain other terrible consequences, which the Apostle indicates in the body of this second chapter.

Let us now take a bird's eye view of the chapter. Paul puts it to us like this: first and foremost, the Jew was resting on the fact that he was a Jew. Then if you argued with him about that, and showed him how that was not enough, he would say, 'Ah, but I have a second argument. God gave us the law, and the fact that He has given us the law is absolute proof that we are His people and that we are saved. We have the law; nobody else has it'. That was their second mistake. And thirdly, they said, 'We have a still greater argument – circumcision! How can you say that we and the Gentiles are one? What do you mean by saying that the gospel is the power of God unto salvation to every one that believes, to the Jew first, and also to the Greek? We do not need your salvation. You must not lump us together with the Greeks like that. We have nothing to do with them, we are absolutely separate. You must not say that we are guilty as they are, and that we need justification by faith only. We are Jews, and we can prove we are Jews'.

That was the position. The Jews thought that they were in an entirely separate category, and that therefore they must never be considered together with the Gentiles. Now see how the Apostle deals with these three positions. In verses 1 to 16 he takes that first argument that they were all right as they were, simply because they were Jews. There are subdivisions to this section, and we will consider them. Then from verses 17 to 24 he takes their argument about the law, and from verse 25 to the end of the chapter he takes their argument based on the fact and the sign of circumcision. He works out these three arguments separately and in detail, and that is what you and I have to do.

But before we do that I want to apply all that we have been considering to ourselves, for the Scriptures, as you know, have been written for an example, for our instruction. That is the glory of the Word of God: it is always up to date, it is always relevant. This is not only a position that confronted Paul when he was preaching nearly two thousand years ago. It is as true now as it was then, and it may be true of us, alas! We must examine ourselves; and we must do so in the light of our understanding of Romans 1 : 16–32. There are certain terrible lessons here, it seems to me.

Let me put it in general first: Paul here is proceeding to unfold to us the terrible character of sin. In that first chapter we seemed to be walking through the gutters of life, and felt we needed a bath afterwards, with all those terrible, unnatural perversions, and all those other things that are almost unmentionable and yet were nevertheless there. Indeed, he has dealt there with the vileness and foulness of sin. What is he going to do now? Well, here in chapter two he is going to deal with what we may well call the subtlety of sin, and the subtlety appears in the way that I have already indicated to you. You see it perfectly in the case of the Jew. Here they were, listening to Paul, and saying that they were one hundred per cent in agreement with him, that what he was saying about those wretched Gentiles was nothing but the truth. It was because of the subtlety of sin that they ever said such a thing; they did not see the real statement, they did not follow the argument, and they failed to see its application to themselves.

Now that is the thing we must consider. Let me put it to you like this, to show how this affects us all, and how constantly we have to guard ourselves against the very same pitfall into which the Jews of old fell. Do not forget that these were God's people; they had been called by God. They were the people who had the Scriptures, who read and studied the Scriptures, and gloried in them. Yet in spite of all that, they crucified their own Messiah. They did their best to prevent the Gentiles being saved and they did their best to exterminate Christianity. What a terrible position! What a terrible possibility!

But let me divide it up like this: we see here how sin introduces, or can introduce, a prejudice into our listening to the gospel, or into our reading of the gospel. It does it in this way – full of our prejudice, we come to the Scriptures, pick out what we like and do not notice what we do not like. That is exactly what these Jews had done; all they heard, when Paul spoke so strongly, was that God's wrath was upon the Gentiles. 'Hear, hear!' they said. But they did not listen to the rest. You see, they were blinded by their prejudice. Jew and Gentile – this was the one big thing, and this governed everything, so that when they read their Scriptures they saw this alone, and nothing else at all. And is it not still a possibility? How easy it is to listen to a sermon or an address or to read the Scriptures and just pick out what we like and leave the rest. Some people do that even in their regular reading of the Bible; they only read certain parts of the Bible, and they say they find it very comforting, very nice. It never disturbs them, of course, because they want only comfort, that is what they go for, and they get nothing else. They take parts of the Scripture and leave the rest.

Or yet again, is it not a terrible danger that some of us, sometimes, tend to read the Scriptures, not so much to be enlightened and to be taught, as to confirm our own theories, our own ideas, and our own prejudices? Now I want to make that a universal statement. We are all guilty of it. For instance, it is the danger of the Calvinist, who looks for one thing only and ignores difficulties. It is equally the danger of the Arminian, who looks only for what he wants, and does not notice the other stresses and emphases. Each one sees only the part he wants to see, and ignores the rest. We are all guilty. – 'What is your view of prophecy? What is your view of sanctification? What is your view of all these doctrines?' – In the name of God, I say, let us be careful that we do not go to the Scripture with such a prejudice that we pick out only what agrees with our theory and ignore and forget the rest! Let us come to it with an open mind and an open heart and learn of it, whatever it may have to say: let us look at it in every detail, and beware of prejudice.

The second danger is that so many tend to make us put ourselves into special categories and compartments. That is the outcome of the first, is it not? 'I am a Jew. He is a Gentile'. We are all given to these labels. They are terrifying things, these labels, and we should avoid them as the very plague, but people are very fond of putting labels on us and we sometimes like them! How often we hear people say, 'I am a Methodist'; 'I am a Salvationist'; I am this or that or the other. No. We are Christians primarily and we must not put the label first. We tend to put ourselves into categories and compartments and then, of course, we go on doing what I have already been saying – we find statements in Scripture to confirm us and to buttress our position.

And then there is a third way whereby the subtlety of sin makes us apply the truth to which we are listening to other people but not to ourselves. 'Quite right', we say. 'These abominable sins!' We see them as we walk along the streets in London, we read about them in the newspapers, and we are impatient with those people, we feel they all ought to be blasted out of existence. We see it so clearly as it applies to others, but never in the case of ourselves. We tend to be blind to our own sins. All this was true of the Jews, as we shall see. But there is no point in our going on to consider what was wrong with the Jews if we fail to see it in ourselves. That was the very error of the Jews. So I cannot take you further until we all realize that we are looking at ourselves in the mirror that was here provided. How easy it is to say, 'I do hope so and so is in the service this morning; it was just for him'. Yes, and we tend to fail to see that it was just as much for us! That is exactly what these Jews were doing. We protect ourselves. We can easily apply the truth to others. 'Obviously!' we say. 'Wonderful. Wasn't that a great sermon?' And we have not seen that there was anything in it applicable to ourselves.

Fourthly, we see here the many subtle ways in which sin makes us deny the cardinal foundational doctrine of justification by faith only. That is the great theme of this Epistle: chapter one, verse 17 reads '. . . the righteousness of God revealed from faith to faith: as it is written, The just shall live by faith'. This is the theme, and Paul is now going to show us how everybody is trying to avoid it and run away from it, armed with some other theory or explanation, and he brings us back to it. We are all experts at running away from it. How do we do that? Well, we run away from the doctrine of justification by faith only when we rely upon anything or anyone except the Lord Jesus Christ and His perfect work. I do not care what it is! If you rely on your country, if you say, 'I must be a Christian, I was born in Great Britain – a Christian country', if you are relying on that kind of thing, you are denying justification by faith, as the Jew did. If you are relying on the fact that your parents were Christians or saints; if you have any reliance upon your birth and ancestry; or if in any way you are relying on any form of moralism, on your good life, and your respectability, and your good works; if any of these things is true of you, you are denying justification by faith.

This was the curse of the Pharisees. It was this that our Lord had to fight them on, and Paul was constantly fighting with them over the same issue: moralism in any shape or form, smug self-satisfaction, and contentment with one's state. There are people who say, 'You know, I really cannot honestly say that I have ever felt I am a sinner!' Well if that is really true of you, you are not justified by faith, because you have not seen any need of it. You are all right as you are, as the Jew thought he was. And the same applies to ritualism, which is one of the great menaces at this present time. There is a recrudescence of ritualism, even in nonconformity; they are all bringing it in, to a greater or lesser degree. And in the end it comes to this, that as long as you have performed the ritual or the ceremony, as long as you have gone to your Communion, you may do what you like for the rest of the day, for this puts you right – you rely upon the form and the ceremonial and the ritual. That is the sort of thing Paul is talking about, and every time we are guilty of any of these things, whether it is circumcision or anything else, we are denying justification by faith.

But let me show you one other very subtle sin, and this is perhaps the most important of all, for it leads us to separate doctrine from life. That, as I am hoping to show you, was the cardinal error of the Jew. The Jew, you see, did not take daily living into consideration at all, either in the case of the Gentile or in his own case. His attitude, quite simply, was: 'Because I am a Jew I must be all right, I must be saved'. He did not consider how he was living. This is what made Paul say, '. . . thou art inexcusable, O man, whosoever thou art that judgest: for wherein thou judgest another, thou condemnest thyself; for thou that judgest doest the same things' [*Romans* 2 : 1].

But the Jew seemed to say, 'It does not matter what I do. I am a Jew, and because I am a Jew I am all right. As for the Gentile, of course . . . !' Now that is separation of doctrine and life, and it is a terrible danger and a most subtle one. It does not matter whether you have little doctrine or much doctrine, it is equally dangerous. There are people who say, 'I have believed on the Lord Jesus Christ, therefore I am all right. I want no more. I do not want your doctrines. I do not want that deep teaching. I have believed in Christ. I am saved. I went forward and I have taken my decision'. And they go on living more or less as they did before. That is a separation of doctrine and life. They somehow think that because they say they believe on the Lord Jesus Christ, everything is all right, and they pay very little attention to their mode or manner of living.

There are others who are very interested in doctrine; they like to read books on doctrine and on theology, and nothing gives them greater joy than to be arguing about these things – the Reformed doctrine, or whatever it is. They show great enthusiasm for this, and to them this is *the* thing. Yes, and sometimes even as they are arguing about it they may be losing their tempers, and what then is the value of their doctrine? Sometimes these people seem to know all the doctrines in their heads, but look at their lives – are they living as Christians? My friends, the more doctrine you know the greater is your responsibility, and the more is expected of you.

Let me give you some quotations to show that this is not my own theory. Listen to the Lord Jesus Christ speaking to such people: 'If ye know these things, happy are ye if ye do them' [*John* 13 : 17]. 'Not every one that saith unto me, Lord, Lord . . . but he that doeth the will of my Father which is in heaven' [*Matthew* 7 : 21]. You remember what He said to some people one afternoon: 'If ye continue in my word' – they said that they had just believed on Him – 'If ye continue in my word, then are ye my disciples indeed; and ye shall know the truth, and the truth shall make you free' [*John* 8 : 31–32]. Free from what? Free from sin! The Jews said that they were not sinners; our Lord replied, Your works prove that you are sinners. And the business of the truth is to set us free and free from sin. There you have our Lord's own teaching.

But listen to the Apostle Paul saying the same thing in his Epistle to Titus: 'For the grace of God that bringeth salvation hath appeared to all men, teaching us that, denying ungodliness and worldly lusts, we should live soberly, righteously, and godly, in this present world; looking for that blessed hope, and the glorious appearing of the great God, and our Saviour Jesus Christ; who gave himself for us . . .' Why? '. . . that he might redeem us from all iniquity, and purify unto himself a peculiar people, zealous of good works' [*Titus* 2 : 11–14]. It may surprise you that I should say this, but I must say it: I do not care what your knowledge of doctrine is, it will avail you nothing unless it has led to that, unless it has purified you, and is purifying you, from these dead works, and making you a person 'zealous of good works'. Oh, the terrible danger of imagining that because we have a knowledge of truth, all is well, and we can ignore our life and conduct and behaviour. That was the very essential error of these Jews of old. And here is another thing: the persistence with which we tend to do all this in defence of ourselves. We start with one position, then the argument knocks it down, and we jump to another. The Jews started with the fact that they were Jews, then they relied on the goodness and the mercy of God, then on the law, then on ceremonial. We will clutch at any straw. Like the lady I once heard of who, having been brought up under Reformed doctrine, suddenly one day heard an Arminian preaching, and said at the end of the service, 'Thank God there is something for us to do after all!' She was glad there was something for her to do. That is the attitude. You see, the subtlety of sin! Man in sin is so self-centred and so proud and so blind that he will clutch at any kind of straw to justify himself, and thereby reject God's glorious scheme of salvation and justification by faith only.

And finally, one thing emerges from all this, and that is the importance of studying the Scriptures in the right way. Our method should not be simply to rush at them, and to say, 'Here we come to chapter two of Romans. What have we here? Ah yes, three points, three divisions – there is number one, number two, number three. Right, we have finished chapter two!'

No. The Apostle will not have it, and we must not have it. He calls us to stop for a moment. He says, 'We have finished chapter one'.

'Ah', you say, 'I have got chapter one. I have got my notes in full, I know all about it.'

Do you? Are you content merely with an analysis of chapter one, or have you seen the message of that chapter? Are you content simply with having a kind of intellectual division of the Scriptures so that you can divide up the whole of the Epistle to the Romans in one night, as I once heard a man doing? It was so simple, you see. Chapter one, verses 1 to 15: General introduction. Verse 16: Statement of theme. Then right away to the end of chapter five: Justification by faith. Chapters six, seven and eight: Sanctification. Chapters nine, ten and eleven: The position of the Jews. Chapter twelve to the end: General application in a moral sense. Finished the Epistle to the Romans!

But you see the Apostle will not allow us to do that. He pulls us up: 'Thou art inexcusable, O man, whosoever thou art that judgest another'.

You say, 'I agree with what he has been saying in chapter one – these horrible things that people are doing all around us today', and you pass on.

No, I have not been talking only about the people living in the gutters of life, says Paul. I have been talking about *you*: 'To the Jew first, and also to the Greek . . . There is none righteous, no, not one'. It does not matter who you are, or what you are, or what you know, or what you are ignorant of – we are all included here, we are all together. Have we understood chapter one? We have seen the dangers, have we not? What I mean is that the Scripture must always be applied, so that when you have read your portion of Scripture in the morning, or whenever you read it, you do not just say, 'Ah, yes, I have read the Notes and I have got the analysis'. No, you must stop and say, 'Now, what does this say to me? Where do I come in?' I may have been reading about the Pharisees and our Lord's arguments with them, and His final denunciation of them – and I think to myself, 'What terrible people the Pharisees were!' But I must go on from there and say, 'Am I a Pharisee, I wonder? Is there anything of that in me? It may not be blatant always, it can be there in a very small form, but is there anything of that in me?' Always apply it.

Oh, I say it again – there is no such thing in my opinion as 'lecturing' on the Bible; the Bible must be preached; it must be applied; it must be brought home. The Apostle insists upon that. He will not pass on until he is clear and satisfied about it all. He wants it to be perfectly clear to these people who think they have got an understanding of it when they have not; so he works out the argument. And, God willing, we shall follow him as he proceeds through the Epistle. But above all, I do pray that we will be examining ourselves the whole time, seeing its relevance and application to us. We must always put ourselves under the Word and look up to it and listen to it as it speaks to us. We must never study the Bible academically. Never become theoretical!. That has been the curse of theological seminaries. Men who have gone in full of life have come out dead, and all because of this academic interest in the Scriptures. Beware of it! It can even be a danger of studies like these. It is a danger whenever we read the Scriptures, whenever we listen to a sermon. It must always be applied: applied to ourselves, not to the other person, and we must pray that we may all have grace to apply it as it comes to us.

Two

*

Therefore thou art inexcusable, O man, whosoever thou art that judgest: for wherein thou judgest another, thou condemnest thyself; for thou that judgest doest the same things. But we are sure that the judgment of God is according to truth against them which commit such things. And thinkest thou this, O man, that judgest them which do such things, and doest the same, that thou shalt escape the judgment of God?

Romans 2 : 1–3

So far we have been introducing the theme, the subject that is put before us here by the Apostle, and we have seen how important it is that we should consider it in the light of what Paul has been saying in the previous chapter. We have also seen that here, primarily, he was dealing with the case of the Jew who was so wrong in his view of himself and his own position. The real trouble with the Jew, in the last analysis, was that he did not understand this doctrine of the wrath of God 'against all ungodliness and unrighteousness of men', and for that reason he could not see the need of justification. Then we went on to draw some general lessons from all that, showing what a subtle thing sin is, and that just as these Jews were unconsciously able to put themselves into this appalling position, so it is possible for us to do the same unless we truly grasp the biblical teaching.

There, then, is the setting. The Apostle imagines the Jew, as it were, breaking in at this point and saying, 'What you are saying about the Gentiles is all right, but it has got nothing to do with us'. But the Apostle is concerned to show that it has everything to do with them. What he is setting out to prove ultimately, as he says in the third chapter, is that there is none righteous, no, not one, that every mouth has been stopped, Jew as well as

Gentile, and that the whole world is guilty before God – again Jew as well as Gentile. So at this point he has to establish this, he has to convince and convict these Jews of sinfulness, of the fact that the wrath of God is upon them, and they must hasten to hide themselves under the blood of the Lord Jesus Christ as the only way of salvation. That is what he now proceeds to do, and he does it in detail.

The first thing he does is prove, in verse 1, that the Jew is entirely without excuse, because he really condemns himself: 'Therefore thou art inexcusable, O man, whosoever thou art that judgest: for wherein thou judgest another, thou condemnest thyself; for thou that judgest doest the same things'. This appears, in a sense, to be simple, and yet if we are not careful we can easily miss the point. Here were these Jews condemning the Gentiles and the kind of life that the Gentiles lived, while they were actually guilty of the same thing themselves. We must look at this in two different ways. The Jews *were* actually guilty of these things. Sometimes people seem to forget that, and while they have an idea that the Gentiles were guilty of those terrible things recorded in the second half of the first chapter, they think that the Jews were entirely free. But they were most definitely not.

The Jews, as you can read in the Old Testament, frequently sank into some of the foulest and most horrible sins; their moral condition frequently became deplorable. You will find prophet after prophet outlining this, and giving a list of their sins, and it was very much the same even when our Lord was in this world. The Apostle says it quite explicitly in verse 24 of this second chapter, in these words: 'For the name of God is blasphemed among the Gentiles through you'. In other words, here were people claiming to be the people of God, claiming to be in a special relationship with Him, claiming to be different from everybody else on earth, and yet, says Paul, because of the kind of life that they were living they were causing the other nations to blaspheme the name of God. The other nations looked on and said, 'Well if this is what it means to be God's people, if this is what happens when people claim that they are the unusual object of God's blessing and benediction, then we do not want to know God, and we do not want to be blessed by Him'. So there, it seems to me, it is stated quite clearly and explicitly that the

Jews were actually guilty of these things themselves. That is what Paul means, therefore, when he says, 'For thou that judgest *doest the same things*'.

But, of course, it is not necessary for us to say that all the Gentiles or all the Jews were guilty of every one of the terrible things that the Apostle has been recording in the first chapter.

What the Apostle is really convicting the whole world of is what he says in chapter one, verse 18. He says, 'The wrath of God is revealed from heaven against all ungodliness and unrighteousness of men, who hold [down] the truth in unrighteousness'. This is very important because there are people who evade this argument by agreeing that, of course, there is nothing to be said for anyone who is guilty of those foul perversions – men who 'burned in their lust one toward another', women with women also, and all these other things: 'Being filled with all unrighteousness, fornication, wickedness, covetousness . . .'.

'Of course', they say, 'there is nothing to be said for that sort of thing, but we have never been guilty of such things'. And because they are not guilty of these things they imagine that they are no longer sinners, and have never been sinners.

So you see how important it is for us to realize that there is a difference between being guilty before God and under the wrath of God, and the commission of particular sins. What the Apostle says is that the wrath of God is upon all ungodliness of men. You can be a highly respectable person morally, and yet be ungodly. As we saw in chapter one he puts ungodliness first. Ungodliness means anything in us that fails to glorify God and to worship Him and to make Him supreme in our own lives, and in the lives of others. That is ungodliness. Indeed there is no more terrible instance of ungodliness than the case of a person who does not see any need for the righteousness of Jesus Christ. The most ungodly people, the people whose ideas of God are most tragically wrong, are those who have never really felt that they are sinners, and who cannot see why Christ had to die, because they think that as they are they can satisfy God. So, when you see it like that, it is easy to understand how all these Jews were guilty of ungodliness, and also, of course, of unrighteousness, because the Apostle does not stop at the foul perversions. He talks of 'envy, murder, debate, deceit, malignity; whisperers, backbiters, haters of God, despiteful, proud, boasters, inventors of evil things, disobedient to parents, without understanding, covenant-breakers, without natural affection, implacable, unmerciful', and so on. The Jew, you see, had missed the significance of all this. But it is very important that we should press the principle that the Apostle here is convicting the Jews of ungodliness and of unrighteousness. Though they said they were the people of God, and used the name of God, and went regularly to the temple, they were guilty of ungodliness, and he does not hesitate to assert that – it was ungodliness and unrighteousness. In other words, the principle here, in a sense, is that it is not the form of the sin that matters, it is the essence of sin, which is to refuse to give to God the glory that is His right, that is His due. And it makes no difference how we fail to do it – it is the very essence of sin.

Now it took the Apostle Paul himself a long time to understand this. Indeed, when he was Saul of Tarsus he did not see it at all. He himself tells us that he thought he was blameless as regards the law, until he discovered that the law said, 'Thou shalt not covet'; and the moment he realized that the law said that, he was slain by the law. Of course, this was the great difficulty with the Pharisees, and it was the point, therefore, that our Lord had to elaborate in the Sermon on the Mount. The Pharisees' idea of these matters was that as long as you do not actually murder a man you are not guilty. Not at all, said our Lord. If you say in your heart about a man, 'Thou fool!' you will be in danger of hell fire. The Pharisees said that as long as we have not actually, literally, committed adultery, we are free from adultery. Not a bit of it, says our Lord; if you look on a woman to lust after her you have already committed adultery with her in your heart. So, you see, there are most highly respectable people who are guilty of murder and adultery, according to our Lord's teaching. That is what the Apostle is saying here. It is not the mere act that matters, it is this attitude, this spirit. The actual commission makes it worse, of course, but in your heart you can be guilty of it. And thus the Apostle convicts the Jew of condemning himself. He condemns these things in others and does not realize it is equally true of himself. But in his actual condemnation of the other, because he does the same thing, he is condemning himself, and his whole argument has collapsed.

Let us turn aside for a moment to show what an extraordinary result of sin this is. I have sometimes thought that there is no more extraordinary manifestation of sin, or consequence of the Fall, than the very thing with which the Apostle is dealing here. Is it not astounding that we can see these things so clearly in others, and yet find it so difficult to see exactly the same thing in ourselves? And even if it is pointed out to us, we are always ready to excuse it or to explain it away, and to show that somehow or other in our case it is not the same thing. Now we probably do this quite sincerely and honestly; we are not aware of what we are doing. That is one of the appalling results of the Fall and of sin.

Let me give you one or two very obvious illustrations of what I mean. There is a contemporary illustration that puts it perfectly. We see it in the realm of politics: look at the division of politics in this country into two main parties. Have you noticed how both these parties are really saying the same thing? The Labour Party says during its conference that the Tories are all out for themselves, that they are 'against us', as it were. Then at the Tory Party conference we are told the exact opposite – these Labour people are utterly selfish, and they never think of anybody but themselves. Now each one sees it absolutely clearly in the case of the other, but does not seem to be able to see it as far as he himself is concerned. Each one claims that he is out for the good of the country, that really he is not selfish at all, he is quite altruistic, and the real concern of his party is the well-being of the vast majority of the people. They both say it and they both say it with the same sincerity. And each one sees only the utter fallacy of the other's claim.

So we are familiar with it, and we not only find it in politics, but in industry as well. Both sides are saying the same thing. So many today maintain that the problem in this country at the moment is that the working man no longer works; he wants to get something for nothing; he wants more and more pay for less and less work; he wants to get all he can out of it for his own ends. Then go and listen to the working man; he will say that the trouble with the owner, the capitalist, is that he is really not interested in the business at all, except as a means of getting money to live the life of a gentleman and enjoy himself. He is simply taking out of it; he is putting nothing into it.

Then the owner says, 'Don't you see how they are making the week shorter and shorter, coming down to five days? It will be four days next'.

Listen to the other man replying, 'Who began the long weekend habit? It was the owner, the master'.

Each one sees it so clearly in the case of the other, and all this pother and argument and debating is in a sense so futile and so childish. But, you see, it is simply a repetition of what the Jews were doing at the time of the Apostle Paul. We can see it with absolute clarity in the case of the other, but when we look at ourselves we somehow do not see it, the truth being, of course, that we do not like looking at ourselves.

In 2 Samuel 12, there is a classic statement of the problem in the record of the prophet Nathan dealing with King David. You remember the story. Nathan told the king of a cruel, rapacious man who, to spare his own flock, killed the one ewe lamb of a poor man in order to entertain an unexpected guest. And David was filled with righteous indignation and said, 'This is terrible; it is impossible! Fancy a man doing a thing like that! It is inhuman, it is unnatural. That rich man must be put to death, and the lamb must be repaid fourfold to the poor man'.

Now David believed this, he was absolutely sincere and honest. But then the prophet looked at him and said, 'David, the man I have been talking about is you. Thou art the man!'

When it was a question of taking a lamb, David could see it clearly, but when it was a matter of taking another man's wife, he could not see it at all because he was the man who had done it. David was not being a hypocrite, he was not being dishonest, he really had not seen it. There is always something different when you and I do the wrong thing. That is the trouble. That is where sin not only blinds us, but perverts us, and twists us. So we come to this extraordinary result – we can see these things so clearly in others, but cannot see them in ourselves.

Not only that, we are so ready to denounce others and to judge them and condemn them, that we do not realize, as we are doing so, that we are in reality simply condemning ourselves. Our Lord put it very clearly at the beginning of Matthew 7: 'Judge not', He says. Be careful. 'Judge not, that ye be not judged. For with what judgment ye judge, ye shall be judged: and with what measure ye mete, it shall be measured to you again'.

Be careful therefore; let us all be careful. In passing judgment upon others we may well be condemning ourselves; and with the very same measure that we have used it shall be measured to us. There is no need to argue about this, is there? The Apostle very rightly puts it as a blunt assertion. We have only to look at this, we have only to examine ourselves, to know perfectly well that it is nothing but the simple and the startling truth. We are absolutely without excuse; we have already condemned ourselves in condemning somebody else. You see, we confine the words 'lust' and 'coveting' to just one thing, and because we are not guilty of that we think we are all right. We have forgotten that we can lust in our mind, we can lust in our imagination, we can lust in a thousand and one ways. And we can murder with our mouths and in our hearts. Because we confine it to one form we think we are innocent, but by condemning that thing in others we are condemning the same thing in ourselves. That is Paul's first argument.

But let us move on to the argument of verse 2, which is a tremendous statement: 'But we are sure', says the Apostle, 'that the judgment of God is according to truth against them which commit such things'. Now the translation here is very important. In the Authorized Version it reads: 'We are sure that the judgment of God is according to truth'. I believe the Revised Version is the same. But the Revised Standard Version not only goes wrong here, it misses the whole point. They translate it like this: 'We know that the judgment of God rightly falls upon those who do such things'; not 'judgment according to truth', but the judgment 'rightly falls'. Now that is quite wrong, as I must show you. It misses the whole point in this way. What the Apostle is saying here is that God's judgment is not like man's judgment. Man's judgment is never a true judgment, it is never according to a great eternal standard of truth. Man's judgment is not only fallible, it is always false. The judgment of God is always according to truth. And Paul has to say this because these Jews were ready to wriggle out of it at any point which they thought they could discover. They disliked this declaration that the wrath of God was upon them, and they were setting out to prove that it was not true of them. 'You may be making general statements', they said, 'but *we* are Jews and therefore we are in a different position'.

[22]

Wait a minute, says Paul. The judgment of God is always according to truth, and you cannot wriggle out of that. God's judgment is always the same, therefore, and God's judgment is eternal.

Now I am not stopping to emphasize the fact that God does judge; in chapter one, verse 18 we saw the wrath of God, the judgment of God. And, as Paul proves in the rest of that first chapter, He has revealed it and manifested it by what He has done among the Gentiles, and indeed among the Jews. Rather, I want to concentrate on this principle that God's judgment is always according to truth, for this is one of the most fundamental principles of the Christian faith. Notice, therefore, how Paul puts it: 'We are sure', says the Authorized Version. A better translation is, 'We know'. Who are the 'we'? Everybody. Everybody who has any knowledge of God knows always that this is a fundamental postulate which needs no argument or discussion. God's judgment is always according to truth.

Let me show you how concerned the Apostle was about this. Look what he says in chapter three, verse 4, where he again takes up this same kind of point. In verse 3 he says, 'For what if some did not believe? shall their unbelief make the faith of God without effect?' Then he answers, 'God forbid'. It is unthinkable. 'Yea, let God be true, but every man a liar'. God is true, and God alone is true, and what Paul is setting out to do, in the whole of this section, is to show this eternal truth of God over against man's lying and equivocation. And, indeed, when you come on to chapter three, verses 24 and following, you will see that he is doing the same thing there. He is putting up his tremendous defence of the justice and righteousness of God, which is, indeed, nothing but the truth of God.

I emphasize this because if we do not grasp this teaching that the judgment of God is always according to truth, we shall, of course, not believe in the doctrine of the wrath of God. There are many today, as we saw, who do not like the doctrine of the wrath of God. And they do not like it because they have not realized that the judgment of God is always according to truth. Again, if we do not accept this, we shall not accept the doctrine of justification by faith only, and shall not see any need for it. But what is still more serious, as I want to show you, is that if we do not grasp this teaching we shall never really understand the doctrine of the atonement, which is the very bedrock of our whole position.

Another reason why it is important is that if we do not realize that the judgment of God is always according to truth, we shall, for certain, fall into the terrible sin of antinomianism, which says that because we are God's people it does not matter what we do. 'Of course', such people say, 'if we were not God's people these things would be tremendously important. But after all I am a child of God and therefore I am right with God, my salvation is assured, it does not matter what I do'. But this is putting the grace and the love of God over against the law, the justice and the righteousness of God. Antinomianism! It is a belief which is denounced in the New Testament, and which has often wrought havoc in the history of the church. And people fall into that terrible pitfall because they do not realize that the judgment of God is always according to truth, that it does not matter to God whether you are His child or not, if you sin against Him it is sin, and He will punish you. What a terrible thing it is not to realize this!

And then, lastly, it leads to this: there are many people in the Christian life, I believe, who are not enjoying the full blessings of salvation simply because they have not grasped this principle. Because they are disobedient to God, or are sinning against Him in some way, they are causing God to withhold His blessing from them. He will not bless while we disobey. While we are sinning against Him we have no right to ask blessing. There is a condition to every single promise in the Bible, and if we do not keep the conditions we have not much right to expect the blessings. So, then, you see what a tremendously important doctrine it is, and how important it is that we should know and be sure that the judgment of God is according to truth. Why? Well it must be because God is God; because of the character of God.

Now the Bible is full of this teaching. There is, in a sense, nothing which is taught more regularly in the Bible from beginning to end than just this, that God's judgment is true because He is God, because God is true. You find it way back in Genesis: 'Shall not the Judge of all the earth do right?' said Abraham in his magnificent confession. He said, 'I know that you can never do anything wrong. You are the Judge of all the earth and all that you do is always right, it is always true'. This is the whole point of the Ten Commandments and the moral law, which you will find in Exodus chapter twenty. That is what God was revealing there – His judgment upon sin, and that it is a righteous judgment. What is the teaching of the Book of Leviticus, and parts of Numbers, and the remainder of Exodus, about the burnt offerings and the sacrifices and so on? Why was all this necessary? It was because God's judgment is always a judgment according to truth, and it had to be done in that way, and without argument. God had revealed it.

Then there is a great statement of this truth in Psalm 11. It is one of the most notable statements of all, and the psalm is worthy of our careful consideration. Verse 4 says: 'The Lord is in his holy temple, the Lord's throne is in heaven: his eyes behold, his eyelids try, the children of men'. What a tremendous statement! Can you see it? His eyes *behold*, His eyelids *try*. He looks in general, and then He concentrates his gaze by narrowing the focus, as it were.

The psalmist continues: 'The Lord trieth the righteous: but the wicked and him that loveth violence his soul hateth. Upon the wicked he shall rain snares, fire and brimstone, and an horrible tempest: this shall be the portion of their cup. For the righteous Lord loveth righteousness; his countenance doth behold the upright'.

What a wonderful statement of this truth! And, further on in the Old Testament, this is really the whole argument of that great book of the prophet Habakkuk. It is called a theodicy – a vindication of the ways of God. What the prophet was concerned about was that whatever might be happening, whatever might be going on, there was one thing that was absolutely certain, God would never do anything wrong. God's judgments are always according to truth.

But of course you have it still more clearly in the New Testament. John, in his first Epistle says: 'God is light, and in him is no darkness at all'. Or hear our Lord saying it in the way He addresses God, His Father – He addresses Him as 'holy Father', or 'righteous Father'. No one knew this doctrine as clearly as He did – that the judgments of God are always according to truth.

Now the important thing for us is to see how this works out in practice. This doctrine means that because the judgments of God are always according to truth, then God never has any varying standards. This was the point that the Apostle was pressing upon these Jews, because they thought that God did have varying standards – one standard for the Jew and another for the Gentile. No! God's judgment is always according to truth, and if it is always according to truth there can never be any varying standards. Our standards, of course, do vary. We tend to have our favourites. One standard for our children, another one for other people's children. One for our nation, another for another nation – varying standards! That is why we are such poor judges. Secondly, there is no changeableness nor variableness in His standard, and for this reason: He is 'the Father of lights, with whom is no variableness, neither shadow of turning' [*James* 1 : 17]. If God is condemning you in one thing, you cannot run round behind Him, as it were, and find a different face or a different attitude. No, you can try to do that to evade His judgment and His righteousness, but you will always find the same blazing, eternal light – no variableness, neither shadow cast by turning. What a tremendous thing this is! The standard is always the same, ever, always, in every century, in all continents, in all conditions, under all circumstances, never a change, always according to truth.

And the reason for this, as we have already seen, is God's character. If there were any variation in the standard of judgment it would imply a variation in God. Now you notice how I am putting it, and I do that very deliberately. Even Dr R. W. Dale of Birmingham fell, I think, into error at this point, when he spoke in his book on the atonement about some 'eternal law of righteousness that guided God', as if God has to conform to an eternal law of righteousness. But where did that come from? Who put that into position? What is this law that God is subservient to? It is wrong! The Scripture does not say that. The eternal law of righteousness is in God Himself – it is God! The judgment of God is according to truth because God is God, and He cannot deny Himself, He cannot change in any sense, at any point. His judgment is constant, and without variation.

But even further than this: because the judgment is always according to truth, it follows that God in His judgment is always equally penetrating, by which I mean that He never judges

merely by the outward appearance. You remember how our
Lord put that to the people? You will find it in John 7 : 24 –
'Judge not according to the appearance, but judge righteous
judgment'. Ah, He said, you Pharisees, the trouble with you is
that you judge only by the outward appearance. Never do that.
Judge righteous judgment, which sees the inside as well as the
outside, and takes account of the whole. Again, He put it still
more explicitly to the Pharisees, when He said to them – you
will find it in Luke 11 : 39 – 'Now do ye Pharisees make clean [so
punctiliously] the outside of the cup and the platter; but your
inward part is full of ravening and wickedness'. God sees the
inside as well as the outside, and it is unthinkable that God's
judgment could vary in that way, unthinkable that He could
only see the outside and not the inside! No, it is always
according to truth.

Or, to put it in the other form, God not only sees the external
manifestation, He sees the heart. One of the most alarming
things our blessed Lord ever said is to be found in Luke 16 : 15,
'Ye are they which justify yourselves before men; but God
knoweth your hearts: for that which is highly esteemed among
men is abomination in the sight of God'. You Pharisees, He said,
can 'justify yourselves before men', because men are poor
judges, they do not judge according to truth, but God 'seeth your
hearts'. His judgment penetrates, it is true right through, it sees
through everything. Truth is that which brings to light.

Or again, you can take it from Hebrews chapter four, verses 12
and 13: 'For the word of God is quick, and powerful . . . piercing
even to the dividing asunder of soul and spirit, and of the joints
and marrow, and is a discerner of the thoughts and intents of the
heart'. There is nothing hidden from Him for, 'all things are
naked and opened unto the eyes of him with whom we have to
do'.

Then – and I must emphasize this because of its terrifying
importance – God as a Judge can never be bought. He can never
be bribed. You can never get round Him, as it were, or somehow
or other mitigate the judgment, or influence it by doing
something that is pleasing to Him. The classic statement of this
you will find in 1 Samuel 15 : 22–23 in the case of that tragic
man Saul, the first king of Israel. Saul thought, you see, that
though he had disobeyed God, if he now brought his burnt

offering and sacrifice, all would be well, but this is what God said to him through the prophet Samuel: 'Hath the Lord as great delight in burnt offerings and sacrifices, as in obeying the voice of the Lord? Behold, to obey is better than sacrifice, and to hearken than the fat of rams. For rebellion is as the sin of witchcraft, and stubbornness is as iniquity and idolatry'.

You see there the whole teaching that we are handling here in Romans. It is exactly the same thing; they denounced idolatry, yes, but stubbornness 'is as iniquity and idolatry'. If you are stubborn in your will against God it is as bad as being a sexual pervert, it is as horrible in the sight of God. 'Rebellion is as the sin of witchcraft, and stubbornness is as iniquity and idolatry. Because thou hast rejected the word of the Lord, he hath also rejected thee from being king'. What a terrifying statement that is! You see, we cannot buy God with our burnt offerings and sacrifices. He will not have them! He wants our obedience. He wants our hearts and not merely the gifts.

We find the same argument again in Amos 5 : 21–27: 'I hate, I despise your feast days, and I will not smell in your solemn assemblies. Though ye offer me burnt offerings and your meat offerings, I will not accept them: neither will I regard the peace offerings of your fat beasts. Take thou away from me the noise of thy songs; for I will not hear the melody of thy viols. But let judgment run down as waters, and righteousness as a mighty stream. Have ye offered unto me sacrifices and offerings in the wilderness forty years, O house of Israel? But ye have borne the tabernacle of your Moloch and Chiun your images, the star of your god, which ye made to yourselves. Therefore will I cause you to go into captivity beyond Damascus, saith the Lord, whose name is The God of Hosts'.

My friends, the judgment is always according to truth, and if you want the final proof of it here it is: I know that it cannot be said, but if you ever tried, by any stretch of the imagination to say that God ever had a favourite, I suppose that King David would have been that favourite. And yet you remember what happened to him when he sinned? God has no favourites. As Peter said to Cornelius, 'God is no respecter of persons' [*Acts* 10 : 34]. James in the third chapter of his Epistle teaches that wisdom must be 'without partiality'. True judgment, the wisdom that comes from God, 'is first pure, then peaceable, gentle, easy to be intreated . . . without partiality'; always true; no favourites; no special concern for one person; no winking here and punishing there – always the same for everybody.

And so, though the children of Israel were God's own chosen people, whom He had made and created for Himself, He cast them out. As Paul tells us in Romans chapter eleven, they were the 'natural branches' of the olive tree, but because they sinned and rebelled, He plucked them out, and has grafted in this new, unnatural branch, the Gentiles. 'But be careful', says Paul to the Gentiles, 'if He did not spare the natural branches, how much less will He spare you if you fall into sin'. While it is very right for us to talk about the goodness of God, let us never forget that with the goodness of God there is also the severity of God; so these things must always be taken together.

And thus, you see, in his second argument the Apostle brings it right home to these Jews. God, he says, is not as you are, with your varying standards and favouritism, and special people and special positions. No! Because God is God, His judgment is always according to truth. So He may have a man who has been a great servant of His for many years and has done marvellous things, but if that man falls into sin, it does not matter what he has done, he shall be punished. I do not mean by that that he is lost, but he will suffer loss, he will be punished. You cannot backslide without suffering. You cannot play fast and loose with God. It is no use saying, 'Because I am saved, it does not matter what I do'. God's judgment is always according to truth, whether you are a believer or an unbeliever. Sin is sin.

Do you not think, in the light of all this, that perhaps one of the main explanations of the lifeless state of the Christian church today is just this unconscious antinomianism? We have become guilty of this because we are for ever talking about 'taking it by faith', and saying we must never examine ourselves and never look into ourselves. We are saved and we are all right, and thus we become slack and loose in practice and in conduct, forgetting that God's judgment is always according to truth.

Three

*

But we are sure that the judgment of God is according to truth against them which commit such things. And thinkest thou this, O man, that judgest them which do such things, and doest the same, that thou shalt escape the judgment of God? Or despisest thou the riches of his goodness and forbearance and longsuffering; not knowing that the goodness of God leadeth thee to repentance?

Romans 2 : 2–4

Now we must remind ourselves that here the Apostle is bringing home, especially to the Jews, the fact that they, like everybody else, were under the wrath of God, and that the only hope of salvation open to them, as to all others, was in this righteousness provided by God in the Lord Jesus Christ, a righteousness which is received by faith. The Jews were trying to argue that this did not apply to them in either respect, negative or positive, and in this chapter the Apostle is bringing the argument home to them and convicting them of their sin and of their entire helplessness to save themselves. We have seen that the argument hitherto runs like this: first of all, in the first verse he proves to them that they are convicting themselves; they are guilty of the same things that they condemn in others and therefore they are condemning themselves. In verse 2 he says that they are guilty of the fallacy of forgetting that God's judgment is always according to truth. They think that God's judgment is like their judgment, and human judgment is not only fallible, it is always unworthy; it is never entirely according to truth, even at its best. But God's judgment is different, as we all know. Paul says that everybody who believes in God at all must believe that God is perfect in every respect and therefore His judgment must always be according to truth – and we have worked out in detail what that means. Finally, we showed that the ultimate proof of all this was the case of the Jews themselves, because, though they were His own chosen people, God actually did judge them and punish them more than once.

That, then, is the point at which we have arrived – God's judgment is always 'according to truth against them which commit such things'. But before I leave this, there is just one thing I must add. There is a kind of deduction which we make from all that, which is both significant and important. We shall find the Apostle taking it up himself in the third chapter, but I must note it at this point. Earlier on, in introducing this question of God's judgment according to truth, I said that a failure to understand and grasp that fact accounts for many a heresy that has appeared in the life of the church; and in a very special way it accounts for the reason why so many people are in trouble about the doctrine of the atonement. I think you will agree with me when I say that no doctrine is more crucial than the doctrine of the atonement. There is no better way of telling where a man stands with regard to evangelical truth than to know his opinion on the doctrine of the atonement. I suggest that there are many who not only are not clear on that doctrine, but who in particular reject the substitutionary aspect of the doctrine of the atonement simply because they have never grasped the great statement that God's judgment is according to truth.

How does that work out? We can only deal with this briefly now, but the first thing that we see is that God *will* judge, and that God, because He is who and what He is, *must* judge. God would no longer be God if He did not judge sin, so there will be and must be a judgment upon sin. But there are many whose view of the atonement is that what was really happening on the cross on Calvary's hill was that God was announcing, through the death of His own Son, that He is nothing but love, that there is no judgment, and that He is ready to overlook sin. That, you see, is because they do not realize that God's holy character and God's justice and righteousness insist upon a judgment of sin.

Secondly, this judgment of sin must always be according to truth. In other words, God has said that He will punish sin. He said it repeatedly in the Old Testament, especially, perhaps, in the Ten Commandments and the moral law, but in many other places also. It is there in Eden even before the giving of the law and it is there, too, in the writings of the prophets. He told Adam, in his state of perfection, that if he sinned he would die, and because he sinned he did die. Now that is because God's judgment is always according to truth – the punishment must fit the crime. God has said what the punishment is, and God always insists upon that punishment being carried out. I am sure that you see the significance of that for the doctrine of the atonement? There are those who regard the death of Christ in this way; they hold that what God is saying there on Calvary is that if you only say that you believe on the Lord Jesus Christ, God forgives you. That is their understanding of what happened there. They believe it is an announcement, a proclamation, that God is love and that He is prepared to forgive the sins of anybody who repents and who says that he is sorry. Now if you hold that view of the atonement you are denying the statement that God's judgment is according to truth, for that statement means that the punishment God has said He will mete upon sin must be meted out, otherwise He is no longer true to His own word, He is not any longer judging according to truth.

So the right way of viewing the doctrine of the atonement and the death on the cross is that God has said that He is going to punish sin, therefore God must and does punish sin. But how then can He forgive me? How can He possibly forgive me? To this there is, of course, only one answer: it is because He has punished my sin in the person of His own Son. And so we see that this doctrine about the judgment of God according to truth introduces the great doctrine of the atonement, and it insists upon our viewing the atonement in a penal manner, in an expiatory manner, in a piacular manner – it does not matter which of the terms you use. It insists upon the fact that God cannot forgive anybody without punishing the sin. God cannot say to me, 'Ah well now, because you say you are sorry I am going to forgive you'. No. God must punish sin, for His judgment is according to truth. And we believe that that is exactly how we are saved by the death of Christ; that God has judged our sins according to truth and in so doing it meant the death of His only Son – for my sins, for my guilt, to bear the punishment that I so richly deserve. So any view of the atonement which does not include the fact that God's judgment is according to truth is a denial of this Scripture.

Now I need not stay with this any longer, because we shall find that Paul elaborates this subject in chapter three, from verse 24 onwards. He says there: 'Being justified freely by his grace through the redemption that is in Christ Jesus: whom God hath set forth to be a propitiation through faith in his blood, to declare his righteousness for the remission of sins that are past, through the forbearance of God; to declare, I say, at this time his righteousness: that he might be just, and the justifier of him which believeth in Jesus'. If you have a view of God's forgiveness of sin which in any way derogates or detracts from the justice of God, it is a denial of the Scripture. Therefore you see the importance of observing every one of these phrases as we proceed. It is because God's judgment is according to truth that it was necessary for the Son of God to come on earth from heaven, and especially was it necessary for Him to go to Calvary and there be so dealt with under the wrath of God that He cried out, 'My God, my God, why hast thou forsaken me?' It is all just an exposition of this tremendous statement that God's judgment is according to truth, always, everywhere, even when His own Son is the sin-bearer. He spared Him nothing because His judgment is always according to truth.

In the third verse the Apostle is really just applying that, so we need not stay long with it. 'Thinkest thou this, O man, that judgest them which do such things, and doest the same, that thou shalt escape the judgment of God?' In other words, if you yourself condemn this sort of thing when you see it in others and thereby condemn yourself, how much more must God condemn it because He judges according to truth. So if you accept the first conclusion, that you have condemned yourself, then you must accept the second, that there is no way of escaping the judgment of God. There is no argument, no subterfuge, no cleverness, nothing that will avail.

It is a terrible word, this word 'escape'. If you look through your New Testament for it, you will find it frequently. 'Thinkest thou, O man, that thou shalt escape the judgment of God?' The world is as it is tonight because men still think that they can escape the judgment of God, and they have many ways in which they think they can do it. The psalmists understood them; people have always been like this, and speaking through one of the psalmists, God says: 'Thou thoughtest that I was altogether such an one as thyself' [*Psalm* 50:21]. And how common that is! Oh, men display their ingenuity in trying to escape the judgment of God. They think that God does not see, or that He is going to make an exception, or this or that or the other, and thus they are constantly persuading themselves that somehow or other they are going to escape. And, therefore, the question the New Testament keeps asking is: How shall we escape if we neglect this only way? How do you think you can escape, O man, in the light of what we have just been seeing, which you cannot refute? There is no escaping the judgment of God.

And this truth is one of the first things that the gospel proclaims. The message of John the Baptist was that men should 'flee from the wrath to come'. When he saw the Pharisees coming to him to be baptized he said, 'Who hath warned you to flee from the wrath to come?' Our Lord repeats the same message. Paul in 1 Thessalonians 1:9–10 says that 'ye turned to God from idols to serve the living and true God; and to wait for his Son from heaven . . . *which delivered us from the wrath to come*'.

The terrible thing is that the world goes on with its laughter and its joking, paying no attention to this, not interested in this question of the wrath and the judgment of God, and saying that in general it believes in God while fondly imagining that it is going to escape the righteous judgment of God according to truth. This is the great motive for evangelism. This is the first reason why we should ever talk to man about his soul and present the gospel to him. Before we begin to tell him anything about the benefits of Christian salvation and Christian living, we must tell men and women that, as they are, they are under the wrath of God and that they cannot escape it, do what they will. They know they have got to die, they cannot escape that: 'It is appointed unto men once to die, but after this the judgment' [*Hebrews* 9:27]. Now, Christian people, do we all realize this as we should? Is this our motive? Does this urge us? Does this give us a concern about the souls of men and women? The terrifying thing that is proclaimed here is that the whole of mankind is under the judgment and the wrath of God, and that there is no escape apart from the way that God Himself has provided through our Lord and Saviour Jesus Christ.

But let us proceed. Man in sin believes in the depth of his being that he can escape, and he puts up an argument. When you knock that down, he puts up another; you knock that down, and he will take up yet another – and that is exactly what these Jews were doing. So the Apostle goes on to the next argument that they put up, and that is stated in verse 4. Here is a very clever, and apparently a very subtle, argument that mankind thinks up in order to show how it can escape the judgment of God: the argument about the goodness of God. You see, when you establish that man condemns himself because he condemns the same thing in others, he has no answer, so he then tries to argue that he is in a special position in the sight of God. And when we show that this is not so – that God's judgment is always according to truth – after a moment's thought, he comes back with yet another argument: What about the goodness of God?

Now the Jews were constantly bringing this particular argument forward. They did it in the time of our Lord Himself, and they did it against the Apostle Paul. Their argument was this: 'Look back', they said, 'across our long history. Is there anything more plain and clear than the fact that God has blessed us, that God loves us? We do not say we are perfect, but look at the way He has blessed us, look at the way He has led us, look at the way He is still blessing us now. He has not only done it through the centuries, He is still doing it and He always will do it'.

When John the Baptist preached to them, he knew their case so well that he said, 'Begin not to say within yourselves, We have Abraham to our father: for I say unto you, That God is able of these stones to raise up children unto Abraham' [*Luke* 3:8]. He knew that they were saying that they were Abraham's children, and that because of that they were by-passing all this doctrine about the wrath of God and fleeing from the wrath to come. Do not fall back on that, said John the Baptist, that is not going to help you. God is not going to be good to you simply because you are the children of Abraham.

But that was their argument. They put up the goodness and kindness of God towards them, and said that a God who had always treated them like that could not possibly punish them in the way that Paul was suggesting.

Now here, I think, we see very clearly the terrible blinding effect of sin. Sin is something that affects the whole of man; it has ruined him. It affects our intellects as well as every other part of us, and what it does is to blind us. See how it had blinded these Jews. It made them misread their own Old Testament, of which they were so proud and which was the thing that differentiated them from all other nations – the oracles of God. They were proud of the fact that they had got God's Word and that it was read to them every Sabbath in the synagogues. They said, 'This is how we live, this is our life, this is the thing that we enjoy, the Old Testament Scriptures'. But you see, because they had been blinded by sin, they had completely misread and misunderstood their own Scriptures. The Old Testament had told them quite clearly what God's character was. God had revealed Himself and His character to them in the Ten Commandments and in the moral law and in the writings of the prophets. It was perfectly plain and clear that He is a righteous and a holy God who always judges according to truth. They had read the very Scriptures but they had been blind to that; they had misread them. They were twisting the Scriptures to suit their own case.

Not only that, but sin had blinded them to their own history. This is almost incredible, but it is a fact. If you read the story of the children of Israel in the Old Testament you find that because of their sin, God Himself had punished them by raising up the Chaldeans who came and destroyed them and carried them away captive to Babylon. It is there in their own history. And yet they read the history and they could not see it. Now this is not a theory; let me give you proof of it. One afternoon our Lord was preaching and we know He was preaching with unusual tenderness and authority because we read that as He spake these words many believed on Him. Then our Lord looked at these men who had just believed on Him and said, 'If ye continue in my word, then are ye my disciples indeed; and ye shall know the truth, and the truth shall make you free' [*John* 8 : 31–32]. What a wonderful thing to say! But did they shout, 'Hallelujah and Amen!'? Nothing of the sort! They stood back on their dignity and said, 'We be Abraham's seed, and were never in bondage to any man: how sayest thou, Ye shall be made free?' They said, in effect, 'Do you not realize that in promising us that we shall be set free, you are insulting us? Do you not know that we are Abraham's children and have never been in bondage to any man?' So said these creatures whose own history told them that they had been in bondage in Egypt and in bondage in Babylon! But that is what sin does; they were reading the history in their national pride. 'We have never been slaves', they said, while their own history proved that they certainly had been slaves. Sin blinds. It blinds us to fact as well as to teaching.

But not only that, it blinded these Jews to the signs of the times. It blinded them, at that very time, to the things that were happening round and about them. Again let me quote our Lord's words; you will find them in Luke 12 : 54-57. He turned upon the people on that occasion and said to them that He did not quite understand them: 'When ye see a cloud rise out of the west, straightway ye say, There cometh a shower; and so it is. And when ye see the south wind blow, ye say, There will be heat; and it cometh to pass. Ye hypocrites, ye can discern the face of the sky and of the earth; but how is it that ye do not discern this time? Yea, and why even of yourselves judge ye not what is right?'

What does He mean by that? In effect, He is saying, 'You people are so expert in the signs in the heavens and the earth, and in every other respect, so why is it that you did not see the significance of John the Baptist and his preaching? Why is it that you do not recognize who I am and the significance of my coming and my preaching? The signs of the times – there they are and you do not see them'. And they did not see them because they were blinded by sin. Sin does that.

Another thing it does, therefore, is to give us a false sense of security. Here were the Jews saying these things at the time of John the Baptist and our Lord, and continuing with the same argument when the Apostle Paul was writing this letter to the Romans some twenty years later at the very least, it may be even more than that. Paul is now preaching and the other Apostles are preaching, and the Jews are still saying, 'Nonsense, this cannot happen to us, what about God's goodness? What about His forbearance and longsuffering? We are all right, we are Abraham's seed, God's people. He has always blessed us, He is still blessing us, He is always going to bless us.' They were saying that right away up to A.D. 70, and you remember what happened then? Well, the Roman armies came and routed them, and sacked their city and destroyed their temple, and the Jews as a nation were cast out of their own land and have been scattered among the nations ever since. They said until the last moment, 'It will never happen to us, the goodness of God is covering us'. That is how sin blinds. They could not see it in their own history, they would not listen to the preaching of John the Baptist or even the Son of God, let alone the Apostle Paul, and then the judgment came, they could not escape it after all, it descended as an avalanche upon them.

There, then, is the argument that the Apostle is employing in this passage, 'Thinkest thou . . . that thou shalt escape?' But it is still the same, you see, and God forbid that any of us should think that we are simply considering the case of the Jews nearly two thousand years ago. No, it is happening now as much as it happened then, and, alas, I am sorry to have to say, it happens with many who are in the church as well as with that great crowd that is outside the church. No argument is put up so frequently against these truths – the doctrines of the wrath of God, and the judgment of God, and the righteousness of God, and the absolute necessity of the death of the Son of God as One bearing the punishment of sin – no argument is brought up and adduced and advanced against them so frequently as this argument of God's goodness and God's kindness and God's love.

You are familiar with this, and it is important that we should know how to answer it. This is the thing on which people are relying, and this is how they put it: they pit God's goodness and His love and His kindness against His holiness and His righteousness and His justice. Indeed, they go further. Many of them do not hesitate to go so far as to say that to talk about the wrath of God is blasphemy! Now they say that in books, they call it 'that old tribal idea of God that you get in the Old Testament'. They go on to say, 'Jesus came and taught us something better than that. Jesus teaches us that God is love and that therefore He is no longer only holy and righteous, and so we must never speak of the wrath of God against sin. No', they say, 'that is absolutely wrong, it is a libel on God's character'. They not only pit these qualities of goodness and love and mercy against the others, they do it to such an extent that they get rid of the others, and they take those attributes out of the character of God. It is being done very freely, as I said, not only outside the church but even inside the church. That is one form the argument takes.

But here is another form: they argue that because God does not strike us down immediately we sin, and punish sin the next second after we have committed it, He will never do so. It sounds a very clever argument, does it not? This is how they put it: 'You tell me that God is just and righteous and holy, that He cannot look upon sin. Very well, I fall into sin, and if God is what you say, He should immediately punish me and strike me, but he does not do that. We know He does not do that – He does not do it with us individually, He does not do it with nations, He has not done it with the world. Obviously He does not do it because God is good and full of goodness and mercy and love and compassion. What you are saying about Him is wrong. God does not do, and never will do, that sort of thing'. You see the logic?

And then another argument which they use is this: 'If what you say is right and God does take that view of sin and of man in sin, is it likely that God would ever grant any blessing at all to such sinners? How would it be possible for such a God to bless anybody at all unless he is a believer in Him and a true Christian? But the fact is', they continue, 'God obviously grants blessings to many people who do not believe in Him, and we can understand that, because God is One who is full of goodness and love and mercy and compassion, and really these other things you are talking about, they are not true of God'. So they use the fact that so many people are enjoying good health, and perhaps worldly material prosperity, and many other things. People who do not believe in God at all take that as absolute proof that God is full of goodness and love and mercy, and that He will never do to anybody what you are suggesting He is going to do to all who are not believers.

And then, finally, they put it like this – there are many other arguments, I am simply picking out some of them – they argue that the long history of the world is a proof in and of itself that God is never really going to judge the world. You will find all this in 2 Peter 3. There the Apostle says that 'there shall come in the last days scoffers . . . saying, Where is the promise of his coming?' 'You Christians', they say, 'and your preachers especially, have been talking about a judgment of God, and that Christ

[39]

is coming back to judge the world in righteousness. Ha!' they ask, 'Where is the promise of his coming? for since the fathers fell asleep, all things continue as they were from the beginning of the creation'. In effect, they say, 'You know, you had better change your argument, you had better admit and confess that you are wrong. Are you asking us to believe that the God whom you say is righteous and just and holy, and who must punish sin because He hates it with a holy and divine hatred – do you mean to say that God would have allowed a world of sin such as this to go on for six thousand years? It is monstrous! These things cannot happen'. That is the argument. Peter presents it there and we hear it constantly today.

There, then, are some of the arguments which men bring forward in order to try to escape this whole idea of the judgment of God according to truth against all sin. And what has the Apostle got to say about it? He answers very plainly and very bluntly; he says there is only one thing to say about people who talk like that – they are all despising the goodness of God. Now the form in which he puts it adds to it. He puts it in the form of a rhetorical question which answers itself: 'Or despisest thou the riches of his goodness and forbearance and longsuffering; not knowing that the goodness of God leadeth thee to repentance?' What you are doing, says the Apostle, is to despise the goodness of God.

Here is one of the most serious and one of the most solemn charges that can ever be brought against man. What Paul is saying is that there is nothing more reprehensible than to persist in a life of sin while talking about the goodness and the mercy of God. I say that this is a very serious and solemn thing, because up to a point we are all guilty of it. We all try to excuse sin in ourselves in some shape or form, falling back upon the goodness of God, so that when we do fall into sin our repentance is not always true, it is not always thorough. We heal ourselves a little bit too quickly. We want to get rid of the pain; we jump to what we know to be true of God's love. But that is to abuse it.

But however it may be true of us in that way, there is nothing more terrible in the world today than to think of men and women who are going on in a life of sin and who do not submit to God and who do not believe in the Lord Jesus Christ because of their misunderstanding of the goodness of God. Now, my friends, I am emphasizing this because it is such a common attitude, such a common condition. I am sure you all meet it as you talk to people about these matters. This is the argument of arguments against becoming a Christian, against the necessity of doing so, against the necessity of the death of Christ, and against all that we say about the miraculous and the supernatural. And the whole of their argument is about the goodness of God and the love of God. It is put up against this great doctrine of His wrath that is expounded in the Scriptures. That is why I say that for our own sakes and for the sake of others who are in this most appalling state, we must know the way to deal with it and to answer it – and the Apostle does that here for us. He makes the blunt assertion, he proffers this most specific charge, that this is to despise, to make light of, to regard as something cheap, the very goodness of God Himself.

He brings home the charge in this way: he says that the very conduct of these people, their very attitude towards the thing about which they are speaking, is a proof that they are guilty of despising it, and he proceeds to establish that. Let me suggest to you how he does it. A man who goes on talking in this way about the goodness and the mercy and the love of God, but at the same time continues in sin, is a man who is showing quite clearly that he has never really studied or contemplated or understood the goodness of God as he should have done, and thereby he despises it. He is the sort of man who talks glibly and lightly and loosely about the goodness and the love of God, but who has never taken the trouble really to examine it and to work it out and to stand before it and meditate upon it. Rather, what he says is, 'Ah, I believe in the goodness of God', and then he goes on to commit his sin, or continue the life he has been living. He has never really contemplated God's goodness – and is not that to despise it?

We all, of course, can see this very clearly when we do it with one another. Sometimes, for example, you have the privilege of being introduced or presented to some great man, and sometimes you may have this sort of experience – when your turn comes to shake hands with this great personage, and you hold out your hand and he holds out his, you notice that while he is holding your hand he is looking at the next person in the queue. Then you feel that he is despising you; he is not interested in you. He pretends to be, but he is not. If he were really interested in you and glad to meet you, he would look you straight in the face, and he would pay a little attention to you. Or perhaps you are good at drawing or painting and you have a piece of work which you think is rather good. An expert comes along and you feel you would rather like to show it to him, wondering what he might think of it. But he takes a sort of casual glance and moves on; he has despised your painting or your drawing.

Now what the Apostle is saying here is that these people are guilty of doing that very thing with the goodness and love and mercy of God about which they talk so much. They have never really considered it. Paul says, 'Or despisest thou the riches of his goodness, and the riches of his forbearance, and the riches of his longsuffering?' They know nothing about 'the riches'. Their estimate of the riches of God's grace is very small. They have never taken the trouble to read right through their Bibles and to know it and to seek it out, and they have never ended by saying, 'Oh! How good God is and how kind and how longsuffering!' Not at all. They have never read it. They think, 'I believe in the goodness of God', and then off they go to do just what they want whether it is wrong or not. Do you not see how they are insulting His goodness? They know nothing about it; they have never considered it.

But let me show you how Paul brings out his terms. First, the *riches* of God's goodness. Now that is a term he is very fond of, as you know. In a sense, it is a term which really tells us everything. Whenever Paul uses this word 'riches' he wants you to think of a treasury which has endless wealth in it; you can never exhaust it – it is the riches of God's goodness, it is eternal in its extent. That is the word he uses, the richness of it all, the riches of it all. And these people know nothing about this.

Then what does he mean by *goodness*? Well, he means God's kindness in a general sense. There is a perfect statement of this by our Lord Himself in the Sermon on the Mount in Matthew 5 : 45, where He says that God 'maketh his sun to rise on the evil and on the good, and sendeth rain on the just and on the unjust'. That is an illustration of the riches of God's goodness – even to the evil, who are unjust and who hate God and who blaspheme His name and break His commandments and delight in doing so. Yet God, in the richness and the riches of

His goodness, causes the rain to fall upon their fields and their crops to fructify them, and sends the sun with all its warmth, and its life-giving power. He does it to the unjust as well as to the just; to the unrighteous, the evil, as well as to the good. But do these people stop to consider that? Of course they do not. They like to use the argument that He will not punish them because He is good, but as they look at their fields in late August or early September and see these marvellous crops they never stop to say, 'What has produced this?' They just begin to think of how *they* ploughed and harrowed and sowed, and so on. Ah yes, but all that would have availed nothing if it had been bad weather, if God had not sent the rain and the sun. They should surely say, 'Oh, how good God has been!' But they do not do that, they have never examined it. They only talk about the goodness of God when they are challenged, and they know nothing about it. They just, as it were, take a passing glance and say, 'All is well', and off they go to sin again. They are despising it, the very thing they claim to believe in!

But let me give you another illustration. When the Apostle Paul preached at Lystra he was talking to a company of pagans who thought that he was a god because he had healed the man who had been lame since he was born. 'Stop!' Paul said in effect. 'You do not realize what you are doing. I am no god. There are no gods except one, the living God. You do not know Him and you do not worship Him, but you are without excuse because he left not himself without witness, in that he did good, and gave us rain from heaven, and fruitful seasons, filling our hearts with food and gladness' [*Acts* 14 : 17]. They had never considered that, they had never examined it. 'You know nothing about it', said Paul, and he says the same thing here in our text.

There, then, you see something of the riches of God's goodness. There are people alive by the million in this world today who have had the gift of life from God, the gift of health from God and the gift of families and loved ones from God. They have not provided any of these things, God has done it all – protection, home, food, clothing, shelter – all these things; God is the Giver of every good and every perfect gift. These people know nothing about it. They know nothing of 'the riches', they have never thought about it. And yet they talk about the goodness of God, and their very talk about it is an insult to it.

They are despising it by not thinking about it properly, examining it and working it out, as they ought, and seeing it in all its glory.

But let me conclude with the next term which Paul uses. The third term is *forbearance* – the riches of His forbearance! This means the way in which God bears with us in our sins. Why does God not punish us and strike us down the moment we sin? It is because of His forbearance, His patience. Though He is who and what He is, and though He hates this sin, and though He has pronounced His wrath upon it, He does not immediately punish. Why not? Because of His forbearance. We will come later to see why He is forbearing, but we are dealing now with the fact of His forbearance; were it not for this we would all be undone. We promise God a great deal sometimes and then we forget all about it; or perhaps we even break our promises or fall into sin. Why does He still have any patience with us at all? It is His forbearance, my friends, and oh, the riches of His forbearance! He bears with us as He suffered the evil manners of these children of Israel down the years. I do not know how He did it – we would never do it. We are not like this, but God is rich in forbearance. These people who presume upon it know nothing about it, they have never analysed it, and they have never seen it.

And the last word is *longsuffering*. This means that His forbearance continues over a long time. He continues to be forbearing, He postpones the punishment. As Psalm 103 has put it, He is 'slow to anger, and plenteous in mercy'. Or, as you read in 2 Peter 3 : 9, He 'is longsuffering to us-ward, not willing that any should perish, but that all should come to repentance'. Oh, the riches of the longsuffering of God! Do you know that it is the only explanation of why the world is still in existence? It is the only explanation of why God did not destroy the world in the Garden of Eden. It is the only explanation of why we are now in the twentieth century, though there has been this long history of sin. It is the longsuffering of God – the riches of His longsuffering.

Before we go on to the further arguments the Apostle works out, shall we pause here and ask ourselves a question? Am I a student of God's goodness? Am I a student of God's forbearance? Am I student of God's longsuffering? I am talking to Christian

[44]

people. Do you take your forgiveness as something that you have a right to, that you are entitled to, without remembering God's goodness and forbearance and longsuffering? Do you heal yourself very easily and very quickly? It seems to me that we have not really accepted forgiveness truly from God unless it brings us to the point at which we stand in amazement at His goodness, at His forbearance, at His longsuffering. God forbid that we should be guilty of just looking in a glancing manner at these things, and passing on to what we are interested in, we who claim His name and who know Him and who receive so much from Him. God forbid that we should be so unconcerned about those who are outside, those who are much more guilty of the same thing, infinitely more so. For they are in a sense producing their own damnation by their references to the love of God, because in their talk about it they are simply despising it.

Four

*

Or despisest thou the riches of his goodness and forbearance and longsuffering; not knowing that the goodness of God leadeth thee to repentance?

Romans 2 : 4

Let me begin by reminding you that in these opening verses of Romans chapter two Paul is dealing with the position of the Jews who were so ready to condemn the Gentiles and who felt that they themselves need have no fear of the wrath of God because they were His chosen people. We have dealt with Paul's first two arguments – that while condemning others they were condemning themselves, and that God has no favourites, but that His judgment is according to truth. We are now dealing with Paul's third argument, in which he deals with the position which holds that because of God's love and goodness He can never really punish sin.

The first part of this argument shows that people who talk glibly like that are actually despising God's goodness and that they have never really examined or studied it. Because if they really knew what it meant, they would spend their time in looking at it, and they would end by being amazed at it and worshipping God. But they do not do that.

Let us now come on to the second part of the argument. This attitude of despising God's goodness and longsuffering is guilty also in that it obviously regards God's goodness as something which, as it were, gives us licence to sin and to go on sinning. In other words, it regards God's love and mercy and compassion and forbearance as being something weak and flabby, something which has no element at all in it of righteousness or of justice. It is just a sort of indulgent idea. Perhaps the best way to explain this is to take up that word that the Apostle Peter uses in his Second Epistle, in chapter 3, verse 9, where he says, 'The Lord is not *slack* concerning his promise, as some men count slackness . . .'. Now that is the word. These people interpret God's goodness and forbearance and longsuffering as if it were nothing but slackness, something which looks very imposing on paper but in reality has no substance and no body at all.

I need not elaborate this because I think it should be quite obvious to all of us. And there is no doubt but that this is precisely the view that so many people do take of God's goodness. It is just some sort of slackness, something which pretends it has not seen our sin, or, if it has seen it, says, Oh well, after all that is not desperately serious, and though there is such a thing as justice and righteousness it must not be pressed as far as that. Let us just ignore it, and go on as if it had never happened. No, that is slackness. And there are people, as the Apostles say, who regard God's goodness and forbearance and longsuffering in that light, and that, I need scarcely prove to you, is to despise it. That attitude is utterly despicable. It really is not ennobling or uplifting at all. It is something that simply cannot be excused. Slackness is a moral weakness; it is something dissolute and has nothing to be said in its favour. And if we so view the goodness of God as to put it into some such category as that, we are patently guilty of despising it.

But that leads me to my third point, which is still more serious: to hold that view of God's goodness and forbearance and longsuffering is really, in the last analysis, to despise God Himself, because these attributes of God cannot be separated from God Himself, from His personality; they are expressions of God. So to hold this view of God's goodness is tantamount to despising the very character of God, it is to say that God Himself is indulgent towards sin – and again, that is precisely what so many people do say. You see, what it amounts to is that they say, 'Of course, God talks about righteousness and justice and so on, but in actual practice He does not do that; He says one thing but He does another. It is impossible that God should really punish, and you know He does not because God, after all, is love'. And so, you see, they imply a kind of central contradiction in the character and being of God Himself. It is to say that though God, through the law and through His servants, has constantly made these things perfectly and abundantly plain and clear, yet He does not really intend to do them at all.

Now there is surely nothing more insulting to God than just that very attitude, and what it leads to is that God's justice and righteousness are put on an even lower plane than the law of the land. It makes His justice something weaker even than that which is to be found in a father or a mother worthy of the name who really has the interests of the children at heart. But that is what it comes to. You know what you think of the kind of parent who is always telling the children what should be done and what should not be done, and what will happen if they do the wrong thing, and then, when the children do the wrong thing, smiles at them and takes no notice at all! Have you any respect for such a parent? What would you think of the law of a country which did that kind of thing? There are countries where that happens. On paper they have a very fine legal system, but they do not put it into practice, they have ways of avoiding it. Surely we tend to despise any such system.

Now, to regard God's goodness and forbearance and long-suffering in that kind of way; in a way which puts His justice and righteousness entirely out of court, and to feel that we can more or less do what we like, because God is so good and God is so kind; I say it is to represent God in terms in which we would not like to be represented ourselves as parents, and which we would not like to be true of the government and the judiciary of our own country. Let me put it like this: it is generally said that this biblical teaching about the justice, the righteousness and the wrath of God (as taught especially by the Apostle Paul) is something that is quite wrong, and one reason why it is wrong is that it represents God as a kind of Victorian father. That is something that has often been said during the past fifty to sixty years. They say, 'You know, that old theology, that view of God, was nothing but a sort of projection of the Victorian father, the stern Victorian father who, when he said to a child, "If you do that I will punish you", most certainly did punish him and perhaps punished him even more than he said he would. Now that is a misrepresentation of God'.

My reply is that if the God of the Bible is like the Victorian father, then the God of the modern man is like the modern father, and we know what that means. It means practically no discipline at all, no discipline in the home, and as a consequence, no discipline in the schools, and as a consequence, juvenile delinquency and all our modern troubles and problems. So if they do really want to argue in terms of natural fatherhood, there it seems to me is the complete answer. You see, the modern child, in the last analysis, does not have any respect at all for its parents, because they say something and do not do it. And though the child is very glad that it is not punished, it has lost its respect for the parent in the process. This illustrates how these ideas about God's goodness and forbearance and longsuffering are from every point of view guilty of despising the goodness of God. They make of it something small and cheap. As the child of that indulgent parent, who does not do what he said he would, loses its respect for the parent, so men who have such a view of God's goodness ultimately have a poor and debased view of God Himself. And that, of course, is precisely what is happening at the present time.

Or, fourthly, let me put it to you like this: this view of the goodness and the forbearance and the longsuffering of God is guilty, is it not, of using what it regards as the truth about God to serve its own ends, and I suppose there is no greater insult that we can offer to God than that. These people are primarily concerned about going on with the sinful kind of life which appeals to them. So they are unconsciously constructing a god for themselves who will allow them to do that. They are using God's goodness as a licence and a liberty, a cloak and an excuse for their own sin. And that is simply to use God – even God – to serve our own ends. I can imagine nothing more appalling than this, and yet it seems to me to be the controlling idea amongst people today with respect to God. They are manipulating, or trying to manipulate, even the character of God to serve their own ends. Man is in the centre. What man wants to do, what man likes doing, must be supreme; and God has got to be modified to fit in with what I want to do, and what I like. In other words, modern theology, liberalism, is thoroughly subjective. It starts with man, and everything has to be accommodated to suit man. It is not God-centred. It does not start with God. And the appalling result is that it despises God and insults Him to His face, even while it claims an allegiance to Him, and professes Him to be the God who has been revealed by our blessed Lord and Saviour Jesus Christ.

But now we come to the final argument, and this is the one that the Apostle puts before us most prominently at the end of the verse: 'Not knowing that the goodness of God leadeth thee to repentance'. Now this is the final way of despising God's goodness, and it is to fail completely to understand the object and the intent and the purpose of God's goodness. We have seen what they think the end of God's goodness is. It is the exact opposite of what God intends. And, of course, it is this that really accounts for all the other errors that I have been pointing out.

We must examine the second half of this fourth verse rather carefully because it is an important statement and one that can be easily misunderstood. It is a statement that for all who are interested in true doctrine and theology is one of the most fascinating statements in the whole of the Scripture. It is not an isolated statement – there are parallels to it, which I shall draw to your attention – but it is very significant.

So let us look at Paul's terms. First of all – *not knowing* – 'Not knowing that the goodness of God leadeth thee to repentance'. Now this term does not mean 'not considering'. Of course, it includes that: they do not consider it; but it does not only mean that. Neither does it mean simply 'not acknowledging'. Again, it includes that, but the term itself means more than that. It means 'not understanding', 'not comprehending the true nature'. But it goes even further than that. There is in this term 'not knowing' a suggestion of a wilful character. Someone has translated it as 'a contemptuous unconcern about it'. 'Not knowing that the goodness of God leadeth thee to repentance' – not caring that the goodness of God is designed to lead you to repentance.

Now, let me show you a parallel to it, and again I take you back to 2 Peter 3 : 4–5. The Apostle, you remember, is depicting there these people who continually say, 'Where is the promise of his coming?' These 'scoffers' who will be in the world in the last days, and who, when they are told about the coming of the Lord Jesus Christ to judgment and to wind up the affairs of this world, will keep on saying, 'Where is the promise of his coming?' And Peter says, 'For since the fathers fell asleep, all things continue as they were from the beginning of the creation'. 'It is no use saying that to us', people say. 'You cannot frighten us. You know, we are living in the twentieth century, and we have heard this sort of thing before. But look at history, it is still going on! Where is the promise of his coming?' Now this is the trouble with them, says Peter, 'For this they *willingly are ignorant of . . .*'. They are not only ignorant, they are willingly ignorant – there is a deliberate element. Now that is what we have in our statement here – 'not knowing'. The fact of the matter is that they ought to know, that there is no excuse for their not knowing, because the evidence is there, the facts are before them. And they do not know them because they do not want to know them. It would be very inconvenient for them to know them. So that they do not know them deliberately – they are deliberately, contemptuously ignoring the statements and the facts. Willingly ignorant.

I think you will see at once what a tremendous castigation this is. And, of course, it applies to men and women today, especially all those who live in a country where the gospel is being preached freely. Indeed, as the Apostles and others argue in various places, and as we saw in Acts 14, where Paul preached to the heathen at Lystra, even the heathen, the pagans, are left without excuse, because God has not left himself without witness. So this ignorance is a deliberate thing which is without any excuse at all. It is a contemptuous unconcern, for they have no reason for being ignorant. And why is it that they have no reason? Because God's goodness 'leadeth thee to repentance'.

There, then, is our second term, *leadeth*, and here we arrive at what has often proved to be a very difficult statement, which has often led to a good deal of discussion and debate and confusion. The Apostle's statement is that God's goodness leads them to repentance, and we need to know what he means by this. Why does he use this particular term? In Romans 8 : 14, he says, 'For as many as are *led* by the Spirit of God, they are the sons of God', and that is exactly the same word as we have here, where we are told that the goodness of God 'leadeth thee unto repentance'. Now this term does not, of course, mean forcing; it does not mean driving or bludgeoning. What it obviously means is a constraining influence. That is what you do when you lead a horse, or a dog, or any other animal. You are bringing to bear a constraining influence if you are holding the reins or the halter, or whatever it may be. There is no force of necessity, but there is a sense of constraint, there is an influence, a constraining influence, and what the Apostle says is that God's goodness exercises this kind of constraining influence on men to bring them to repentance.

In view of that, then, we again have to ask what exactly he is teaching here. It is important that we should be clear about our terms, and the first thing we notice is that he is talking about unbelievers. These are the people who are not brought to repentance, therefore they are the unbelievers. And what the Apostle says is that they are without excuse because they are despising the goodness of God which was meant to bring them to repentance.

Now you see where the difficulty arises in the realm of theology. Here are unbelievers who die unrepentant, and yet the Apostle says that the goodness of God leads them, exercises this constraining influence upon them, to bring them to repentance. And it is not surprising that this has often been a bone of contention, and has engaged the attention of those who desire to have a truer understanding of God's way of salvation and of how any single one of us ever does come to believe on the Lord Jesus Christ.

So what do we make of this? We must go back again to 2 Peter 3, this time to verse 9. Is it not interesting to notice the parallel between these Apostles? Always where you come across a difficult place in Scripture the thing to do is to compare Scripture with Scripture, to find another one, a parallel statement, something that is similar, and here it is: 'The Lord is not slack concerning his promise, as some men count slackness; but is longsuffering to us-ward, not willing that any should perish, but that all should come to repentance'. You notice it is saying almost precisely the same thing. And do you know that there are other statements in the Scriptures which speak to the same effect. You will find in Ezekiel 33 : 11, for instance, that God says, 'I have no pleasure in the death of the wicked'. And you will find other statements in the Scriptures in which God, as it were, appeals to them, to the nation of Israel, and beyond the nation of Israel to all people, with the word 'Oh!' And you remember how our Lord Himself wept over Jerusalem and said,

'O Jerusalem, Jerusalem . . . how often would I . . . and ye would not!' [*Matthew* 23:37].

Now all these statements are parallels with the statement in this passage and therefore I must ask this question: What, then, is God's goodness meant to do with regard to the unbeliever? For it is the unbeliever with whom we are dealing. There are people who have tried to evade this difficulty by saying that this statement means that God has shown His goodness to the unbeliever to render him without a single excuse; that He causes His sun to rise on the evil and the good, and sends His rain on the just and the unjust, so that at the day of judgment they will have nothing to say. God's goodness will be the answer to their every excuse. And yet, you see, we cannot accept that as an explanation, because if the Apostle had meant to say that, he would have put it in that way, and he would never have used the word 'leadeth'. This word is too active and positive a word for that. If that had been merely God's object, it would have had no effect upon them, it would not have been designed to have an effect upon man. But you cannot use the word 'lead' without getting this idea of a constraining influence. When you talk about somebody leading somebody else or of being led by a truth, it is very positive. That other idea just leaves it there on the wall, as it were, passive and negative, there merely to rob me negatively of any chance of excusing myself. But this is an active word.

What then, does it mean? It seems to me that there is only one conclusion we can come to, and that is that God's goodness is meant and designed to bring men to repentance and salvation; and when I say 'men' I mean all men, unbelievers as well as believers. We are dealing with unbelievers here. The Apostle is arguing with men who will not repent and he says, even to them, that God's goodness leads you, was meant and designed to lead you, to repentance. So the Apostle here is teaching that God manifests a positive favour even to the unbeliever – and that is where the importance of being clear about these matters comes in.

It is, as I have shown, a parallel with what our Lord teaches in the Sermon on the Mount: '. . . for he maketh his sun to rise on the evil and on the good, and sendeth rain on the just and on the unjust' [*Matthew* 5 : 45]. At that point, you remember, the Lord is talking to the disciples, and He tells them that they are to be perfect even as their Father which is in heaven is perfect; He tells them to love their enemies, and to do good to them that hate them. He says, you should do it because God does it. So we are to love our enemies as God loves His enemies. He loves the unbeliever and He shows that love in this goodness through the sun and the rain. There is the parallel.

We find the same again in Paul's sermon at Lystra in Acts 14. But indeed it seems to me to be parallel also with what the Apostle has already been saying in chapter 1 : 20, where he says, 'For the invisible things of him from the creation of the world are clearly seen, being understood by the things that are made, even his eternal power and Godhead; so that they are without excuse'. So the teaching must be that this goodness of God is a manifestation of God's grace to all men, sinners and unbelievers included. By these things He would lead all men to repentance and therefore to salvation. For as I have already quoted from 2 Peter 3 : 9, He does not wish that any should perish but that all should come to repentance.

Now then, where have we landed? 'Does that mean', says someone, 'that you are completely denying the doctrine of predestination and election?' It sounds like it, does it not? But I am not. How, then, you may ask, do you reconcile these things? In this way: this is the manifestation of *a* grace of God, but it is obviously not efficacious grace; it is not effectual grace; it is not a constraining grace; it is not the irresistible grace. Because, although God manifests this grace to these people, it does not lead them to repentance. It is meant to, and it is designed to, but it does not do so. Why not?

Well, the answer is – and here we come up against a great mystery which we shall never solve in this world – there is clearly a difference between what God desires and what God wills and brings to pass. What God wills He performs and brings into being. But – and this is the astounding thing that we are told – God does not wish that any should perish. He wishes that all should come to repentance. There are some who are brought to repentance, there are some who are not. It is *God* who brings to repentance, for no man left to himself would repent – this text proves that once and for ever with an unusual clarity. Though God manifests His goodness and His forbearance and His longsuffering, men despise it, they use it to serve themselves, their own ends, and their sins. They pass it by, they do not trouble to look at it. Though God has manifested His grace, and though He meant it to bring them to repentance, it does not do so. No one would repent if God did not bring us to repentance by an act of His will and by His constraining and effectual grace.

Now let me try to elaborate that a little, because it is important if we want to be clear about the Scriptures we are studying. We shall find the same thing again as we go on in this Epistle – it is at the very heart of chapter nine. It is there, as we have seen, in 2 Peter 3 : 9, it is in 1 Timothy 2 : 6, and so on. It is in many places in the Bible, and it is our business as Bible students and those who are anxious to glorify God, to come to an understanding of these things.

So consider yet another example of this in Acts chapter seventeen. The Apostle Paul, preaching at Athens, said, 'The times of this ignorance God winked at; but now *commandeth* all men every where to repent'. That is an absolutely universal statement; you cannot imagine anything more all-inclusive than that. In other words, the gospel is to be preached to all creatures. The offer of salvation is to be made to everybody. Not to some, but to all.

Now if you want to know what hyper-Calvinism means, it is the teaching which says that the gospel is only to be offered to some. And I have had the distinction of being called a dangerous Arminian by people who hold that belief, because I say that the gospel should be offered to all. God commandeth all men everywhere to repent, which means that if you repent, then you come to salvation, it is the first step in it. Yes, and therefore the offer of salvation, the offer of Christ and His perfect work, should be preached to all men without distinction. And that message is to be preached in order that men may come to know God's goodness and in order that they may yield to it. I say, therefore, that God wishes that all men should come to repentance and to salvation, but it is equally clear that He does not will it. Then that leads me to say that this extraordinary statement here in the second half of Romans 2 : 4 gives the lie directly to all who try to argue that what the gospel does is to persuade us to repent. It is an absolute proof that we cannot be persuaded. God has manifested His goodness, His forbearance,

His longsuffering. He has commanded that all men everywhere should repent. There is all the moral suasion that you can ever get.

But what it leads to in the case of the unbelievers is that they despise it. That is what the natural man does with it. Moral suasion will never save anybody. No man is saved simply by the influence or the general effect of the appeal of the gospel upon him. No man can repent or believe until he has a new nature. He must be *born again*, because 'the natural man receiveth not the things of the Spirit of God: for they are foolishness unto him: neither can he know them, because they are spiritually discerned [1 *Corinthians* 2 : 14]. The natural mind is enmity against God; it is not subject to the law of God, neither indeed can be. So when God commands such a man to repent, he defies God and says he does not want to repent. When God showers His goodness upon him to lead him to repentance, he despises it. It is God alone who saves, by the mighty operation of His Holy Spirit in the depth of the soul and of the personality.

If ever a text, which on the surface seemed to be saying the opposite, proved that, it is this text – the goodness of God is designed to lead men to repentance. It does not do so. It never has done so. Man will always use God's goodness to serve himself. He will trade on it. He will make merchandise of it. The last thing he does is so to see it that he repents. That is not what makes a man repent. It is the operation of the Holy Spirit in giving a man a new mind, a new outlook and a new understanding. The first proof that a man has been born again is that he repents and believes the gospel. That is the order of salvation. I commend to you the wisdom of working out this text again. Study it, take it with its parallels, and I think you will see that it will bring you to that inevitable conclusion.

Very well, then, that brings us to our last term, which is the term *repentance*. This is the grand New Testament term, and all I want to say about it here is this: it is the term that is always found at the beginning. 'The goodness of God leadeth thee . . .' he does not say to salvation, he does not say to accept Christ as Saviour. No! 'The goodness of God leadeth thee to repentance' – first. It is the thing he puts in the forefront. And you know the whole gospel, does the same. Who is the first preacher in the New Testament? He is John the Baptist. What did he preach?

The baptism of repentance for the remission of sins. That is the first note always in gospel preaching. The first business of the preacher of salvation is to call men to repentance.

Look further: it is not only true of John the Baptist, our Lord did the same thing. Read in Mark the account of the beginning of our Lord's ministry and you will find that we are told that he went and preached everywhere that men should repent. Repentance! You start with it. Obviously you do not see the need of a Saviour unless you have seen yourself as a sinner and in the wrong relationship to God. It must be repentance first, otherwise you are not interested in salvation – at least not in New Testament salvation. If I mean by salvation just having a nice, happy feeling, or hoping to get rid of certain physical ailments or something like that, then, of course, I can have it without repentance, but if I want to know God, which is salvation, I must repent first. There it is in our Lord's ministry.

And then, you remember the first sermon ever preached under the auspices of the Christian church, Peter's sermon on the Day of Pentecost at Jerusalem? He was preaching, and the effect of his preaching was such that men began to cry out, saying, 'Men and brethren, what shall we do?' And this is the answer: 'Repent, every one of you'. He did not say, 'Come to Christ and you can repent later'; he said, 'Repent and be baptized every one of you in the name of Jesus Christ for the remission of sins, and ye shall receive the gift of the Holy Ghost' [*Acts* 2:38]. Repentance is always the first.

What of the Apostle Paul? It is still the same. In that lyrical account in Acts chapter twenty the great Apostle, saying farewell to the elders of the church at Ephesus, says to them: You remember my ministry, 'I . . . have taught you publickly, and from house to house . . . by the space of three years I ceased not to warn every one night and day with tears' [vv. 20, 31]. What did he preach? The repentance that is toward God, and faith toward the Lord Jesus Christ [v. 21]. But you notice the order – repentance first. And here it is in this verse that we are looking at together – 'not knowing' – not paying attention to the fact, deliberately ignoring, contemptuously and wilfully being ignorant of the fact that 'the goodness of God was designed and meant to lead you to repentance'.

In studying this verse, we have not only been handling a

rather difficult subject, but have been looking into something marvellous and wonderful, something inscrutable, something, I take it, that we will never fully understand throughout eternity, and it is this: how God, being who and what He is, could ever show any grace or love or kindness to those who have not only sinned and rebelled against Him, but whom He knows will remain finally impenitent. But He does so, and He addresses them like this, 'Oh that ye had known!' I do not pretend to be able to put these things into such intellectual order that no difficulties are left. There are difficulties. But, my dear friends, we are talking about God and we are but human beings! We are looking into the eternal, the character of God, and our business is to accept our Scriptures, not to try to evade a problem like this by saying, 'Ah, it is just there in order to render them without excuse'. No. The word 'leadeth' is active and positive, we have had to face it. And there, it seems to me, is the only answer – He wishes the salvation of all, but He does not will it, for what God wills He brings to pass. But here, to me, is the mystery – that He wishes this, that He wishes their salvation and proves it by His goodness and forbearance and longsuffering. He wishes that even those who are impenitent should finally have repented and come to salvation. 'Oh the depth of the riches both of the wisdom and knowledge of God! how unsearchable are his judgments, and his ways past finding out!'

Let us therefore, my dear friends, tread carefully. Let us approach these high and great and abstruse matters with reverence and with godly fear. Above all, let us be careful of passing judgment upon God and what He does. That is what these people do who are without excuse, these despisers of His goodness. Let us, then, in a spirit of adoration and worship look at the words that the Holy Spirit gave to the Apostle, let us give them their full content, and let us always beware of pressing any statement by our own logic beyond its own meaning and its own context. But above all, let us always be careful to compare Scripture with Scripture, lest in our ignorance and haste we be guilty of so describing God as to make Him contradict Himself, and, indeed, of having a contradiction at the very centre and heart of His own life and eternal being. What a privilege to be allowed to look into these things! Let us thank God.

Five

*

Or despisest thou the riches of his goodness and forbearance and longsuffering; not knowing that the goodness of God leadeth thee to repentance? But after thy hardness and impenitent heart treasurest up unto thyself wrath against the day of wrath and revelation of the righteous judgment of God.

Romans 2 : 4–5

We are still dealing, you remember, with Paul's arguments against the position of the Jews. The first was that they were guilty of the very things that they condemned in others, but were unconscious of their utter inconsistency in so doing and did not see that they condemned themselves in condemning others. The second was their failure to remember that the judgment of God is always according to truth. And now we are considering his third argument, which is their complete misunderstanding of the biblical teaching concerning the goodness of God, and the forbearance and the longsuffering of God, and especially as he puts it like this – 'not knowing . . .'. And that is wilful, remember, choosing not to know, regarding with contempt: 'Not knowing that the goodness of God leadeth thee to repentance'.

We have looked in detail at the word 'leadeth', and now therefore we must consider this great and all-important word *repentance*. Let me emphasize again that it is of very great importance for us to observe that this is always the first note in gospel preaching. First and foremost the gospel calls us to repentance. I have given quotations, and shown how John the Baptist preached the baptism of repentance for the remission of sins. There is the herald of the gospel. Our Lord went and preached everywhere that men should repent. Peter on the Day of Pentecost brings it out like a thunderbolt – 'Repent', he says, 'and be baptized every one of you in the name of Jesus Christ'. And, as we saw, the Apostle Paul, in saying farewell to the elders of the church at Ephesus, reminds them that his ministry was to preach the repentance that is towards God, and the faith that is towards the Lord Jesus Christ.

Now this question of order is very important. Obviously it is one of those determinative points in the whole matter of evangelism, and I think you will agree that this is surely something that we are tending to forget at the present time. The idea seems to have come in that the business of preaching is to bring people to Christ and that later on they will repent. Now it is no accident that in the Scriptures themselves the order is always put otherwise, and, surely, it is very dangerous for us if, purely for the sake of results, we vary and reverse this clear scriptural order, which has always characterized the preaching of the church in every great period of revival and reawakening. It is not surprising that there is but little evidence of a sense of sin these days, or that it is a rare thing to see anyone weeping under conviction; it is not surprising that it is a rare thing to hear anyone going through an agony of soul because of his or her consciousness of sinfulness in the presence of a holy God. If we do not preach repentance, of course, we cannot expect to see such things. If we go back and read the great story of the Christian church in every period of revival and reawakening, we will find that this note of repentance has always been central and it has always been primary.

However, I leave it at that and pass on, because we must consider what, exactly, repentance means: 'The goodness of God leadeth thee to repentance'. Now a very convenient way of looking at it is just to take two words, the Latin word, which is the one from which our word repentance comes, and also the Greek word which covers this term. The Latin term 'repent' means 'think again', you think – again. In other words, you have normally thought in a given manner, and the effect of the call to repentance, which is the effect of God's goodness, should be to cause us to stop and think again.

There are many illustrations of this in the Scripture, but the one that invariably appeals to me is the one which we find in Matthew 21 : 28–32, where our Lord Jesus Christ Himself, in the so-called Parable of the Two Sons, spoke on this very matter of repentance: 'A certain man had two sons; and he came to the first, and said, Son, go work to-day in my vineyard. He answered and said, I will not: but afterward he repented, and went. And he came to the second, and said likewise. And he answered and said, I go, sir: and went not. Whether of them twain did the will of his father? They say unto him, The first. Jesus saith unto them, Verily I say unto you, That the publicans and the harlots go into the kingdom of God before you. For John came unto you in the way of righteousness, and ye believed him not: but the publicans and the harlots believed him: and ye, when ye had seen it, repented not afterward, that ye might believe him'.

Now it is this first son who is the important one, because here we see that the first thing about repentance is that we 'think again'. Here is a young man whose father tells him to go and work in his vineyard. He says he will not, but then we see him going to the vineyard. What, then, has happened to him? Well, obviously, he must have thought about the question a second time – he thought again. It is always an essential part of repentance. There are certain things we all seem to have made up our minds about before we came into this world! For instance, the natural man does not believe in Christianity; he is already against it. He does not turn against it, he *starts* by being against it, and no man becomes a Christian, therefore, without thinking again. The average man in this country today has made up his mind about these things, and he will not listen to them. So, if ever such a man becomes a Christian it means of necessity that he must have thought again – and repented.

But obviously merely thinking again is not enough by itself, and that is where the Latin word from which our word comes, is really not sufficient. You see, that first son in our Lord's parable may have thought again about the command but still have come to the same conclusion. But obviously he did not, he came to a different conclusion. Now the Greek word for repentance is a word that carries the idea of a 'change of mind'. Not only looking at a subject and thinking about it again, but changing your mind about it, coming to a different decision, arriving at a different conclusion. So there is the second element.

[61]

And the third element is equally obvious: repentance involves action, because a man acts according to his thinking, and this first son, having said to his father, 'I will not', had not gone to the vineyard. But then, when he thought again and changed his mind, he repented and went, and that going was a part of the repentance. In other words, repentance is not something detached and theoretical and academic. Repentance does include the idea of not only a change of mind but a change of a course of action, a change in the whole direction and habit of one's life.

What, then, are the things about which we do change our mind and our course of action when we repent? First and foremost, we do this with respect to God Himself. That is clear in the immediate context of these verses in Romans chapter two. Here are people who look at the goodness and the forbearance and the longsuffering of God, and they come to a certain conclusion. But it is wrong; and, in coming to a wrong conclusion about that, they are coming to a wrong conclusion about the very character of God Himself. And that is the teaching of the Scripture everywhere. The natural mind is enmity against God, its thoughts about God are wrong and unworthy. The natural man either does not think about God at all, or if he does, he thinks of Him as some great tyrant who is set against man, someone who is unfair. We hear a lot of this during these present days – 'Why does God allow this and that?' That is the question; there is the enmity. You see the view of God that is expressed by these questions – 'If God is a God of love, why does He allow spastics? Why does He allow war?' . . . And so on. That is man's attitude towards the character and being of God, towards God's greatness, His justice, His love, His mercy and His compassion. The natural man has a totally wrong view of God and of His purposes and plans, and that was the trouble with the Jews.

The first thing, then, that happens when a man repents is that he begins to think differently about God. Repentance is the exact reversal of what happened in the Garden of Eden, when the devil tempted Eve and then Adam. The first thing insinuated into the mind of Eve was wrong thoughts: 'Hath God said?' Is God fair in saying it? Is not God against you in saying such a thing? And there, at the beginning, they accepted it, and the wrong view of God first came into the world. Repentance just reverses all that. We begin to realize that all our ideas of God have been totally wrong.

The sense in which repentance leads to action can be seen in what Job did when God Himself had spoken to him. In Job 40 : 4 we read that the first thing he did was put his hand upon his mouth. He had been talking wildly and loosely, but when he came, as it were, into the presence of God and God revealed Himself to him, Job put his hand upon his mouth, he did not want to speak, he was afraid to utter a word. He saw then how wrong he had been in so many of his ideas. That is an essential part of repentance. The Jews were constantly sinning in this respect, and the great purpose of Paul's preaching was to bring them to this new conception of God.

We must emphasize this, for some people seem to think of repentance only in terms of actions. They think repentance means that a man stops getting drunk or being an adulterer or whatever else it may be, and begins to live a different life. But that is the end of repentance, not the beginning. The beginning is this changed attitude towards God, this new thinking about God Himself; thinking about God in terms of the scriptural revelation rather than in terms of our own ideas and our philosophies and our arguments from man to God, instead of from God to man. That is the first thing.

But obviously it also means that we think differently about ourselves, and this is quite inevitable. It is our thinking about God that controls our thinking about ourselves. And so, secondly, we, who are 'in sin', need to think about ourselves in a different way, to think again and to change our minds about ourselves. By nature we all think that we are very good and very nice people. We think that God is not really very fair to us, that we are having a very hard time, and that if only we were given an opportunity, the world would be perfect. But the moment we begin really to know ourselves we begin to say, 'Vile, and full of sin I am! I am *all* unrighteousness!' 'In me (that is, in my flesh) dwelleth no good thing'. That is how the repentant man speaks. He changes his view of himself. Having admired himself and praised himself, having found no defects in himself, though many, always, in others, he begins to see, as one of the old Puritans, I believe, put it, that he is 'nothing but

[63]

a mass of corruption', that he is, in other words, a festering sore!

Now that is the language which Scripture itself uses with respect to man in sin, and it is a tremendous thing when we begin to get this new view of ourselves, when we no longer say, 'God is not fair to us!' What amazes us, now, is how God tolerates us at all! We no longer feel that we have any claim on His love and we are reduced to tears when we realize that, in spite of our being what we are, and God being what He is, He nevertheless has had mercy and compassion, and there is such a thing as grace. That is repentance! And you see how important it is to define it like this? It is not only a matter of actions, it is a man's view of himself as well. Do we abhor ourselves? Job did and he said so. He hated himself. Indeed, you cannot read the Bible without seeing that all these men who have come to know God have felt like that. Furthermore, when you read Christian biographies you will find that these people, too, have all said that they have hated and despised themselves. I am not arguing that we should all feel this to the same intensity as the greatest saints, but I am arguing that surely we cannot claim to have repented unless that is to some degree our view of ourselves. Self-defence goes when we repent, when we feel we deserve nothing but punishment. We realize that we are paupers, that we are vile. Man, then, changes his view about himself.

And, of course, thirdly, he changes his view about everything else. His whole view of life is different. Before this, his idea of life was, really, what the world is enjoying today, or what it persuades itself that it is enjoying. But the moment a man repents, he has an entirely different view of life in this world. He sees himself in the light of God and before God. He now sees life as a journey in the direction of God, not as a place into which you come to settle down and just have a so-called good time, and let yourself go, and live like an animal obeying the lusts of the flesh, and so on. No! He sees man now as someone with a great and glorious destiny. Like those great men depicted in Hebrews chapter eleven, he sees life as a journey, as a pilgrimage. He is but a sojourner in this world, he is travelling home to God, and his whole view of life and of death and of everything that happens to him becomes different. That is a part of repentance.

Of course, as a consequence of all these things his conduct undergoes a very profound change. But – and this is what I want to emphasize again – the conduct and the behaviour are the *end result* of repentance, not the beginning and not the whole of it. The conduct and the behaviour must of necessity change, because of the changed view of God and man, of life and death and judgment and eternity, and all these tremendous things. This, then, is what the Apostle is arguing – that the goodness of God and His forbearance and His longsuffering were meant to lead us to repentance, and that, patently, if we fail to arrive there, we are entirely misunderstanding the goodness of God – indeed, we are guilty of despising the goodness of God.

Now God reveals this goodness and forbearance and this longsuffering in order that we may ask questions. We should say, for example, 'I wonder why God does that? Do we deserve it?' We begin to think again, and having done that, we should change our minds about all these things. And we should end by saying, 'Is it not wonderful that God ever blesses this world at all – the world that He made and which rebelled against Him and sinned against Him? Why does He send the rain and the sunshine? Why does He not blast us all out of existence and immediately condemn us for all eternity?' That is the kind of question that the goodness and the longsuffering of God should lead us to ask. And as we question we should end by being amazed at His mercy, His compassion, His forbearance, and His longsuffering, and we should end by worshipping Him. But, says the Apostle, these people do not know – 'Not knowing that the goodness of God leadeth to repentance'.

But Paul does not leave it at that, because that is not the only thing which they do not know. Indeed, it seems to me that at this point the Apostle is gathering together a number of things which the Jews, particularly, and all who are in their position and who have that attitude, do not know. We have looked at the first. But let us now consider the others that he elaborates in the fifth verse. He has shown that they despise the goodness and the forbearance and the longsuffering of God, and now here he tells us that they also do not realize *why* they despise it; they do not realize what it is in them that accounts for the fact that instead of being led by this goodness to worship God and to repent, and to yield themselves to Him, and to believe in His Son, they do the exact opposite. Why is this? And that, says Paul, is what they are ignorant of; they are ignorant of *their hardness and their impenitent heart*.

This again is a profound matter of doctrine. I take first the word 'heart' because this can well be translated like this: 'But after thy hard and impenitent heart'. The hardness applies to the heart as much as does the impenitence. According to the Apostle here – and we find the same teaching everywhere in the Scripture – the trouble with man in sin is in his heart, and here by heart is meant the centre of personality. It does not merely mean the emotions or the affections. It includes that. But the heart stands for the very seat and centre and throne of personality and there, according to the scriptural teaching, is the seat of sin. The essence of sin is to be found there and nowhere else. I need not dilate here on how completely that is in contrast with the modern view of sin, which says that a man is really all right in his heart, but that he goes wrong in this respect or that respect. It is exactly the other way round. It is the heart, says the Bible, that is wrong, and men are only right in patches on the surface.

Let me demonstrate this from Scripture. We have, indeed, already seen the same truth in the first chapter, in verse 21, where Paul says, 'Because that, when they knew God, they glorified him not as God, neither were thankful; but became vain in their imaginations, and their foolish *heart* was darkened'. We find the same again in Hebrews 3 : 12 where the author warns the people to whom he is writing against 'an evil heart of unbelief', and Jeremiah, too, has already said it in chapter seventeen, verse 9, of his prophecy: 'The heart is deceitful above all things, and desperately wicked: who can know it?' The heart is the trouble, you see. And our Lord Himself has said, 'Out of the heart of men proceed evil thoughts, adulteries, fornications, murders . . .' The whole source of trouble with mankind, says our Lord, is this evil heart which is in man: 'Whatsoever thing from without entereth into the man, it cannot defile him . . . That which cometh out of the man, that defileth the man' [*Mark* 7 : 18, 20]. Now this is obviously fundamental for us. The trouble with man is not in his intellect and not merely in his mind, though there is trouble in his mind. Alas, the trouble with man is very much deeper than that.

That is where all who are not Christian go wrong; and it is, of course, at the basis of the pathetic belief, especially in the last hundred years, that you have nothing to do but educate men and women and they will live a good life. You see, it has been believed. But we are living, today, in a world which shows how nonsensical it is. The world, in a sense, has never been as highly educated as it is now, but here we are almost on the verge of war again. What is the matter? There is only one answer; it is the evil heart that is in man. 'Why are there wars among you? It is because of your lusts and your passions', says James. Man is not just an intellect; there is something in him which is much more powerful than his intellect, and that is what is called his heart. It does not matter how brilliant a brain a man may have, nor how highly educated he may be, he is governed much more by his instincts and by that which is elemental in him, than by his higher senses. If that were not so, educated people would never pass through the divorce courts, and they would never behave as cads, and there would be no such thing as infidelity and immorality. But it does not matter what the brain is like, there is something more fundamental – this flesh that the Apostle talks about, this 'law in my members warring against the law of my mind'. And that is the most powerful thing in man. It is deeper than his brain; it is his heart, says the Apostle, this hard and impenitent heart.

Now the more we grasp that truth, the more we shall see the absolute necessity of an operation by the Holy Spirit of God before a man can ever be a Christian. I have already quoted what the Apostle says about this in chapter eight of this great Epistle. The natural mind, he says, (and there he is including the whole man again), 'is enmity against God.' The trouble with man, again, is 'enmity against God'. It is not simply that he does not believe in God; he hates Him! And it is no use disputing it; it is a fact. Man in sin *hates* God. There is a vituperation, there is an antipathy, there is a veritable hatred in the heart of man. That is why men are always hoping that at last somebody, some scientist or other, will succeed in proving that there is not a God. How delighted the whole world would be! Why? Because they hate Him. It is something very deep. So we must emphasize this word 'heart'.

And then I take up the word 'hard' – 'after thy hardness . . .' –

after thy hard heart. Here, of course, the picture is a perfectly clear one. It is a sort of callosity, a corn, if you like; as, for example, the skin of the hands may become hardened by manual labour. But let us look at this hardness in a different way. Take a lump of clay, which you can mould and fashion almost as you like. Put it out in the blazing sunshine and it will become as hard as a brick. I think there is something of that idea here, and I look at it like this: the goodness and the forbearance and the longsuffering of God are shining down upon mankind like the sun, and they are meant to soften and to melt us, but what they do to these people is to harden them. The sun does both things – it melts butter, but it hardens clay. And, according to the Apostle here, it is always one or the other. That is why the preaching of the gospel and listening to the gospel both carry such a tremendous responsibility – they either soften or they harden. They are bound to do one or the other. And what Paul says here is that these people, because of their completely wrong attitude, are hardened by the very thing that was meant to melt them, and to soften them. Hardness!

Again, you find this running right through the scriptural teaching. Turning once more to Hebrews, we read in chapter three, verse 13: '. . . lest any of you be hardened through the deceitfulness of sin'. Sin in its deceitfulness hardens us, it hardens our hearts. That is a terrible process – for process is what it is. Every time we refuse to listen to God's voice we are correspondingly harder, and it is going to be more difficult next time. It is a process of hardening: '. . . lest any of you be hardened through the deceitfulness of sin'. And in the life story of an individual you can often trace this process of hardening as it goes on. It is a terrible and a very realistic term. And the terrible thing is to contemplate the fact that it is the love and the mercy and the compassion of God that, as it were, produces the hardening. If you do not respond to it, it will harden you.

And that brings me to the word 'impenitent', and you notice how these terms which he uses are the opposites, as it were, of all that he has been saying in verse 4: 'Despisest thou the riches of his goodness and forbearance and longsuffering' – shining like the sun, in other words – 'not knowing that the goodness of God leadeth thee to repentance?' Ah! But they do not; they do the exact opposite – they lead to an 'impenitent heart'. And an impenitent heart is a heart that is so hard, with such callosities upon it, that it cannot repent. You remember we are told about a king in the Old Testament who was on the point of being punished, but when the prophet spoke to him he accepted the teaching, and God said to him, 'Because thine heart was tender . . .' [2 *Kings* 22 : 19]. God forgave him because his heart was tender, a softening had come in. 'Saviour', says the hymn, 'while my heart is tender, I would yield that heart to Thee . . .'. That is it. And it is only the man who has a tender heart who ever desires to yield to the Lord. But as for these people, their hearts are hard, and so they are incapable of repentance.

Now this again is a great truth in Scripture. Work it out for yourselves. What we are told is that this is what happens to us in regeneration. God says, through the prophet Ezekiel, 'I will take the stony heart out of their flesh, and will give them an heart of flesh' [*Ezekiel* 11 : 19]. The stony heart can never be softened, it is set and fixed and you can do nothing with it. It cannot respond, so we need a change of heart, a new heart, and we are given a heart of flesh which can respond. The stone, as it were, is taken out and the flesh is put in.

But the kind of man whom Paul is describing does not realize that he has this hard impenitent heart. As we have seen, he does not know *why* he is as he is. He thinks it is a matter of knowledge, he thinks it is a matter of learning; he does not realize that his trouble is deep down in the very depths of his heart, and it is the business of preaching to convince men of that.

But let us look at the third thing which such a man does not know. He does not realize either, says the Apostle, what he is doing, quite inevitably, by despising the goodness of God. What is he doing? Well, Paul says, he is treasuring up for himself wrath: 'But after thy hardness and impenitent heart treasurest up unto thyself wrath against the day of wrath and revelation of the righteous judgment of God'. Now this, in many senses, is an extraordinary and, indeed, a terrifying statement. Again you notice a contrast with verse 4. In verse 4 Paul talks about 'the riches of his goodness and forbearance and longsuffering', and here, in a sense, he is talking about 'riches' again. There God has treasured up His goodness, here man is treasuring up wrath for himself! You notice the play on words? Paul is bringing out the antithesis. We can put it like this: man in refusing the stored up riches of God's goodness is storing up for himself wrath. This word 'storing up' is interesting. We talk about a thesaurus, and that is the very word – something where meanings of words are stored up. And that, the Apostle tells us, is just what is happening.

Now this is the most terrible thing to contemplate. Think of the unbeliever, think of a person at this moment who is not a Christian. Here he is, he is misunderstanding and ignoring God's goodness and longsuffering and forbearance, and he does not repent. He just goes on and makes use of it to suit his own ends. What is he doing? Well, he is storing up something for himself. Think of the picture of a man treasuring up something. He is a collector – of pearls, if you like. He finds one, and takes it home. Then he unlocks his cabinet, puts the pearl inside, and locks it up again. Then he gets another, and he puts that one in too. He is 'treasuring up', he is 'storing up'. That is exactly what the unbeliever is doing, says the Apostle. He does not realize it, but he is doing it nevertheless. In this way he is treasuring up wrath. And the terrible thing is that it is the man himself who is doing this. Paul does not say that God is doing it – 'But after thy hardness and impenitent heart treasurest up *unto thyself* wrath'. This is the truly alarming and terrifying thing. It would be terrible if every time we were guilty of this, God, as it were, put a mark down; but according to this teaching it is the man himself who is doing it; he is treasuring up for himself. *He* is the one who is locking up all this for himself. Each time he despises God's goodness this kind of individual is simply storing up for himself this wrath of God against sin, and he does not know it.

But the last thing which he does not know is this. He does not know, he does not realize, what finally awaits him. And what is that? It is the day of wrath, the day of the revelation of the righteous judgment of God. Here again is something which we surely need to put before the whole world at a time like this. We are living in a century of wars, a century of judgments: it is the only explanation.

That is the meaning of these wars, they are a part of God's punishment upon sin. We saw that earlier when we considered the end of Romans chapter one. God is giving the world over in its sin and in its arrogance. He is giving it over to a 'reprobate mind'. He is allowing it to reap the consequences of its own false attitude towards Him. But all these things, the two world wars, what is happening at the present time, are but pale adumbrations of something which is to come, and that something which is to come is the day of wrath: '[Thou] treasurest up unto thyself wrath against the day of wrath and revelation of the righteous judgment of God'.

If you are familiar with your Scriptures you will know that everywhere in the Bible we are taught that there is to be a definite *day* of judgment, a particular day. The Apostle Paul, when preaching in Athens, said: 'God . . . now commandeth all men every where to repent: because he hath appointed a day, in the which he will judge the world in righteousness by that man whom he hath ordained; whereof he hath given assurance unto all men, in that he hath raised him from the dead' [*Acts* 17 : 30–31]. He has appointed a day. It is a day that is already determined by God. The Lord Jesus Christ said that He did not know the day, and neither did the angels. It is God alone who knows it. But He *does* know it. In God's eternal calendar there is a day of judgment.

You will find this truth in many other places. The Apostle in talking about himself and Apollos, in 1 Corinthians chapter three, says: All right! every man is building upon this one and only foundation; some build wood, hay and stubble, and others gold and precious metals. But, he goes on, 'The day shall declare it' [1 *Corinthians* 3 : 13]. Every man's work shall be judged, the day will declare it – the day of judgment. Paul refers to the day of the Lord again in 2 Thessalonians 4. Some people were teaching that the day of the Lord was at hand or had already come. It has not, says Paul, certain other things have got to happen first. But it will come. 'He which hath begun a good work in you', he says again, to the Philippians, 'will perform it until the day of Jesus Christ' [*Philippians* 1 : 6]. It is the same day in all these passages. It is the day of the return of the Lord Jesus Christ for the final judgment of the world.

And, indeed, we read about it in the Book of Revelation, particularly in chapter six, verse 17: 'The great day of his wrath is come . . .'. Read the Book of Revelation again, keeping your eye on this day and the manifestation of the wrath of God. It is the whole of the scriptural teaching. The whole world, the

whole of history, is heading up to this great day of judgment. It is
to be a day of revelation of something. And this word 'revelation' is important. The judgment of God is going on *now*. It is
going on day by day. 'Some men's sins are open beforehand' says
Paul to Timothy [1 *Timothy* 5 : 24], and they get their punishment. Some are not, and they will get their punishment too. But
a great deal is revealed now. We have already considered that, in
chapter one. Much has happened – much is happening. God's
judgment is being revealed, but only at that day shall it be
revealed and unfolded in all its fulness.

In 2 Peter 2:4 the Apostle Peter puts it like this: 'For if God
spared not the angels that sinned, but cast them down to hell,
and delivered them into chains of darkness, to be reserved unto
judgment . . .'. They have already been judged, in a sense; they
were driven out of heaven. Yes, but they are being reserved in
chains for the judgment of the last day. And, indeed, in
1 Peter 3 : 19–20, Peter again refers to this when he says that our
Lord in spirit 'preached unto the spirits in prison, which
sometime were disobedient . . . in the days of Noah'. They are in
prison now; they are spirits in prison waiting. They have already
received a good deal of judgment, but the great day is the day
when the final sentence will be promulgated, and God will
announce His verdict upon all men, every single individual. In a
sense, this is the most tremendous fact in the whole of
Scripture.

Let us, finally, look at one more passage, Revelation
20 : 11–15: 'And I saw a great white throne, and him that sat on
it, from whose face the earth and the heaven fled away; and
there was found no place for them. And I saw the dead, small and
great, stand before God; and the books were opened [Ah, here,
you see, the books were opened, the books which sinners have
been marking themselves without realizing it]: and another
book was opened, which is the book of life; and the dead were
judged out of those things which were written in the books,
according to their works. And the sea gave up the dead which
were in it; and death and hell delivered up the dead which were
in them: and they were judged every man according to their
works. And death and hell were cast into the lake of fire . . . And
whosoever was not found written in the book of life was cast
into the lake of fire.'

That is the day. The day the books will be opened and all this wrath that men have been treasuring up for themselves will be produced in evidence against them. They will be punished. And what will be revealed, he tells us again, is the righteous judgment of God. Nobody will have any complaint; everybody will see God's righteous judgment. And that is why the Book of Revelation tells us earlier that some people, when they see it, will say to the mountains and the rocks, 'Fall on us and hide us' [*Revelation* 6 : 16]. There will be no excuse; there will be no plea. God's judgment is always according to truth, and on that great day the truth, the righteousness, the justice will be finally revealed.

Well, there it is. That is what the Apostle says about those Jews who misunderstand the goodness of God. They are ignorant. They do not know that it was meant to lead to repentance. They do not know what it is in them that leads them not to repent. They do not know that by not repenting they are treasuring up wrath against themselves, and they do not know, they do not realize, that they will have to stand before God and give an account of these things, and be confronted by all His goodness, His forbearance, and His longsuffering; above all, by the Lord Jesus Christ, the Lamb of God, the One whom they pierced. For 'every eye shall see him, and they also which pierced him' [*Revelation* 1 : 7]. What an appalling ignorance! Beloved Christian people, our business is to enlighten people about these things, so that as we talk to them about the present crises, we may lead it on to that, and ask them why it is that these things keep on happening, and what it is that is wrong with man. Do not be content merely with discussing newspaper headings or taking a worldly man's view of these things. Make them see what it is all due to. They are ignorant – 'not knowing' – and your business and mine is to give them the knowledge, to open their eyes, to enlighten them, and to exhort them to repent and to flee from the wrath to come.

Six

*

Who will render to every man according to his deeds: to them who by patient continuance in well doing seek for glory and honour and immortality, eternal life: but unto them that are contentious, and do not obey the truth, but obey unrighteousness, indignation and wrath, tribulation and anguish, upon every soul of man that doeth evil, of the Jew first, and also of the Gentile; but glory, honour, and peace, to every man that worketh good, to the Jew first, and also to the Gentile.

Romans 2 : 6–10

In these verses the Apostle takes another step forward in the argument that he is conducting primarily against the Jews, with whose position, of course, he is very familiar, having at one time been in it himself. But, again, it is an argument which not only applies to the Jews of those days; it applies to all others who adopt the same kind of attitude towards the pronouncements of the gospel of our Lord and Saviour Jesus Christ. We have already considered the first three parts of this argument – their misunderstanding about the goodness of God, the fact that they are really despising it and that in doing so they are 'treasuring up to themselves wrath'. But that is not all, Paul says. There is a further argument, which arises out of the previous one. It is something that he has got to tell them about that day of the wrath of God and the revelation of His righteous judgment. Now he knows that the Jews are not clear about these things. They have completely misunderstood some of their own Scriptures which he is going to quote to them and they are therefore tragically ignorant of what will be revealed at the time of the righteous revelation of God. And because of all this, he takes up with them this further point, so that they will be left without any argument whatsoever. Their position is quite untenable, they are governed by a prejudice, and they are not facing their own Scriptures, of which they boast so much. And so Paul goes on, point after point, step after step, bringing home to them this thing which is uppermost in his mind – that they as Jews are as much under the wrath of God as anybody else, and that the only way of salvation for them, as for everybody else, is to believe in and to submit to and receive this righteousness of God which is by faith in Jesus Christ. Let us follow him then, as he takes up the fourth argument and as he shows them what it is that will be revealed in this great day of judgment which, as we have seen so clearly, is certainly coming.

The first thing Paul tells them is that it is to be a judgment which will be upon *all* men. He says that three times in these verses: in verse 6: 'Who will render to every man according to his deeds'; in verse 9: 'Tribulation and anguish, upon every soul of man that doeth evil . . .'; and in verse 10: 'But glory, honour, and peace, to every man that worketh good . . .'. Now the Apostle does not repeat a statement like that without having some very good reason for doing so, and so it is clear that this is the primary point that he is anxious to bring home to these people. So let me divide it up like this: what he is asserting is that this great judgment which is coming will be an individual judgment. Every human being that has ever lived will appear in this judgment. It is universal, and it is a personal and an individual judgment.

In other words, it is not a matter of nations; the world is not going to be judged at the end in national groups and neither are we going to be judged as families. You see the importance of all this? There are many people who think they are going to heaven because they happen to have been born in a certain nation. Indeed, there are still those who believe that anyone born in this country is a Christian. As for the people who are born in pagan nations – they, of course, are not! Paul's answer to such views is that every one is going to be judged separately, individually, and distinctly. 'Every soul of man', he says – and that is an important addition which emphasizes again the particularity.

There are also, undoubtedly, many who still think that they can go to heaven because they belong to a certain family. Many have tried to persuade themselves that you can ride into heaven on the back of a saintly father or mother, or even a grandfather or grandmother. But here is the answer: no! It is an individual judgment, not a familial matter. We will not be admitted as families, with everyone who is in the family going in. Now that is the sort of thing the Jew believed. He believed that because he was a Jew he was safe. But God will judge all men as individuals.

This, again, is something that is taught throughout Scripture. There are some who would have us believe that it is not taught in Matthew chapter twenty-five, where our Lord, dealing with the final judgment, you remember, in His third picture in that great chapter, puts it like this: 'When the Son of man shall come in his glory, and all the holy angels with him, then shall he sit upon the throne of his glory: and before him shall be gathered all nations: and he shall separate them one from another, as a shepherd divideth his sheep from the goats: and he shall set the sheep on his right hand, but the goats on the left' [vv. 31–33]. Now there is a teaching, with which many of us are, no doubt, familiar, which says that this is the judgment of the nations, and that the nations of the world are going to be judged as nations in that great day, according to their treatment of the Jews.

Well, to me the statement we are looking at together here is more than a sufficient answer to that. You will see that the Apostle goes out of his way to say that there is no difference between the Jew and the Gentile. It is an individual judgment. Nowhere in Scripture, apart from that one isolated passage in Matthew chapter twenty-five, is there a suggestion that there is going to be any sort of 'national' judgment on that day – indeed, the whole of Scripture is against that. And it is the simplest thing in the world, surely, in that paragraph in Matthew chapter twenty-five, beginning at verse 31, to see that that is just a term: – 'All the nations of the world' – all the peoples. From that point the word 'nations' is not mentioned and Jesus immediately goes on to deal with these individuals who are going to be divided up as sheep and goats. There is nothing anywhere in Scripture to suggest that nations are going to be judged as nations, and that the determining factor of their fate will be their treatment of the Jews. This is a subject that must obviously be raised at this point because the Apostle says that the judgment is going to be on 'every soul of man', not in blocks, not in groups, but individual and personal.

But not only is that important in terms of correct exposition of Scripture, let us all remember that it is something that speaks to us. If you read Revelation chapter twenty, you will find that the same thing is emphasized there: the dead are all going to be judged – those who are in the graves, those who are in the sea – it does not matter where they are, they will all arise and have to appear and listen to this ultimate sentence. Oh yes, believers as well as unbelievers. And it is because believers are at that judgment that we are told that this second book appears, which is the book of life in which their names are written, and which will announce to them their glorious destiny. But they will have to appear in this great judgment. And therefore, I say, it is important for us always to remember that the judgment is individual and personal.

The second thing is that no distinctions will be recognized – none whatsoever. Notice how the Apostle repeats himself for the sake of emphasis in verses 9 and 10: 'Tribulation and anguish, upon every soul of man that doeth evil, of the Jew first, and also of the Gentile'. The Jews will not be in a special position; that is the whole purpose of this argument. The Jews thought that they were in a special position, and that they would always remain in a special position. No, says the Apostle, this is a universal, individual judgment for the Jew first, and also for the Gentile. Then he goes on in verse 10: 'But glory, honour, and peace, to every man that worketh good, to the Jew first, and also to the Gentile'. Now the point there, too, is that there is no difference at all between the Jew and the Gentile. That difference has gone; in this matter of judgment, especially, it does not exist at all.

And so, indeed, we can even go further and say that the Apostle teaches that far from escaping the judgment because he is a Jew, the judgment is going to come to the Jew first. That phrase, 'to the Jew first, and also to the Gentile' is repeated in verses 9 and 10, by which Paul surely means that not only is the Jew not going to escape this judgment, but that the judgment is going to be particularly severe upon him because of all his advantages: because he had the oracles of God, because he belonged to this nation that God had formed for Himself, and because of all the prophets and all the teaching. To the Jew *first*; not only first in order, but first, as it were, in intensity, because of all the advantages that he has enjoyed.

Here once more we see the treachery of the human heart, the deceitfulness of sin. The Jews had actually twisted the Scriptures to say the exact opposite of what they really say. Not only are the Jews to be judged, it is to the Jew first, and also then to the Gentile. And I want to apply this to ourselves, because as we have already seen many times, there are many in the Christian church today in the precise position of these Jews at the time of Paul and of our Lord. They are relying on the fact that they were born to Christian parents, that they have always gone to a place of worship, and were admitted into membership at a certain age . . . they are relying on those things alone as proof of the fact that they are Christians. They have no spiritual experience; they often do not know what they believe; they are relying simply upon church membership, or some accident of birth or of upbringing. And it is to such people that the Apostle Peter says, 'Judgment must begin at the house of God' [1 Peter 4 : 17]. As it is right to say 'to the Jew first', it is equally right to say 'to the house of God first'. There is no question but that judgment will begin among those who make a profession of Christian faith. There are many instances of that in the Scriptures, and I shall probably be quoting them later. But I would say that the general message, at this point, is that as the Jew could not rely upon his nationality, or his privileged position, so we must rely upon none of these external things. We shall not be judged in churches, or in groups, in any sense. There is no privileged position. Every one will have to stand on his own, and he will have to face the same judgment.

That, then, is the first point, but let me go on to the next. The second statement is that this judgment will be according to our deeds. Paul says in verse 6, 'Who will render to every man according to his deeds', or, if you like, his works. At this point the Apostle is, incidentally, displaying his brilliance as a debater, because what he says there is nothing but a quotation from Psalm 62, verse 12. It is also an exact quotation of Proverbs chapter twenty-four, verse 12. There are other passages which say the same thing in slightly different words, but this is a direct quotation from those two verses. So you see the brilliance of the argument as he conducts it; he is quoting to them the Scriptures of which they boast, and pointing out that the Scriptures which they rely upon say that God will judge every man in this very way – according to his deeds.

This, then, is an important statement, and it is a statement that has very frequently been misunderstood. I once heard a man expounding these verses, and his teaching was that there were some people who were going to be justified by works after all! There, you see, is the danger. Here is a categorical statement – 'who will render to every man according to his *deeds*'. How, then, do we interpret it? Now, the best way to approach a difficult passage is always to take it, I think, like this: First of all, take the exact statement which the Apostle makes. Before we jump to any conclusions, before we begin to argue, let us notice particular statements; then, having got them perfectly clear, and having discovered exactly what he says, we can see how they fit in to his major argument.

What exactly does the Apostle mean, therefore, when he says that every man is going to be judged according to his deeds? Well, what he goes on to say is that there will be two groups of people, the righteous and the unrighteous, and their fates will be correspondingly different. There is a fate which awaits the righteous; there is a fate which awaits the unrighteous. Then he says that each of these two types can be described in detail, and he describes each one of them in a threefold manner, so that as we listen to what he is saying we are in a perfect position to be able to examine ourselves and to judge ourselves. Here we are – we know that we have got to stand in that great judgment before God, we know we are going to be in one of these two groups, and there is nothing in the world more important for us than to know to which of these two groups we belong. The Apostle, I say, very fortunately gives us a threefold division of each of them, and you notice that he makes the same points about them. First of all, he considers the general attitude of the two groups to God, and to the things of God in general. Secondly, he examines them in terms of the general bent or tenor of their life and living. And, thirdly, he examines them in terms of their actual conduct and behaviour.

So, then, let us look at the two groups – the righteous group, and the unrighteous group. I have three things to explain about them both, the same three points to examine, but we shall see where they differ. Let us look at the righteous first. To start with, what is the attitude of this person towards God and the things of God? The answer is that he is a person who is seeking for glory and honour and immortality. You find that in verse 7: 'To them who by patient continuance in well doing seek for glory and honour and immortality . . .'. That is their general attitude. And my question to myself should be, 'Am I seeking for these things?'

Now by 'glory' Paul means everything that God Himself is and represents, and everything that God has for His own people. Oh, how often is that term used for this in Scripture! We read about 'the glory of God' being manifested. You know, the old theologians of three and four hundred years ago used to say that the thing which makes God *God*, is His glory. Everything else that is true of God – all His attributes – are summed up in His glory. So, then, what we are told about these people is that they desire to be with God and to behold His glory, and to spend their eternity in His glory.

Now the Apostle is very interested in this truth. In chapter 5:1–2 he says that because we are justified by faith, we have peace with God, through our Lord Jesus Christ: 'By whom also we have access by faith into this grace wherein we stand, and rejoice in hope of the glory of God'. That is the characteristic of the attitude of the righteous man; this is what he is looking forward to. He has an understanding concerning God and His being and His nature, and the supreme thing in his life is to know God, to be like God, and to spend his eternity in the glorious presence of God. He is seeking this glory.

The Apostle says the same thing later in the Epistle, '. . . and whom he called, them he also justified: and whom he justified, them he also glorified' [8 : 30]. You see, our final salvation is our glorification. 'Christ is made unto us wisdom, and righteousness, and sanctification, and redemption' [1 *Corinthians* 1 : 30]: and in that redemption is this final glorification. Take what is going to happen to my body; when the Lord Jesus Christ comes back He will change this, the body of my humiliation, that it may be fashioned like unto the body of His glorification. My body is going to be glorified, as well as my spirit. I will be altogether glorious, sharing something of the glory of God and spending my eternity in His glorious presence. These people *seek* for that glory.

The second thing which they seek is 'honour', and this means the honour that God gives us. God, as it were, honours us, He distinguishes us from others, and He places an honour and a dignity upon us. Now the best commentary on this is a word of our Lord Himself, which you will find in John 5 : 44; he turned to the critical Jews one day, and He said, 'How can ye believe, which receive honour one of another, and seek not the honour that cometh from God only?' You see what an important statement that is. He is saying in effect, 'You know the real trouble with you is not your intellects, it is that you are seeking honour from one another. You want to be great in this world and want to have honour from men, and you are getting it and that is all you do get; but because you are so intent on that, you never seek for the honour that can come from God alone, which God alone can give'. But the righteous are seeking that. They do not care very much what the world thinks of them. 'Let the world deride or pity, I will glory in Thy Name', say these people. 'Destitute, despised, forsaken, Thou from hence my all shalt be'. That is the honour these people are after, not the human honours, not the honours that the papers make so much of, and the world with all its boasting makes so much of, an honour that is going to disappear, the honour that Dives, the rich man, had with his sumptuous clothing and his great feasts, and all the rest of it. No, these people were not known by the world, and the world did not respect them nor honour them. But God did, and that was the only thing that mattered with them.

And then the third thing is 'immortality', which can also be translated as 'incorruptibility'. This means, of course, the absence of decay of any kind; it means to be in a condition in which nothing harmful can happen, in which no injury can take place to you at all – incorruptible. Nothing can defile it. The Apostle Peter says, 'Blessed be the God and Father of our Lord Jesus Christ, which according to his abundant mercy hath begotten us again unto a lively hope by the resurrection of Jesus Christ from the dead . . .' To what? '. . . . to an inheritance incorruptible, and undefiled, and that fadeth not away' [1 *Peter* 1 : 3–4]. And Paul, again, says it in the great fifteenth chapter of 1 Corinthians: '. . . for the trumpet shall sound, and the dead shall be raised incorruptible . . . and this mortal must put on immortality'. That is it! Now these people, he says, are seeking that. They are seeking glory; they are seeking honour that God alone can give, and they are looking forward to this state of incorruptibility, this immortality, this state of being perfect and pure that can never end, beyond sin, above sin, eternally perfect in the presence of God. That is the general attitude of these people.

But let me come to the second test. If that is their general attitude, what is the general tenor of their life? Paul here puts it in these words: he says that they are people who, by 'patient continuance in well doing', seek after this glory, and honour, and incorruptibility. And what does this mean? Well, it is almost self-explanatory, is it not? The emphasis, of course, is on the words 'patient' and 'continuance'. If you like, one word will express it – 'perseverance'. By patient continuance in well doing they seek this. In other words, they are not people who take a sudden decision, and seem to be all out for God, making the rest of us feel that we have never been Christians at all. It may last for a month or two and then they drop the whole thing. Those others are the exact opposite of that. Patient continuance in well doing – these do not merely start, they go on. They need patience, because they are in a world that is dead against them. They are subjected to the onslaughts of the world, and the flesh, and the devil. They are tried and tested by things that happen to them directly, things that happen round and about them in their families, in their office, or in the world. They are tried; they are shaken. The devil does his utmost to get them down, and all hell seems at times to be against them, but in spite of it all they hold on and they go on: patient continuance – endurance.

You cannot read the New Testament without seeing that constantly emphasized. Let me put it to you like this: these people are absolutely unlike some of the groups depicted by our Lord in the Parable of the Sower. They are certainly not like those people who are compared to the pathway that the seed fell on, seed which the devil came and took up at once; they are not like that. Neither are they like the people represented by the stony ground on which the seed fell and sprang up, but because it had no root soon withered. Such people do not continue. They are marvellous for a moment, but they do not continue patiently in well doing, they give up. Neither are the righteous like the people who are compared to the soil that was full of thorns. Here again when the seed fell there appeared to be promise of a wonderful crop, but it was all choked. The cares of this world and the deceitfulness of riches choked the word; or when trial, and temptation, and persecution came, they could not stand up to it and nothing came of them.

But the righteous are the exact opposite. Patient continuance in well doing – this is their great characteristic. Read Hebrews chapter eleven again and see how that was their whole secret. Everything was against those heroes of the faith, but still they went on, they held on by faith. They were looking for 'a city which hath foundations', and nothing could stop them. This is also very clear in Hebrews 3 : 14, where the author says, 'We are made partakers of Christ, if we hold the beginning of our confidence stedfast unto the end'. In chapter six he says the same thing, exhorting his readers to give the same diligence to 'lay hold upon the hope set before us'. It is the great theme of the Epistle to the Hebrews.

But it is something that we find frequently in the whole of Scripture. You remember our Lord saying to the people one day that 'men ought always to pray, and not to faint' [*Luke* 18 : 1], because if you faint you fall down, you do not go on patiently. And the only way to continue patiently is to live this life of prayer. It means diligence; it means application; it means reading your Scripture; it means keeping your communion with God. It is the only way to continue patiently and to go on. But those who do not do these things faint, and fall by the wayside. And you remember that Paul, the Apostle of faith, in writing to the Galatians says, 'In due season we shall reap, if we faint not' [6 : 9] – those who faint do not reap, and so we are given all these exhortations to patient continuance.

Now Paul does not mean by this that the righteous never fall, or that they are sinless. He does not mean that they are perfect. If I may borrow an expressive statement out of the Old Testament, the position is this – 'Faint – yet pursuing'. Still going on, stumbling at times, but going on – by patient continuance in well doing. They keep on fighting the good fight of faith. They are not these giddy people who say they never have any temptations or problems, and sing 'Now I am happy all the day'! Not at all! They say it is a struggle and a fight. They go on patiently, with great endurance – sometimes wondering what is happening to them – but persevering with patient continuance in well doing. That is what is asked of us and that is how we must test ourselves.

Then we come to the third test, which is their actual conduct. What Paul says about them I find here in verse 10: 'But glory, honour, and peace, to every man that worketh good'. There you come right down to the particulars. We have seen their general attitude, we have seen the general tenor of their living, and here in actual practice they are living a good life – they are doing good. This means, of course, that they are doing their utmost to keep the commandments. 'Hereby', says John, in his First Epistle, 'we do know that we know him, if we keep his commandments'. This righteous man does not 'abide' in sin, he does not go on sinning; he falls, but he does not abide in it, it is not a life of sin. No, he is living a life of goodness, a life of righteousness. He is keeping the commandments, he is doing good. There, then, is the description of the righteous. Now let me show you the condition of the unrighteous, which is, of course, the exact opposite.

What is the general attitude of the unrighteous? The Apostle puts it in one word in verse 8: 'But unto them that are *contentious . . .*' Another way of putting it would be to say that they are 'factious': which simply means, of course, that they have a malicious opposition to God, because of their desire to please themselves, and because of their desire to live according to their own likes and dislikes. They are contentious! The first man is always waiting upon God, he is reading His Word, he attends upon God and he prays to Him. Nothing is greater in this man's life than this desire to know God, and this glory and honour. But the other man, when God speaks to him, is rebellious, he contends with God, he is factious. He sets up his opinions against God's opinion. He knows what God is going to tell him, but he does not want to obey, he wants to live another kind of life. He is self-centred, and therefore he argues with God. Indeed, it is all there in the third chapter of Genesis, is it not? It was the very thing, you see, that the devil persuaded Eve to do. He came to her and said, 'Hath God said . . . ?' Is it right for God to . . . ? That is contention. It is when someone queries God, queries God's rightness and His justice, and His truth, and contends with Him.

All this is a perfect description of all who are outside Christ. They argue with the Bible, they expurgate it and take sections of it; they do not agree with this teaching about the wrath of God, or about something else. 'Ah, now', they say in their pride, 'is that the right way or is it not?' They are contentious. They defy God, and thus, in their arrogance, they set up their own opinions against His. In other words, they are men of the world, instead of men of God; they are governed by the outlook of this world. Paul puts it so perfectly in Ephesians 2 : 2: 'Wherein in time past ye walked according to the course of this world' – and all the people who are 'of this world' tonight are walking in that way – 'according to the prince of the power of the air, the spirit that now worketh in the children of disobedience'. They are all great critics of the Bible. They are critics, too, of the Christian life. 'Ha!' they say, 'Your life is so narrow!' They cannot abide it. They do not agree with it. And they show their teeth if you begin to talk about godliness. Contentious! What a perfect description of them! They betray what they are by their general attitude.

But what about the general tenor of their life? We are told here: 'But unto them that are contentious, and do not obey the truth, but obey unrighteousness . . .'. There is the description – they do not obey the truth but they do obey unrighteousness. In other words, they do not live according to God's law. How, then, do they live? Well, go back again to Ephesians 2 : 2–3: 'Wherein in time past . . . we all had our conversation . . . in the lusts of our flesh, fulfilling the desires of the flesh and of the mind; and were by nature the children of wrath, even as others'. That is how the children of wrath ever live – the lusts of the flesh, the desires of the flesh, and of the mind. The Apostle is really repeating what he had said in Romans 1 : 18, where he talked about these people who are guilty of 'ungodliness and unright-eousness'. The ungodliness comes in this contentious spirit, and the unrighteousness follows inevitably. That is the general tenor of their life. They come to the law of God and they do not obey it, then they listen to the enticements of the world, and the flesh, and the devil, and they do obey that. That is the thing to which they give their obedience: what they read about in their papers, and see on their films, the things that are always blared out on the radio and television. The way of the world, that is it – unrighteousness. And they obey it, and they go after it, and they spend their money in doing so, and they enjoy it. That is the general tenor of their life.

And then with regard to their actual conduct, Paul again puts it in a single phrase in verse 9: 'Tribulation and anguish upon every soul of man that *doeth evil'*. In Galatians chapter five he talks about 'the works of the flesh'. You read his list – 'Adultery, fornication, uncleanness, lasciviousness . . . wrath, strife . . . envyings . . .' – all those horrible things. There they are – they do evil. And how different they are from the righteous man.

And this, in turn, brings us to the third thing that the Apostle tells us will be revealed in the great judgment. We have seen that it is a judgment on all men individually, and a judgment according to deeds. Now Paul tells us that at the same time this great day will announce one of two destinies for everybody, and the destinies will correspond to the type of life that we have just been looking at. For the righteous, he says, it is 'eternal life': 'To them who by patient continuance in well doing seek for glory and honour and immortality, eternal life'. I do not want to stay with this now but eternal life means eternal enjoyment of God: 'And this is life eternal, that they might know thee the only true God, and Jesus Christ, whom thou hast sent' [*John* 17 : 3]. And what these people will hear on that great day is that their names are in the book of life! They will go on to this endless eternal life. We can have it here. We begin it here. But there we will enter into it in all its glory and its fulness, to be for ever with the Lord, ever in the presence of God: 'Blessed are the pure in heart: for they shall see God'! Eternal life, and it is everlasting. You remember it was incorruption they were looking for, it was immortality? Nothing there will ever die, it goes on for ever, and for ever, and for ever. It is eternal as God is eternal. That is the thing that they will hear announced with respect to them. God will render that to them.

What of the others? Now the learned commentators very rightly point out here that there is a change in the construction which brings out the idea that what we are going to be told about the unrighteous is not rendered unto them – it just happens to them. It is not a gift of God; it is the inevitable consequence of what they have been. What is it that happens to them? We are told here: 'Indignation and wrath, tribulation and anguish'. You notice he is saying two things: first of all, he tells them of God's attitude towards them – and God's attitude is one of settled wrath. They are always under the wrath of God. 'The wrath of God', as we read in the last verse of John chapter three, 'abideth on him': 'He that believeth on the Son hath everlasting life: and he that believeth not the Son shall not see life; but the wrath of God abideth on him'. It was there, and it remains there. That is the wrath of God – God's hatred of evil and of sin; God's attitude of abhorrence towards it. That will abide.

Yes, but it is not only wrath, he says, but indignation also. What is this? Well, indignation, if you like, is the manifestation of this attitude of God towards sin. God's attitude towards all sin at this moment is one of wrath, but what we are told here, as we are told elsewhere, is that at that great day of judgment, God's wrath will manifest itself, it will unfold itself, it will pour itself out. That is what the indignation means. It is a most terrible thought. It is this the Apostle Paul describes in 2 Thessalonians 1 : 7–10: 'To you who are troubled rest with us, when the Lord Jesus shall be revealed from heaven with his mighty angels, in flaming fire taking vengeance on them that know not God, and that obey not the gospel of our Lord Jesus Christ: Who shall be punished with everlasting destruction from the presence of the Lord, and from the glory of his power' – how this man repeats himself and his teaching! It is exactly the same thing – 'When he shall come to be glorified in his saints, and to be admired in all them that believe (because our testimony among you was believed) *in that day*'.

My dear friends, this is something so tremendous that one scarcely knows how to speak it, how to utter it. But it is here, and throughout the Scriptures. The wrath of God is upon sin now. At that day it will be *revealed*, it will be manifest. The wrath will come to expression. And what will be that expression? Paul puts it in two words – 'tribulation and anguish'. Tribulation means trouble, it means affliction, it means pressure. The derivation of the word is this: in the old days, when they wanted to separate the wheat from the chaff, they would put the garnered wheat on a floor, and then they had great flails, with which they used to beat the wheat. In this way they would separate the chaff from the wheat, and in so doing they were, as it were, bruising it. They used a *tribulum* and hence the term 'tribulation' – as if you are being struck. We still use the term in that sense. We talk about being 'struck' by misfortune, being beaten and battered and bruised by the things that happen to us in this life. Well, that is what is going to happen to these people for all eternity – tribulation; this tremendous kind of beating and bruising.

And that leads to anguish. What a word is anguish! It means a suffering in spirit. It means suffering as a consequence of the tribulation. Now the Apostle brings these two words together in a very interesting way in 2 Corinthians 4 : 8 where he says, 'We are troubled on every side, yet not distressed . . .' He uses the identical words that are used here: 'We are in tribulation on every side, yet we are not in anguish'. So you can have tribulation, you see, without knowing the anguish, and if you are a true Christian, though you pass through tribulation, you are never in anguish. We are troubled on every side, yet we are not distressed, but these poor wretches consigned to hell on that great day of judgment will not only have the tribulation, they will have the anguish also.

The story in Luke chapter sixteen tells us exactly what the anguish means. Dives awakens in hell, in the torment of the flames, and pleads with Abraham to send down Lazarus to relieve him – 'This torment', he says, 'that I am enduring!' It is our Lord who spoke those words – not I! And then He talks about that place in which 'there shall be weeping and gnashing of teeth' [*Matthew* 8 : 12] – that is anguish. Intense suffering in spirit, and in mind, and in heart – endless, eternal remorse; a realization of your folly when it is too late! And to endure that is anguish! Tribulation and anguish! That is not life, is it? But it is existence, and what the Apostle says is that the righteous go on to eternal life, but these go on to an existence of this type, and as eternal life is everlasting, so is this everlasting.

If the Bible did not teach this, I would not dare utter it! I know that every natural man in the world hates and abominates this teaching. I know that there are thousands who do not go to places of worship because of this teaching. They are contentious, and I would not dare to venture to assert it if it were not here in the Scriptures, from the lips of the Son of God Himself, the incarnation of God's love. 'Weeping and gnashing of teeth'; Dives, the rich man, in the flame and in the torment. Yes, the Bible teaches that this is going to happen. There is not a word in the Bible about a second chance. What Paul teaches here is that we are going to be judged according to our deeds – the deeds which we work here and now. It is what you and I do in this life and in this world that determines our eternal destiny. There is no teaching about a second chance, a second opportunity, in the Scriptures. Neither does the Apostle say here that it is only going to be for a limited period of time – that they are going to have tribulation and anguish perhaps for a year or two, or perhaps for a century or two, perhaps for a millennium or two, and then they will be annihilated – there is no conditional immortality in the New Testament. He just says that as the one group go to eternal and everlasting life, these others go to tribulation and anguish – they will exist in that condition. And he does not suggest any end to it, neither does the Scripture anywhere else – 'everlasting destruction', as we have just seen in 2 Thessalonians 1.

There it is, then; doubtless the most solemn, the most momentous, the most tremendous thing that men and women can ever consider but that is what we are solemnly told will be revealed on the great day of judgment. We shall all be standing there, we shall all be judged according to our deeds, and we shall all go to one or the other of the two destinies. Are you seeking glory, and honour, and immortality? Can you say of yourself that you are continuing patiently in well doing, and that your greatest desire is – indeed, can you say that you are hungering and thirsting after – righteousness? If you are, if you can, I assure you that the verdict you will hear will be 'eternal life'. But if not, there remains nothing but that other, awful, awe-inspiring picture.

Let us not only think about ourselves, let us think of the teeming masses around us in the world, who are contentious, and are not obeying the truth, but are obeying unrighteousness. Let us realize their fate. That will bring home to us our responsibility for them; that is what will lead us to prayer, to pray for revival, the power of God; that will lead us to speak to them, to do all we can to enlighten them, as God enables us. Let us, therefore, solemnly meditate deeply and continually upon these things.

Seven

*

> *Who will render to every man according to his deeds: to them who*
> *by patient continuance in well doing seek for glory and honour*
> *and immortality, eternal life: but unto them that are contentious,*
> *and do not obey the truth, but obey unrighteousness, indignation*
> *and wrath, tribulation and anguish, upon every soul of man that*
> *doeth evil, of the Jew first, and also of the Gentile; but glory,*
> *honour, and peace, to every man that worketh good, to the Jew*
> *first, and also to the Gentile.*
>
> Romans 2 : 6–10

In our last study we were just considering the actual terms
which Paul uses in these verses. It is his fourth argument with
the Jews in particular, who are not clear about this doctrine of
the wrath of God and justification by faith, and the principle he
is establishing is one which he lays down in verse 6: that God
'will render to every man according to his deeds'. We have seen
how that divides mankind into two groups, according to their
works, and we have considered what he says in detail about the
character, the nature, of these two groups and the corresponding
destinies which are pronounced upon them.

Now we must proceed to consider the doctrine which is
involved here. As I have said, it is a very important point, and
one that has frequently been misunderstood. What exactly is
Paul teaching here? His categorical statement is that God will
render to every man according to his deeds. If that is so, is this
not clear teaching of justification by works? Is he teaching here
that we are saved by what we do, by our actions? That is what
many, alas, have been tempted to say, and, indeed, have actually
said and taught. 'It is no use arguing', they say, 'the statement in
verse 6 is perfectly plain: "Who will render to every man

according to his deeds". You cannot get round that, and anything you may say about it is only your opinion. Here is Scripture and you must take Scripture as it is, and accept it whatever that may do to your views and to your theology'.

How do we answer that? As I say, this is an important matter if only from the standpoint of exposition of Scripture, a matter of importance for all of us as we come to read our Scriptures. Of course, what we can say at once is that such a suggestion is completely impossible because Paul's purpose in this very section is to prove that no man can be justified by works. He starts, you remember, in chapter one, verse 18, and we saw that from that point down to chapter three, verse 20, the Apostle is really dealing with one big issue only – it is all an elaboration of that eighteenth verse in the first chapter.

And we saw, furthermore, that he wrote that verse because it followed of necessity from what he had just been saying in verses 16 and 17: 'For I am not ashamed of the gospel of Christ: for it is the power of God unto salvation to every one that believeth; to the Jew first, and also to the Greek. For therein [in this gospel] is the righteousness of God revealed from faith to faith: as it is written, The just shall live by faith'. And then, Paul continues, 'For the wrath of God is revealed [has already been revealed] from heaven against all ungodliness and unrighteous-ness of men, who hold the truth in unrighteousness' – and then he proceeds to prove that. That is what he has been proving in the second half of the first chapter, and then, as we have seen, he takes it up and goes on with it here in the second chapter. He is dealing with objections, but the theme all along is the same – that no man can be justified except by faith. As that is his theme, he cannot possibly be saying half way through the argument that men can after all be justified by works.

But if there is anybody still in doubt about it, consider what he says quite explicitly further on in this same section. Take, for instance, chapter three, verse 9, where he says, 'What then? are we better than they? [That is to say, are the Jews better than the Gentiles?] No, in no wise: for we have before proved both Jews and Gentiles, that they are all under sin'. That, he says, has been his purpose in this passage. Then follow him as he puts it again in verse 10: 'As it is written, There is none righteous, no, not one'. Now that is a universal statement. There is no such thing, he says, as a righteous person. Therefore it is inconceivable that he should be saying in chapter two, verse 6, that there are some who justify or make themselves righteous, or save themselves, by their works. Finally, he winds it up in verse 20, where he puts it once and for ever in these words: 'Therefore by the deeds of the law there shall no flesh be justified in his sight: for by the law is the knowledge of sin'. Nothing more. The law gives you a knowledge of sin. It does not save. It cannot save. There is none righteous, no, not one. In the light of all this, I say that the suggestion that verses 6 and 7 refer to justification by works is shown to be utterly and completely impossible.

What, then, is the Apostle saying? Here, again, let me make a point with regard to biblical exposition. If we have never had an illustration of such an error before, we surely have here an example of the terrible danger of taking a verse right out of its context, and establishing a doctrine upon it. People are very fond of doing that. It seems to me to be very wrong to pick a verse of Scripture out of its context at any time, under any circumstances whatsoever. If you do that here, and take out verse 6 – 'Who will render to every man according to his deeds' – and if you just look at it like that, out of context, you might well jump to that false conclusion which I have just been dismissing. You see, the way to avoid that is to do what we have just been doing and to make sure that every verse is taken in its context and never divorced from it. And that is why it seems to me that we ought to agree together that the so-called 'Promise Boxes' are thoroughly unscriptural. Not only can they be misleading and introduce an element of chance or almost of magic, but to use them is to violate the Scriptures. We must never isolate a statement in the Scriptures from its own context.

Furthermore, generally speaking you will find that if you are in difficulties about any one statement anywhere, the context itself will be your best guide with regard to your exposition – much more important than a knowledge of Greek or Hebrew or anything like that. The context is the greatest conceivable help to the exposition of any Scripture, because these men, enlightened and used as they were by the Holy Spirit, have themes, and they work out their themes; they are logical, and they reason, and they are clear. There are some points where, perhaps, we may still not be able to arrive at finality in an exposition, but speaking generally you can do so, if you only pay attention to the context.

And so we come back and ask the question, 'If this is not teaching justification by works, what is it teaching?' And the answer is that in the whole of this section, from chapter 1 : 18 to chapter 3 : 20, the Apostle is not considering the question of justification at all, nor is he considering the way of salvation. He has made that truth abundantly clear in chapter 1 : 16–17, and thus this whole section does not raise at all the question of *how* we are justified, nor *how* we are saved; its theme is something quite different. What he is considering here is what it is that condemns us, what it is that damns us. The theme here is the wrath of God, and, as we must always remember, the Apostle is elaborating this for one reason only, and that is that certain people do not like this doctrine of the wrath of God. They try to avoid it, and to get round it in one way or another. The Jews in particular were to blame here, but not only the Jews, it was true of certain Gentiles also, and this doctrine is still being evaded or mistaught by many people today.

And so Paul's theme all along the line in this section is the wrath of God upon sin and that is what he is still considering in this verse. He feels that something is necessary before he can positively elaborate the way of salvation, and that is this difficulty about the doctrine of the wrath of God. Ultimately, as I think we must have seen clearly by now, no man will really seek salvation until he is clear about this doctrine. As long as a man thinks that his works or his nationality or his family or his birth or his associations or his profession or anything else is somehow or other going to put him right with God, he will trust to that and not to the Lord Jesus Christ. Now the Apostle knew that very well, so he is clearing the ground, he is taking away every prop, every excuse, every subterfuge. He wants to prove the point – that the whole world lies guilty before God, that there is none righteous, no, not one. That is his theme.

So what he is showing here is the ground or the terms of judgment and of condemnation, and he is not considering anything else. We have already studied verse 5, 'But after thy hardness and impenitent heart treasurest up unto thyself wrath against the day of wrath and revelation of the righteous judgment of God; who will render [on that day of wrath and of judgment] to every man according to his deeds'. Those are going to be the terms of judgment, not of salvation. He is not considering salvation here, he is only considering the terms of the judgment on this great day of wrath. And what he is telling them is that on that day nothing will be considered except a man's works. It is no use anybody stepping forward and saying, 'But I am a Jew'. The question is, what were your works? It is no use saying, 'I was a Gentile'. The question is, how did you live? The standard in judgment and condemnation is one of works.

Let me, then, put it like this: the Apostle's ultimate object is to show that works cannot save a man, but he is equally anxious to show here that works can condemn a man. And, furthermore, I believe that in addition to showing that we are judged and condemned by our works, he is at the same time saying that our works do actually show whether we are saved or not. In other words, salvation always leads to works of the type that the Apostle has been describing here.

Now at this point, in case anybody should think that we are simply considering Jews and Gentiles at the time of the Apostle Paul, I want to emphasize that this is something which is as relevant today as it has ever been. We have seen, earlier in this chapter, that there is a tendency in all of us to do what those Jews were doing. Let me show you how that comes in here. There is nothing, in a sense, which is more dangerous than to think that mere belief of certain truths, or acceptance of a certain teaching only, or the making of the profession of belief only, in and of itself saves us. I think you will see where the relevance of all this comes in at the present time. There is a tendency in the church today, it seems to me, when people come forward as inquirers, or whatever you may call them, to give them the impression that as long as they say they believe, all is well. During my many years in the ministry, I have come across many cases of that – where people were definitely given the teaching that if they only *said* they believed, that of itself saved them.

I want to show, therefore, in the light of this passage, how extremely dangerous such teaching is. There was a great deal of it in the Christian church about a hundred and seventy, almost up to two hundred years ago, associated with the name of a man called Sandeman – it was called Sandemanianism or

Sandemanism – and that was their teaching. They used to take that verse out of Romans chapter ten: 'That if thou shalt confess with thy mouth . . . thou shalt be saved', and teach that the way to be saved, therefore, was to confess with the mouth the Lord Jesus. 'Do not worry about your feelings', they said. 'Do not worry about anything. The Scripture says that if you say that, you are saved. So if you do say it, then you are saved'.

Now there is a tendency, it seems to me, to revive that grievous Sandemanian heresy, and to tell people, 'Oh, do not worry about your feelings, do not look into yourself at all. All you have to do is to say, "Yes, I believe that", and all is well'. But Paul's whole teaching here contradicts that and shows us its terrible danger. In other words, we must give full weight to all the statements in the Scriptures about works. Let me remind you of some of them. It was our Lord Himself who said, in Matthew 7 : 21, 'Not every one that saith unto me, Lord, Lord, shall enter into the kingdom of heaven; but he that *doeth* the will of my Father which is in heaven'. Let me repeat, those are the words of the Lord Jesus Christ Himself. And that was not merely teaching for the Jews before they rejected the kingdom, it is the teaching for all Christians at all times. At the end of Matthew's Gospel you will find that He told them to go out and to disciple all nations, 'teaching them *to observe all things* whatsoever I have commanded you'. And our Lord's words are as applicable today as they were then.

Or take again Matthew 16 : 27: 'For the Son of man shall come in the glory of his Father with his angels' – He is talking about judgment – 'and then he shall reward every man according to his works'. There, you see, we find our Lord saying the very thing that the Apostle Paul tells us here. But then, of course, there is the tremendous statement which is made in the third picture in Matthew 25 : 31–46 to which I have already referred:

'When the Son of man shall come in his glory, and all the holy angels with him, then shall he sit upon the throne of his glory: and before him shall be gathered all nations: and he shall separate them one from another, as a shepherd divideth his sheep from the goats: and he shall set the sheep on his right hand, but the goats on the left. Then shall the King say unto them on his right hand, Come, ye blessed of my Father, inherit the kingdom prepared for you from the foundation of the world:

for I was an hungred, and ye gave me meat: I was thirsty, and ye gave me drink: I was a stranger, and ye took me in: naked, and ye clothed me: I was sick, and ye visited me: I was in prison, and ye came unto me. [Obviously it was not whole nations that were doing all this; it was individuals, as we have already seen.] Then shall the righteous answer him, saying, Lord, when saw we thee an hungred, and fed thee? or thirsty, and gave thee drink? When saw we thee a stranger, and took thee in? or naked, and clothed thee? Or when saw we thee sick, or in prison, and came unto thee? And the King shall answer and say unto them, Verily I say unto you, Inasmuch as ye have done it unto one of the least of these my brethren, ye have done it unto me. Then shall he say also unto them on the left hand, Depart from me, ye cursed, into everlasting fire, prepared for the devil and his angels: for I was an hungred, and ye gave me no meat: I was thirsty, and ye gave me no drink: I was a stranger, and ye took me not in: naked, and ye clothed me not: sick, and in prison, and ye visited me not. Then shall they also answer him, saying, Lord, when saw we thee an hungred, or athirst, or a stranger, or naked, or sick, or in prison, and did not minister unto thee? [You notice they call him 'Lord'; they thought they were believers, they were interested.] Then shall he answer them, saying, Verily I say unto you, Inasmuch as ye did it not unto one of the least of these, ye did it not to me. And these shall go away into everlasting punishment: but the righteous into life eternal'.

Now there is the teaching once more. And again you will find people who will try to find the doctrine of justification by works in that passage too. 'Surely', they say, 'it is purely a matter of works?' Now such an interpretation suggests that Scripture blankly contradicts Scripture, and there is no need to fall back into such error and heresy. There is a perfectly simple explanation: The three parables in Matthew 25 are parables in connection with profession, and what our Lord is teaching there is that there is no point in saying, 'Lord, Lord', unless your life corresponds to His. There are certain works that always characterize those who have been born again of the Spirit, and if the works are not there, it is no use saying, 'Lord, Lord', it will avail us nothing. This question of works is essential in the matter of judgment.

The Apostle Paul puts the same thing positively in Ephesians 2 : 10, where he says, 'For we are his workmanship, created in Christ Jesus' – His workmanship, quickened, raised with Christ from among the dead, in the heavenly places – 'created in Christ Jesus unto good works, which God hath before ordained that we should walk in them'. Or listen to him writing to Titus, where he puts it like this: 'The grace of God that bringeth salvation hath appeared to all men, teaching us that, denying ungodliness and worldly lusts, we should live soberly, righteously, and godly, in this present world; looking for that blessed hope, and the glorious appearing of the great God and our Saviour Jesus Christ; who gave himself for us . . .' Why? In order that we might still go on sinning and still go to heaven? No! 'That he might redeem us from all iniquity, and purify [separate] unto himself a peculiar people, zealous of good works. These things speak, and exhort, and rebuke with all authority. Let no man despise thee' [*Titus* 2 : 11–15].

Then we must recall what James has to say about it in his Epistle: 'Even so', he says, 'faith, if it hath not works, is dead, being alone'. He also says: 'Thou believest that there is one God; thou doest well: the devils also believe, and tremble' [*James* 2 : 17, 19]. The same point, you see – that merely saying that you believe, without anything else to support it or to demonstrate it, is of no value at all. Furthermore, John, the Apostle of love, as people like to call him, puts it very strongly indeed. In his First Epistle he says: 'If we say that we have fellowship with him, and walk in darkness, we lie, and do not the truth' [1 *John* 1 : 6]. In chapter 2 : 4 he is even stronger: 'He that saith, I know him, and keepeth not his commandments, is a liar, and the truth is not in him' – one of the strongest statements in the whole of Scripture. That is how the Apostle John preached sanctification, you see. He did not appeal to people to accept something which could be given as a gift; he said, 'If you say that you know Him, and do not keep His commandments, I have only one thing to say to you – you are a liar, and there is no truth in you'.

In other words, the New Testament Scriptures teach us everywhere that no greater danger confronts anyone who makes a profession of the Christian faith, than what is called antinomianism. And what does that mean? It means that you rely upon the fact that you make statements, and divorce them from your life. It is the tendency to say, 'Well, of course, as long as I am saved it does not matter what I do!' Antinomianism. Anti-law; anti the whole conception of commandments and doing the will of God, and working out the good works for which He has created us. Or, to put it in its more modern garb, there is nothing, surely, which is more dangerous to the soul than what we may call a glib believism.

And you see how this affects all our ideas of evangelism. If we are so anxious to get people 'through', as we say, instead of leaving the Holy Spirit to do His own work, we tend to say, 'But look here, it is quite simple – here, you see, the Scripture says if you believe you are saved. Do you believe? Yes. Very well, you are saved, it is all right'. But it may be all wrong! It may be terribly all wrong! And it can be an exceedingly dangerous thing to say that to a soul, and to give people the impression that because they have said they believe and accept, all is well. There is a sense in which we have got to say that to them, but we must not stop at that. We must go on – we must say, 'All your good living and all your works can never save you. You have got to see that, and you have got to admit that to yourself and to God. You have got to see that you can only be saved by the Lord Jesus Christ and that His method of salvation is this: He works in you through the Holy Spirit, and the Holy Spirit will act upon you. He will bring into birth a new man within you; He will implant a new principle of life in you, and that will begin to manifest itself'. In other words, we must never stop at just believing – we must always emphasize regeneration – the re-birth – the new man. Otherwise it seems to me we are leaving souls in a very dangerous position.

And therefore I would argue that part of what the Apostle is saying here is this: it is no use the Jews saying, 'I am a Jew and therefore I am all right'. No, your works are going to decide whether you are all right or not. It is no use a man coming in this Christian era and saying, 'But I am a church member, and I have always said that I believed these things'. That alone will not save you! What is the record? What is your life like? We have already considered what Paul has told us about these works: patient continuance in well doing; seeking for glory and honour and immortality; and, as he puts it again in verse 10, 'to every man that worketh good'. So, then, we can put it like this – there is no contradiction, obviously, between the Apostle Paul and the Apostle James. They are both saying the same thing but are looking at it from a slightly different angle.

However, here, in this second chapter, it seems to me that the Apostle Paul is saying precisely what James is saying in the second chapter of his Epistle. Paul is concerned ultimately to show that no man can justify himself by his works. The method of salvation is justification by faith only. Yes, but the Apostle is also very anxious that we should see that faith is real faith, and faith always leads to works – exactly as James says, 'Faith without works is dead'; 'As the body without the spirit is dead, so faith without works is dead also'. It is the simplest thing in the world for a man to say, 'I believe all that'. I have known men who have said they believed it who lived in drunkenness. I have known men who were living in adultery, and who went on in adultery, say they believed it all. Yet all they had was an intellectual apprehension of it. But the Scripture speaks very plainly about such people. The Apostle John says that such a man is a liar. In other words, if this new life is in us it will show itself, there will be a patient continuance in well doing. The man who is born again is a man who, however feebly, is nevertheless seeking for glory and honour and immortality. In his folly he may backslide at times, he may allow the world to entice him for a moment, but the bent of his life is this seeking after glory and honour and immortality. We can test our faith by this. These are the works which are going to count. We shall not be judged in the judgment by a standard of absolute perfection – obviously not. But what will be looked for, what will be expected of us, is this kind of work which is always the result of salvation.

So the Apostle, it seems to me, is doing these two things at one and the same time. His primary objective is to show that judgment is always in terms of works, and by that he is going on to prove that there is none righteous, that all are under condemnation, because all have sinned. But at the same time there is that further sense, and we avoid it at our peril, in which he teaches, as the other Scriptures, which I have quoted to you, teach so plainly and so clearly, that unless we have got some evidence of new life within us we are in a most dangerous position. The fact that we once said, 'I believe, I accept', is not enough. If we are saved we are regenerate, and you cannot have the new life of God in you without its leading to certain results. As we have seen, the Apostle puts it quite specifically: 'For we are . . . created in Christ Jesus *unto* good works, which God hath before ordained that we should walk in them' [*Ephesians* 2 : 10].

So I come back to what I have said before – the thing we ask ourselves is just this: 'Am I seeking glory and honour and immortality? What is the thing that is uppermost in my life? What do I want? Which way am I facing?' Those are the questions. There are people who say they believed, and they are members of churches, but they seem to be living worldly lives, according to a worldly outlook; their interests seem to be those of the world. You are almost shocked when you find that they are in a place of worship occasionally. In other words, there is no evidence in the life. And that evidence will be looked for on the day of judgment.

That, then, completes our consideration of this section, which runs from verse 6 to verse 10. And that, you notice, leads on quite inevitably to the next section, which we must proceed to study. But it was necessary for us to emphasize the teaching which we have been considering because of the terrible dangers which attend any misunderstanding of it. Let us, then, never forget what the Scriptures say about works, even to the believer.

Eight

*

For there is no respect of persons with God. For as many as have sinned without law shall also perish without law: and as many as have sinned in the law shall be judged by the law; (for not the hearers of the law are just before God, but the doers of the law shall be justified. For when the Gentiles, which have not the law, do by nature the things contained in the law, these, having not the law, are a law unto themselves: which shew the work of the law written in their hearts, their conscience also bearing witness, and their thoughts the mean while accusing or else excusing one another;) in the day when God shall judge the secrets of men by Jesus Christ according to my gospel.

Romans 2 : 11–16

We come here to the next argument which the Apostle develops in this section with regard to the whole matter of the wrath of God. He is anxious that all should realize that they are under the wrath of God, in order that they may hasten to hide themselves under the righteousness of God in Jesus Christ. He is dealing with every conceivable objection which people may have, and this is the fifth. He has hinted at this in the last two verses of the previous section, in verses 9 and 10, where he says, in dealing with the punishments and rewards, 'Tribulation and anguish, upon every soul of man that doeth evil, of the Jew first, and also of the Gentile; but glory, honour, and peace, to every man that worketh good, to the Jew first, and also to the Gentile'.

Here, then, he takes up this statement of his, 'to the Jew first, and also to the Gentile', which he has made twice, because he regards it as so important. He has, indeed, been carrying this idea in his mind from the very beginning, but now he deals with it in a more direct and specific manner. Then, having done so, he will proceed to make direct and explicit charges against the

The Righteous Judgment of God

Jews, starting in verse 17 and continuing until the end of the chapter.

It is important, therefore, for us to know how to read this particular statement and it does seem to me that the Authorized Version is most helpful here. It is more helpful than the Revised Version or the Revised Standard Version, because the Authorized Version puts the statement that is found in verses 13, 14, and 15 in brackets, indicating that it is a kind of parenthesis, and I have no doubt at all but that this is absolutely right. The statement in verse 16, 'In the day when God shall judge the secrets of men by Jesus Christ according to my gospel', really cannot be linked directly with verse 15, because there we are told about the Gentiles: 'Which shew the work of the law written in their hearts, their conscience also bearing witness, and their thoughts the mean while accusing or else excusing one another'. Now, obviously, that is no reference to what happens on the day of judgment, whereas verse 16 does tell us what is going to happen on that day. The Apostle, in verse 15, is saying what is true of the Gentiles now, not what is going to be true of them then. They will not be 'accusing or excusing one another' on the day of judgment. It will be too late for that then. They will all be so overwhelmed by the promulgation of the sentence, that there will be no arguing with themselves or with one another. It is quite inappropriate, therefore, to connect verse 15 with verse 16, and it is a pity that these Revised Versions do not indicate clearly, for the aid of all readers, that this is a parenthesis.

But then there has been a dispute also as to where exactly the parenthesis begins. Granting that there is a parenthesis, and that verse 15 does not lead directly to verse 16, the question is, where does the parenthesis begin? The Authorized Version, as we see, puts it at verse 13, but there are some who have argued for verse 14. They think that the parenthesis starts there, so that they read the main statement like this: [12]'For as many as have sinned without law shall also perish without law: and as many as have sinned in the law shall be judged by the law; [13]For not the hearers of the law are just before God, but the doers of the law shall be justified, [16]In the day when God shall judge the secrets of men by Jesus Christ, according to my gospel'.

Now there again it seems to me that the Authorized Version is absolutely right. You cannot link the end of verse 13 with the statement of verse 16, because the statement of verse 13 is that 'not the hearers of the law are just before God but the doers of the law shall be justified'. But we know perfectly well that there is no such thing as a 'doer of the law'. No man keeps the law, or ever has kept the law, so that there is no question of that being decisive on the day of judgment. So, clearly, verse 13 does not lead directly to verse 16. No! The Authorized Version is right – it is verse 12 that connects with verse 16, so we read it again like this: '¹¹'For there is no respect of persons with God. ¹²For as many as have sinned without law shall also perish without law: and as many as have sinned in the law shall be judged by the law; ¹⁶In the day when God shall judge the secrets of men by Jesus Christ according to my gospel'. Notice that in verses 12 and 16 the theme is that of judgment and therefore the parenthesis runs from the beginning of verse 13 to the end of verse 15. The main statement, therefore, is the statement in verses 11, 12, and 16; while in the verses in the parenthesis Paul elaborates a little on his main contention.

And not only that, he deals with possible objections that someone, whether Jew or Gentile, might bring forward, and having disposed of them, he completes the statement from which he broke off at the end of verse 12. So then, I think the simplest thing for us is to take it as it is put before us. We must look at the main statement first and then consider the little argument of the parenthesis, which has often made people stumble because it seems to tell us something about the situation of the Gentiles who are not only outside the law, but who have never heard the preaching of the Christian gospel.

Let us, therefore, look at the main statement, considering it first just as it stands, and then looking at its doctrine, at its teaching. Verse 11 states the real principle: 'There is no respect of persons with God'. That phrase, 'respect of persons', is interesting in itself. The literal meaning is that there is no lifting up of face where God is concerned, that as people stand in the presence of God, with downcast heads and faces because of a sense of shame, He does not show favouritism, and He does not lift up the face of one more than another.

Now you must have noticed many times in reading through

the Scriptures how constantly this particular statement is made about God. God is contrasted with man. It is very difficult to find a man who is not guilty of respect for persons. That is one of the things that has happened to man as the result of the Fall. It is very difficult for any human being to give an honest or impartial judgment. We are influenced by other considerations. We are not only more lenient with ourselves than we are with other people, we tend to shield our families and our relatives and our friends, or people who belong to the same social circle, the same class, the same group or the same country. We are biased, we are prejudiced, and because we are like that, we tend to think that God is the same. And that is the whole point with which the Apostle is dealing here. He lays it down as an absolute and fundamental postulate that God is not like that. There is no respect of persons whatsoever where God is the Judge. That is something which we must never lose sight of. God is always just; His judgment, as we saw in verse 2, is always 'according to truth', and one of the ways in which we see the working out of God's judgment according to truth is that He is never prejudiced, He is never influenced by these considerations that weigh so much with us in our assessments and in our judgments.

There is nothing we can add to this, it is simply a statement of fact. But observe its application as the Apostle elaborates it in verse 12: 'For', he says, connecting it up, 'For as many as have sinned without law shall also perish without law: and as many as have sinned in the law shall be judged by the law'. Now there he makes a universal statement. Mankind was classified into two groups – you were either under the law or else you were not. There is a famous statement about that in 1 Corinthians 9 : 20–21 where the Apostle shows how it comes into his evangelizing. When he speaks to those who are under the law he says, 'I became . . . as under the law', and when he speaks to a man who is not under the law, he says he became 'as without law'.

In other words, the world was divided into Jews and Gentiles. The law had been given to the Jews, it had not been given to the Gentiles, so the Apostle takes that up here and he just makes these plain and direct statements. The Gentiles, who have not been given the written law through Moses as the Jews have been, shall not be judged according to that written law, they shall be judged as they are. This is very important and it shows us God's fairness and His impartial dealings. If a man is a Gentile and has sinned 'without the law', without the possession and understanding of the written law as given through Moses, he will be judged and he will be punished as one who has not had the benefit of that written law. That is the statement with regard to the Gentiles.

Now we can add to that and say that a man who has never heard the gospel and has never had an opportunity of hearing it, will not be judged as if he had heard it. Observe what I am saying. I am saying no more than that. I am not saying that he is saved by that fact; I am saying that if he has never had an opportunity of hearing it he will not be judged as if he had heard it. I am entitled to say that because the principle is that a man is judged according to the situation in which he is; if he is outside the written law he will be judged as one who is outside it. On the other hand, as many as have sinned 'in the law' (or under the law) shall be judged by the law.

The Jews had had the written law through Moses. It was a great advantage and a great blessing. The Apostle is going to take that up in the next chapter, when he asks, 'What advantage then hath the Jew? or what profit is there of circumcision?' And he answers, 'Much every way: chiefly, because that unto them were committed the oracles of God'. The Jew has received the written law, this explicit statement of God's law, and he is going to be judged accordingly. There, then, is the simple statement in verse 12 which elaborates the principle laid down in verse 11.

What, therefore, is the teaching and the argument? Once more there is nothing more vital than that we should emphasize that this has nothing whatsoever to do with justification or salvation. We must keep on repeating that, because the havoc that men have made of this particular passage has always been due to the fact that instead of observing what it says, and its context, they have just taken it right out and have tried to say that here we are being taught that a man can be saved and justified by his own actions. The Apostle does not begin to deal with that, it is not in his mind at all. What he is still concerned about is judgment: '. . . as many as have sinned without law shall also perish without law: and as many as have sinned in the law shall be judged by the law'. And, of course, what he is saying is that what matters in the judgment is not our possession of the law, or our lack of possession of the law, but sin.

He meets the whole position of the Jew. The Jews' tendency was to say, 'Ah, well, after all we are the people who have got the law, and because God gave us the law we are all right, we are not under judgment, we have nothing to fear, and we need not believe in this doctrine concerning Jesus of Nazareth'. They really believed that, and this is the point which the Apostle has to argue in so much detail. They believed that the mere fact that they had the law given to them, somehow or other saved them. And what the Apostle is saying, therefore, in these two verses is this: 'Listen to me, judgment is not in terms of whether you happen to belong to a nation that has the law or to a nation that does not have the law; the one thing that matters is sin'. That is the thing that is common to both: 'For as many as have sinned without law . . . and as many as have sinned in the law'. Once you come to this question of judgment nothing matters but that.

And that is where God's impartiality comes in. The Jews are not favourites because God had given them the law. No, in the judgment, the one question that will be asked is, 'What about sin? What of your life? What have you done?' The judgment is concerned and interested only in this question of sin. And it does not matter who you are if you have sinned. It does not make any difference whether you are a Jew or a Gentile. It does not matter whether you are a member of a church or have never been a member of a church, or whether you come from the most saintly family in Great Britain. If you have sinned, you have sinned and you will be judged according to your sin. That is what he is saying. And therefore it will be no use turning to God and saying, 'Ah, but you are forgetting who I am, you are forgetting the profession I once made, you are forgetting the church I belonged to, you are forgetting the family, you are forgetting the nation'. It is irrelevant. There is no respect of persons with God, and whether you are one who has the law or one who has not the law it makes not the slightest difference. Judgment, as Paul said in the previous section, is according to works, and here he especially emphasizes the aspect of the sinful character of the works.

That, then, is the Apostle's main argument. But we must also observe the terms that he uses. You notice how the Apostle keeps us to this and how he goes on repeating these things. I am referring to the word 'perish' in verse 12: 'For as many as have sinned without law shall also perish without law'. That is always the punishment of sin. You will find it everywhere in your Bible. I know that modern man does not like it and therefore he takes it out of his Bible, but what has he got left when he has taken it out? Take out all the verses that mention it and where are you? What have you left? This is the categorical statement that is made about the Gentiles, 'As many as have sinned without law shall perish without law'. Perish! And perish means perish; it does not mean go out of existence. It is the opposite to eternal life; it is the same as everlasting destruction. It is the same as that place where their 'worm dieth not and their fire is not quenched'. It is the state of those who are outside the life of God. There is the warning, and we ignore it at our peril.

Now I wonder whether you have observed an extraordinary change of word which takes place in this twelfth verse? 'For as many as have sinned without law shall also perish without law: and as many as have sinned in the law shall . . .' perish by the law? No! 'shall be judged by the law'.

Why this difference, do you think? Why does he say that the Jew, the man who is under the law and who sins, shall be judged by the law? And why does he not say that the other man also is 'judged', instead of saying that he perishes? Here, surely, is an interesting and important point, and there is only one really adequate explanation of it. It is that the standard which God applies to the Jew is a higher and a severer standard than that which He applies to the Gentile. Now that does not make any difference to their ultimate destiny, but it does seem to indicate that there is a difference in the punishment. God demands more of the Jew than He demands of the Gentile, because He has given him the law.

As we work out the parenthesis in verses 13–15 we shall see that the Apostle says that the difference, in a sense, between the Gentile and the Jew is that the Gentile has a kind of fundamental law in his mind and in his heart but that he has never received it in an explicit, external and objective manner. But the Jew on the other hand has received it in that way. God has given it through Moses and therefore the Jew is in a very advantageous position. Sin has been defined for the Jew, it has been codified, it has been made perfectly plain and clear; there is no excuse for him. In the case of the Gentile that has not been done. He does have a knowledge of the law, as we shall see, but not in the same form as the Jew has it, and, therefore, because the Jew has been in a more advantageous position, because he has had teaching and training and instruction and this great help of the external law, the standard applied to him will be a higher standard than that in the case of the Gentile. So that the Jew, far from being saved by the fact that he has the law, is really in the position that his responsibility is altogether greater. Far from escaping judgment altogether because he is a Jew, the judgment in his case will be severer than in the case of the Gentile.

In Luke 12 : 41–48, our blessed Lord Himself draws that very distinction between the two classes of servants about whom He is speaking. He says, 'And that servant, which knew his lord's will, and prepared not himself, neither did according to his will, shall be beaten with many stripes. But he that knew not, and did commit things worthy of stripes, shall be beaten with few stripes. For unto whomsoever much is given, of him shall be much required: and to whom men have committed much, of him they will ask the more'. There, it seems to me, is the perfect commentary upon what the Apostle is saying here. Or, if you like it the other way round, the Apostle Paul is just repeating what his Lord and Master had said before him.

Let us be perfectly clear about this: the sinful Gentile and the sinful Jew will go together to perdition, but there seems to be clear teaching that the punishment and the suffering of the Jew for his sins will be greater than that of the Gentile. And it is perfectly just and equitable. The Jew has had the advantage, the greater opportunity, the greater light, and therefore he is judged according to the light which he had. Now, this is very important not only to an understanding of this particular statement, but because it applies to all of us. You will find that in 2 Corinthians 5 there is a reference to the judgment of believers. There will be as it were, a judgment of rewards. And again, we read in 1 Corinthians 3 of the possibility of our suffering loss. It is a very difficult subject, but it is perfectly clear that it is taught there in those two passages. Read them and study them with care. If the man who is going to be saved has built in a wrong way on the foundation, he is going to suffer loss, yet he himself shall be saved 'yet so as by fire' [v. 15]. But the man who has built well is going to have a greater reward. 'For we must all appear before the judgment seat of Christ; that every one may receive the things done in his body, according to that he hath done, whether it be good or bad' [2 *Corinthians* 5 : 10].

I say, therefore, that every time you and I hear the gospel our responsibility is increased. The more we have heard the gospel, the clearer our understanding of it, the greater is our responsibility. The more we have grown in grace and advanced in the knowledge of the Lord, again the greater is our responsibility; and the principle that is being laid down here is that God in His judgment is going to take all these things into full account. It is perfectly fair, it is perfectly just and right. But surely this ought to affect us all profoundly, and it ought to enable us to see more clearly than we have ever seen before that there is nothing more dangerous to the soul than just to be shouting, 'Lord, Lord', or to be making use of the doctrine of justification by faith as if it put everything right once and for ever. It does in the matter of salvation – in the matter of whether we are saved or lost, but it most certainly goes no further. We are preparing for our eternity.

We read in Revelation 14 : 13, 'Blessed are the dead which die in the Lord from henceforth: . . . *and their works do follow them*'. And they will. Our works are going to follow us. They are not going to determine our salvation, but they are going to make a difference to us. It is going to be a question of suffering loss or of receiving a greater or lesser reward. I do not pretend to be able to understand it more deeply than that. But it is here laid down as a great principle in God's judgment, and, therefore, we ought to pay attention to it and to give it most serious thought and meditation. We cannot leave this particular point without again emphasizing the finality that is expressed in these two words – 'perish' and 'judgment'.

Then we must look next at verse 16, so that we get our general statement complete before we even begin to look at the parenthesis. And in this verse also we notice the emphasis upon this 'day of judgment', this 'day when God shall judge the secrets of men'. I need not go back over that for we have already considered it – that 'day' which the Apostle has been telling us about in the fifth verse. 'The day will declare it', says the Apostle again to the Corinthians. The day of judgment.

But let us note that the next thing he says is that the judgment is going to be exercised by Jesus Christ: 'In the day when God shall judge the secrets of men by Jesus Christ'. Here again is a matter of great importance and interest. The Lord Jesus Christ is not only the Saviour, He is going to be the Judge. You remember He Himself puts this very clearly in John 5:22: 'For the Father judgeth no man, but hath committed all judgment unto the Son'. And again in verses 26–29: 'For as the Father hath life in himself; so hath he given to the Son to have life in himself; and hath given him authority to execute judgment also, because he is the Son of Man. Marvel not at this: for the hour is coming, in the which all that are in the graves shall hear his voice, and shall come forth; they that have done good, unto the resurrection of life; and they that have done evil, unto the resurrection of damnation'.

Now that is exactly what Paul is saying here. Jesus Christ is the Judge, and He is going to appoint the final destiny of the two groups. It is going to be one or the other – the 'resurrection of life' or else the 'resurrection of damnation'. And you notice in what terms – 'they that have done good . . . they that have done evil'. But He is the Judge. The Apostle Paul in preaching at Athens says the same thing. He says, 'God . . . now commandeth all men every where to repent' – Why? – 'Because he hath appointed a day, in the which he will judge the world in righteousness by that man whom he hath ordained; whereof he hath given assurance unto all men, in that he hath raised him from the dead' [*Acts* 17 : 30, 31]. The resurrection of Jesus Christ, in addition to all the other things that it does, proclaims that He is to be the Judge of the world. There, the announcement has been made, the assurance given.

May we speculate as to why this has been done? Our Lord Himself gives us a hint when He says the judgment has been given to Him because He is the 'Son of man'. May I suggest, with reverence, that it is given to Him partly as a reward because He humbled Himself, and because He came down so low. Paul suggests that in Philippians chapter two, where, having described to us how our Lord emptied Himself and divested Himself of His eternal glory and became obedient unto death, even the death of the cross, Paul then continues, 'Wherefore' – because of that – 'God also hath highly exalted him, and given him a name which is above every name . . .'. Yes, He is the Judge as a reward for His humiliation. But there is something further; He is the Judge because He is the Son of man, because He is the Head of this new race of humanity. He is the Judge, because God, as it were, has handed over the affairs of men to Him, and that is why He became man.

That leads to the last point, which is that He is Judge in order that no one might ever be able to say that the judgment is not absolutely fair. We like to think of Him as our great High Priest, because He is 'touched with the feeling of our infirmities', because He is the Son of man, and because He took unto Himself human nature – that is perfectly right, but there is more – He has been here as a man and He has lived as a man. He has been under the law, and His judgment is fair. People are always ready to attack the character of God. They might say, 'How can God judge us, He is so far removed, He is in heaven and we are on the earth? He does not understand human nature and human conditions and life in this world'. The judgment is in the hands of One who has been through it all; He knows all about it – He has lived in this world, as man as well as God, and has suffered under the law and under sin. So, then, He is the Judge in order that every mouth shall be stopped, and God shall be all and in all. The judgment is by Jesus Christ.

Furthermore, I must emphasize what Paul again emphasizes, that in that day the Lord Jesus Christ will judge us and will judge 'the secrets of men'. And he says this in order to remind us that we shall not only be judged according to our actions, we shall be judged according to everything that is true of us. The Pharisee could make a very good show as regards external examination and actions. You are the people, said our Lord to them, who 'make clean the outside of the cup and the platter; but your inward part is full of ravening and wickedness' [*Luke* 11 : 39]. This is a terrifying thought, but it is here. We shall be judged not only by our deeds and actions, but, as the Lord Himself said, by 'every idle word' that we shall ever have spoken [*Matthew* 12 : 36], and not only that, but by every thought, by every imagination, by everything that we have ever harboured or fostered or fondled in mind and in heart or imagination! That is the teaching of Scripture – 'the secrets of men'!

Paul is not saying that it is only according to our secrets that we shall be judged. What he is saying is that in addition to the external actions, our secrets will be disclosed. As the writer to the Hebrews says, 'All things are naked and opened unto the eyes of him with whom we have to do' [*Hebrews* 4 : 13]. God is a discerner of the 'thoughts and intents of the heart'. He can pierce 'even to the dividing asunder of soul and spirit, and of the joints and marrow' [*Hebrews* 4 : 12]. He knows everything. It will be no consolation to us in the judgment to say, 'Ah, I did not actually commit that sin' – the question is, 'Did you play with it in your mind? Did you spend a lot of your time in doing so?' Let me put it like this: How much time do you spend in reading newspaper accounts of the unsavoury details and the un-pleasant proceedings in the law courts and in society at large? If you enjoy it, and if you read it because you like it, you will have to give an account of that. That is part of the 'secrets'. It is all known to God. He knows exactly what we do with our time. He knows exactly how we spend it. Everything we do is known, it is recorded, and we shall be judged according to all these things. The 'secrets of men!' What an exposure it will be! How terrified we are of being found out! 'As long as it is not known', we say. 'As long as it is not known to the press!' How terrified we all are of exposure! If people only knew of the things that happen within us! Well, God does know! And it is all recorded, and it will all come into this question of judgment.

And then we must look at the other phrase in this verse: 'In the day when God shall judge the secrets of men by Jesus Christ *according to my gospel*'. 'But wait a minute', you say, 'Paul, you must have forgotten, you must have been tired when you reached that point. This is not a part of your gospel, surely – judgment! Perishing! Secrets exposed! Sentence promulgated! Is that gospel?' According to the Apostle Paul it is part of the gospel, and an essential part of it. It is, he says, according to the good news 'which has been committed unto me'. In the first chapter he has described himself as a 'called Apostle'. All this has been committed to him. He is going about preaching it, and this is a part of the preaching – the judgment of God upon the secrets of all men.

The gospel is not just simply, 'Come to Christ and have all your problems solved, and walk with a new and a lighter step tomorrow', and, 'Now I am happy all the day'! That is not all the gospel! It is the gospel. But the judgment, too, is a part of the gospel. Indeed, we have seen already that the moment the Apostle announces the theme of the gospel in verses 16 and 17 of chapter one, he at once goes on to say, 'For the wrath of God is revealed . . .'. And unless we preach this wrath of God and the day of judgment, we are not preaching a full gospel, we are holding back something, in order, perhaps, to ingratiate ourselves with men. Of course, the argument is this – we are all familiar with it – people say, 'Modern man does not like that sort of preacher, and if you talk about the wrath of God he will not come to church'. Therefore you leave it out! In other words, in order to be worldly-wise and in order to use your knowledge of psychology, you leave out a part of God's gospel! What a terrible thing it is! How clever we think we are! But how we deny the Word we claim to believe! And, perhaps, we even stand between souls and eternal salvation, for if a man does not realize that the wrath of God is upon him, and that nothing but the death of the Lord Jesus Christ on that cross can save him – not from his particular sin, but from the wrath of God – he really does not have the gospel. This is the essence of the gospel. Read through your New Testament – you will find it everywhere. 'According to my gospel', says Paul, when the modern man would least have expected him to have introduced the very term 'gospel'.

I must say one thing about this little word 'my' – 'according to my gospel'. I would not refer to this but for one thing. I remember reading a sermon about twenty years ago in a well-known religious weekly paper, a sermon by a very popular preacher, and he preached on this phrase – 'my gospel'. He was actually preaching on 2 Timothy 2 : 8 where the Apostle again uses the same expression, as he does also in Romans 16 : 25. Those are three places where Paul talks about 'my gospel'. But this is how this man preached on that expression: 'Now', he said, 'the great thing for all of us to know is this, can I say "my gospel"? There are far too many people who are living on somebody else's gospel – on their father's gospel, their mother's gospel, husband's gospel, wife's gospel, forebear's gospel, the gospel of the church to which they belong. Do you know', he continued, 'they have not really got assurance, they are not able to say "*my* gospel"'. All right! So far we agree with him, but he went further and said this: 'Of course, your gospel may not be the same as my gospel, but that does not matter; the great thing is that you can say "my gospel", that you really have got an experience. You may see it in this way, I may see it in that way, the other man may see it in quite a different way, but that does not matter at all; the great thing is that you can say that the Lord Jesus Christ has really made you happy. Of course, we may disagree tremendously theologically, and so on. One might want to insist upon the penal element in the atonement, and another does not, but what does it matter? The great thing is that you have got an experience, you can say "my gospel"'!

What an utter travesty! That is not what Paul means here and it is not what he means in 2 Timothy 2:8. There he says that 'Jesus Christ of the seed of David was raised from the dead according to my gospel'. He goes out of his way everywhere to say that there is only one gospel; and so he says to the Galatians, 'But though we, or an angel from heaven, preach any other gospel unto you than that which we have preached unto you, let him be accursed' [*Galatians* 1:8]. There is no other gospel. By 'my gospel', he means the gospel which had been committed to him, which he had been privileged to preach. The same gospel as was preached by all the other Apostles. But Paul likes to call it his gospel as well! It was his gospel. He had felt it. He had experienced it. He was preaching it in all its fulness, as the other Apostles were.

I would not have referred to that were it not for the subtle way in which the devil can twist even a little word like 'my' and make it mean the exact opposite of what it is meant to mean. No, what matters is not, primarily, your experience and mine, but this – the truth, the Word of God, the gospel once and for ever delivered and committed to the saints. There is only one, and it is only your gospel and my gospel as we continue steadfast in the Apostles' doctrine, and fellowship, and breaking of bread and prayer. 'Other foundation can no man lay . . .'. This is the *only* gospel. God grant that we may all know it as *our* gospel also!

Nine

*

(For not the hearers of the law are just before God, but the doers of the law shall be justified. For when the Gentiles, which have not the law, do by nature the things contained in the law, these, having not the law, are a law unto themselves: which shew the work of the law written in their hearts, their conscience also bearing witness, and their thoughts the mean while accusing or else excusing one another;)

Romans 2 : 13–15

We now come to a consideration of the parenthesis, which is to be found in the middle of Paul's fifth argument on the great subject of the wrath of God and justification by faith only. We have looked at this argument in general as it is stated in verses 11, 12 and 16 and now we must look at the words which are to be found within brackets in the Authorized Version, in verses 13, 14 and 15. Here, in this parenthesis, the Apostle does two things; he partly elaborates what he has been saying in his general statement, and at the same time he deals with certain objections which he knew many, both Jews and Gentiles, were bringing against his argument. So the object of the parenthesis is to make the truth abundantly clear and to anticipate and to deal with the objections.

Now I think that the best way of dealing with this statement is, first of all, to see the precise terms which he uses, and then to look at the whole question of the doctrine. So, with regard to the exact statement, verse 13 deals with the whole case of the Jews, who thought that the very fact that they had the law and had heard it, somehow or other put them right. They considered that they were in a special category, and that they need not have any fear about the wrath of God. They thought, furthermore, that they, already being God's people and His favourites, were in this peculiar relationship to Him, and that therefore they need not pay any attention to the preaching concerning Jesus of Nazareth as the only way of righteousness in the presence of God.

That is what he deals with in verse 13, and he just tells them quite simply that it is not the hearers of the law who are just before God, but it is the doers of the law who shall be justified. The mere fact that a man has heard it is of no value to him at all. What the law demands is that it should be obeyed. We know that in this country ignorance of the law is no plea, it is no excuse. But it is equally true to say that a knowledge of the law, in and of itself, is of no value either. It does not help a man who is arrested for crossing the traffic lights when they are red, to say that he knew very well that he should not have done that; the point is that he did it. The mere fact that you know the law or are familiar with it will not avail you at all if you have not kept it. Now that is what the Apostle is saying here. To hear the law is not enough. You notice that he says 'hearers' – today you might say 'readers' – of the law. In those days people did not read so much, they sat and listened and the law was expounded to them by their teachers; so he talks about 'hearers' of the law, and that includes anyone who in any way is familiar with the statements and the details of the law. And his principle, I repeat, is that it is not the hearers who are justified, but the doers, those who keep the law are the ones who will be justified in the presence of God.

Then verses 14 and 15 deal with the Gentiles. You see that he takes up both parties – Jews first, then Gentiles. He has been saying, twice over, in verses 9 and 10, '. . . to the Jew first, and also to the Gentile', and in these verses, too, he follows the same pattern. Obviously what he is dealing with is the possibility that somebody might say, 'All right, I understand that about the Jew, but then, what about the Gentile? Is it right that a man should be condemned by a law which he has never heard of? Is it right therefore that he should be condemned at all? If this is purely a question of law – and we admit that, as you put it, the Jews have no excuse and no case, and are under condemnation by the law – then does not that mean that the Gentiles are free?'

Paul's answer is that they are not innocent. It is true that the Gentiles have never received the law that was given through Moses in the way that the Jews had done, but that does not mean that they are free, that therefore they are under no condemnation, and that they are all automatically justified before God. Why not? Well, here are his answers: he says in verse 14 that these Gentiles who do not have the law as the Jews had, are 'a law unto themselves'. By that he means that whereas it is perfectly right to say that they have never heard the law that was given by Moses, and are in no sense, therefore, 'under the law', they nevertheless have a moral consciousness. And it is because they have this that they are responsible – they can be judged in terms of that moral consciousness which they possess. In that sense they are a law unto themselves. In other words, they do not come under the law of Moses but they come under this – we must not call it the law, but this kind of other law which is in terms of their moral consciousness, and which leads to a sense of responsibility.

'That', someone may argue, 'is a dogmatic statement, but can it be proved? Is it absolutely certain that this is the truth about the Gentiles?' Yes, says Paul, there are three proofs at any rate which establish this thing beyond any doubt whatsoever. The first is that they show 'the work of the law written in their hearts'. This is a very interesting statement, which we must look at carefully. You notice that the Apostle does not say that they show the *law* written in their hearts; he says that they show the *work* of the law written in their hearts. Now why did he vary the expression? Well, it is very important that he should have done so because he is not teaching here (as I shall be showing you when we come to deal with the doctrine) that the Gentiles are people who by nature have the law of God written on their hearts. That is not what he is saying.

Let me make this clear. A law is meant to produce certain results, is it not? The law says, 'Thou shalt not kill; thou shalt not steal' and so on. And it tells you, on the other hand, that there are certain things that you should do. So then, what the Apostle is saying is not that the Gentiles have the law itself written on their hearts, but that they show very clearly that the work of the law – these things about which the law is concerned and which it is designed to produce – is written on their hearts. Indeed, he is reiterating in verse 15 what he has already said in verse 14: 'The Gentiles, which have not the law, do by nature the things contained in the law'. In other words, if you observe or read about any pagan race, you will find that they refrain from certain things. The Gentiles, however ignorant they may be, have got ideas about murder and robbery and thieving and such like things, and you will find that this kind of moral sense is very highly developed amongst certain pagan tribes. Now that is what he means by the 'works of the law'. The law says, you must not do this, you should do that. And these people show quite plainly in their conduct that they know something about this, because they punish murder and they punish robbery and theft, and they teach their children that they should not steal, and so on. There are many other illustrations; I am simply picking some out at random.

But, of course, the Apostle has already said this very plainly in the last verse of the first chapter, where, writing about the Gentiles, he says, 'Who knowing the judgment of God, that they which commit such things are worthy of death, not only do the same, but have pleasure in them that do them'. And so you will find that in many pagan tribes and primitive tribes, they actually will punish adultery, for instance, by putting the guilty person to death. They know these things in that way, and yet though they know them, says the Apostle, they do not carry out what they do know; they commit the sins and they try to justify themselves as they do so. There, then, is the first argument – they show very plainly that the work of the law is written in their hearts. That is why they have these rules and regulations, and, without knowing why, they try to attain a certain moral standard and moral conception.

But then he goes on to his second argument, which is that they prove this by their conscience – '. . . their conscience also bearing witness'. Now the conscience is a kind of voice, a faculty, if you like, that is in all human beings. It is an inward monitor which tells us that certain things are wrong and that we should not do them. Whether we like it or not, it is there, and it expresses its opinion and it condemns us when we do wrong.

This is not the place to digress, and to go into the whole question of the conscience. It is an important subject, and we should be clear in our understanding of what the Bible does teach about it, but there, for the moment, it is in its essence. The conscience is something that is mainly negative. Its business is not so much to tell us what is right as to tell us what is wrong and to condemn us if we do it. The conscience is not a perfect instrument by any means, and a man's conscience can vary a good deal during his life. The Apostle Paul himself tells us elsewhere that when he persecuted the church of Christ he did it 'in all good conscience'. Indeed, he says that he had lived until that moment 'in all good conscience', but he came to see that some things which he had thought were right were wrong, and so we must not regard the conscience as a perfect instrument. Nevertheless we should always obey it. 'Ah, yes', you may say, 'but your conscience may be unenlightened'. If that is so, then it is my business to subject myself to further teaching. A conscience can be feeble, it can be unenlightened, and I can educate it, I can teach it and train it; but whatever state my conscience may be in, it is never right for me to do anything against it.

Now you will find that the Apostle makes that abundantly clear in his teaching. For instance, when he writes about the weaker brother, in 1 Corinthians chapters eight to ten, he says that the conscience of the weaker brother is always to be respected, because he must obey his conscience, and you must not be a stumbling block to him. That is not to say that his conscience is perfect, but even as Christians we must never act against the conscience.

So I have digressed a little after all! But what the Apostle is really saying is – and this is the immediate use which he makes of the conscience – that it does not matter how primitive a race of people may be, how ignorant, how unintelligent, how unenlightened, they all have a conscience, they all know what it is to be condemned by it, they all know what it is to be in a state of remorse. There is in every single human being ever born into the world this inward voice and monitor that pronounces its judgment – the conscience. There, then, is a second mighty proof of the fact that these Gentiles are responsible, that the mere fact that they did not know the law of Moses does not mean that there is no standard by which they can be judged. The conscience proves that there is a standard.

And that brings me to the third and last argument, which is this: '. . . their thoughts the meanwhile accusing or else excusing one another'. The word 'thoughts' is not a very good translation here. What it really means is their 'reasonings'. 'Their reasonings also between one another accusing or else excusing one another'. Paul is saying, in effect, 'You know, do you not, that these Gentiles who have never heard the law of Moses often have arguments among themselves as to whether a certain thing is right or whether it is wrong. Not only that, they have disputes and debates between one another as to whether what a certain man has done is right or not. They condemn one another and then they try to excuse themselves. They would not do all this unless they had got a standard'.

And this, again, is universally true. Go to the most primitive tribes in the world and you will find they are always doing this sort of thing – 'Was that right?'; 'Is that man's action right, or is it wrong?' – 'accusing or excusing'. And then, you see, a man will condemn a thing in another and defend it when he has done it himself. 'Ah', he says, 'I have an explanation for it; there was this peculiar circumstance, or feature, you see . . .' – reasonings among one another either accusing or else excusing. And the very fact that people do that is the final proof of the fact that they have this moral sense, this moral consciousness, this ability to differentiate between right and wrong and between good and evil.

And so Paul establishes his case that the mere fact that the Gentiles were not aware of the law of Moses does not for a second mean that they cannot be judged. The Jew is judged as to whether he keeps that law or not, the Gentile will be judged according to his conformity to what he does know, this law unto himself, this moral consciousness. He takes the ground from beneath his own feet in that threefold manner, and therefore there is no difficulty at all about understanding and seeing how it comes to pass that the Gentile is as much subject to judgment as the Jew.

Having made clear the terms which Paul uses we can now come to the teaching. What is the doctrine here? It is essential that we should understand it, because it is very frequently misunderstood, and in a variety of ways. There are those who say, on the basis of this parenthesis, that the Apostle Paul teaches quite plainly that there were certain Jews who did justify themselves by keeping the law. They point to verse 13 where Paul says, 'For not the hearers of the law are just before God but the doers of the law shall be justified'. 'Surely', they maintain, 'you must take the thing at its face value, you must take the words as they stand before you, and they are quite plain. The Apostle is saying that the man who does keep the law is justified by that, and so that means that the Jews who do keep the law are justified by their keeping of it'. That is one misunderstanding.

Another false argument which is developed is this: there are those who say that the Apostle is here teaching that there is a kind of natural law which is written in the hearts of all men; that the same law which God gave to the children of Israel through Moses was originally written in the hearts of all men and remains in the hearts of all pagans who have never heard of the Mosaic law at all. They say that it is quite plainly there in these verses; does not the Apostle say that they show 'the work of the law written in their hearts', and that they 'do by nature the things contained in the law'? That is the second false deduction which is drawn from this parenthesis.

And then the third is this: that the Gentiles, people who have never heard the gospel, can, and do, save themselves, by living up to the light that they have. I am sure that we have all often heard that argument. 'What about the pagans', people ask, 'who have never heard the gospel at all?'

'Ah', the answer is given, 'they are all right. You see, all they have to do is to live up to the light which they have, and that puts them right. God would not be unjust. They are saved, though they have never heard the gospel'. Sometimes that argument is applied to the Greek philosophers who lived before our Lord ever came into this world. It is said that those men were saved because of their excellent moral teaching, and so on. They had never heard of the Mosaic law, they had never heard the gospel, but they had got this light and they lived up to it, and therefore they are saved.

Those, then, are the three things that are said most frequently on the basis of the teaching of this parenthesis; and so we must deal with them. Now it seems to me that the best way in which we can do this is to emphasize, first of all, what this parenthesis does not teach. Let us start, in other words, with our negatives, and the first is that this parenthesis – and this applies to the whole of this section – does not teach in any shape or form the way of justification or salvation for anybody. It does not deal with the way in which the Jew is justified, nor with the way in which the Gentile is justified. That is not what Paul is dealing with. He is dealing with condemnation, with judgment, and with wrath, and he does not raise the question of the way of salvation here at all.

The second thing which it does not teach is that anyone ever has kept, or ever can keep, the law and thereby be justified. Now I prove that statement, first of all, by using an argument which I have had to use several times already in connection with this chapter. Let me remind you of it. The whole object of the Apostle from chapter one, verse 18, to chapter three, verse 20, is to prove that no flesh is justified in the presence of God. The Apostle here is setting out to prove that both the Jews and the Gentiles are under condemnation. He will wind it up by concluding: 'Therefore by the deeds of the law there shall no flesh be justified in his sight'. He says it, also, in these words: 'There is none righteous, no, not one . . . That every mouth may be stopped, and all the world may become guilty before God . . . All have sinned, and come short of the glory of God' [3 : 10, 19, 23]. That is what he is setting out to prove. So if he suddenly says here, halfway through, that there are some Jews who have kept the law and thereby justified themselves, then he is contradicting himself blankly and hopelessly, and saying the exact opposite of that which he is setting out to demonstrate. But the Apostle does not do things like that. He is a most logical thinker; he proceeds from step to step; he takes up objections and answers them; and how vital it is, therefore, that as we are looking at any section we should bear the whole in mind. That is one argument. But there are others.

When we look at verse 13 we see that it is not telling us anything about what anyone does, it is simply telling us what the law demands – 'For not the hearers of the law are just before God'. What the law demands to know is not whether a man has heard it or not; what the law asks is whether he has kept it. Has he put it into practice? That is what the Apostle is talking about. He is not saying that there are certain people who have done this or that, he is saying, in effect, 'Look here, to claim that the mere fact that you have heard the law puts you right in and of itself, is to show that you are ignorant about what the law really says, and what it demands. It does not call for a mere hearing, a mere acquaintance with itself. What it demands is that it should be put into practice'. Paul is not saying that the Jew or anybody else can ever come up to these demands. All he is saying is that for the Jew to maintain that really nothing matters except that he can say, 'Ah, after all, the law was given to us', does not help at all, because that very law says, 'Have you kept my injunctions? Have you carried out my dictates?'

Let me make this perfectly plain, because it is a most important and valuable argument for us as Christian people when we are having a discussion with a moral type of person; the sort of person who is not a Christian and says that he does not see any need for believing in our doctrine about the Son of God coming to earth to die for our sins, and so on. His whole case is that all God demands is that you live a good life. He claims, further, that he has lived a good life, he has not committed certain sins, he does a lot of good – a highly moral person, you cannot point a finger at him. How do you deal with such a person? Well, here is the wonderful argument which the Apostle provides for us. You start by saying, 'But, you see, the law of God demands that a man should carry it out'.

Let me show you how the Apostle says the same thing again in Romans 10 : 5: 'For Moses describeth the righteousness which is of the law, That the man which doeth those things shall live by them'. The law does not say that a man who *hears* these things shall live by them. No, it is, 'The man who *doeth* these things . . .'. It says, 'If you do what I tell you, then you shall live, you shall have salvation'. Let me quote here Dr Moffatt's translation which I think is quite useful at this point. He translates it like this: 'Any one who can perform it shall live by it'. That is the idea. If you keep this law you will be justified in the presence of God.

But what is this law which I have got to keep and which, when I keep it, will justify me before God? That is the question. And our Lord and Saviour Jesus Christ has answered it. When a lawyer came to Him and said, 'Which is the great commandment in the law?' our Lord answered and said, 'Thou shalt love the Lord thy God with all thy heart, and with all thy soul, and with all thy mind. This is the first and great commandment. And the second is like unto it, Thou shalt love thy neighbour as thyself' [*Matthew* 22 : 36–39]. This is the Lord's summary of the law.

So, then, go to the Jew, go to the highly moral person and say, 'You are perfectly correct when you say that if a man keeps the law, he is justified in the presence of God. Do you say that you have kept the law?'

'Well', he replies, 'I have never done this, I have never done that'.

'But', you say, 'that is not what the law demands. What the law demands is that you should love God with all your heart and all your soul and all your mind and all your strength, and that you should love your neighbour as yourself. Are you doing that? If not, you have not kept the law and you are not justified, you are condemned, you are damned, and you are lost'.

Or consider how James puts it in chapter 2:8-9. He deals with this in a most remarkable manner, and it is a vital piece of argument: 'If ye fulfil the royal law according to the scripture, Thou shalt love thy neighbour as thyself, ye do well: But if ye have respect to persons, ye commit sin, and are convinced of the law as transgressors'. Then notice this in verses 10-11: 'For whosoever shall keep the whole law, and yet offend in one point, he is guilty of all. For he that said, Do not commit adultery, said also, Do not kill. Now if thou commit no adultery, yet if thou kill, thou art become a transgressor of the law'. That is, surely, a very definite and final answer to all who imagine for a moment that the Apostle Paul is saying here in Romans chapter two that there are certain Jews who will be found in glory because they have carried out the law and have thereby justified themselves before God. He is saying nothing of the sort. He is addressing these Jews who were foolish and ignorant enough to think that a man ever could keep the law and he is simply saying to them in effect, 'Let me remind you of what the law does demand, and the moment you see that you will see that no man has ever kept, or ever obeyed the law'.

Did you notice, also, the word 'do' in verse 14? 'For when the Gentiles, which have not the law, do by nature the things contained in the law . . .'. Now he is not saying there for a second that these Gentiles have kept the whole law. Of course, the thing is patently impossible. All he is saying is that though they do certain things which the law does demand, they do not do everything. The Gentiles are no more capable of fulfilling the whole law than the Jews were. Nobody can. If you offend in one point you have offended in all: 'Therefore by the deeds of the law there shall no flesh be justified in his sight: for by the law is the knowledge of sin' [*Romans* 3 : 20]. Or, as he puts it in Romans 8 : 3, 'For what the law could not do, in that it was weak through the flesh . . .' – again the same argument, man's flesh is too weak, he cannot keep the law. So, then, there is our argument with regard to that second matter. The Apostle is not saying that anyone ever has, or ever can, keep the law and thereby be justified.

Let me come to a third statement. He is not saying that the Gentiles have the law written in their hearts. Now I pointed out earlier in the exposition that the Apostle does not even say that they have the law written in their hearts; he says that they have the *work* of the law written in their hearts. That argument is enough in itself, but let me give you some further ones. It cannot mean that the Gentiles have the law of God, as such, written in their hearts because the first great obligation of the law is man's attitude towards God – this loving of God with the whole of our being. Indeed, in chapter one he has told us that the only knowledge that the Gentiles have of God is a kind of knowledge of His power as Creator. They have some vague notion of His power and of His deity, but that is not a knowledge of God in His being, and in His character, and in His person. So the Apostle would again be contradicting himself if he suddenly said here that they have this law of God written in their hearts.

Then there is a further vital argument. If it is true that the Apostle is here saying that these Gentiles have the law of God written in their hearts, then it follows that he is saying that they are actually superior to the Jews who only had it written in tables of stone, outside themselves! It is a greater thing to have the law in your heart than to have it on tables of stone, and all that we are told about the Jews is that they had it externally on tables of stone. Paul would therefore be saying here that the Gentiles were superior to the Jews – which is again, of course, to make his whole reasoning ridiculous.

Or a third equally powerful argument is this: if it is true that the Gentiles have this law of God written in their hearts, then they have already anticipated the promise of what is to happen in the new covenant. In the Old Testament God said through the prophet Jeremiah, 'I will make a new covenant with the house of Israel . . . not according to the covenant that I made with their fathers in the day that I took them by the hand to bring them out of the land of Egypt; which my covenant they brake . . . but this shall be the covenant that I will make with the house of Israel . . .' [*Jeremiah* 31 : 31–33]; you will find that quoted in Hebrews 8 : 8–11. What is the great characteristic of the new covenant? It is this: 'I will put my law in their inward parts, and write it in their hearts'. Now that was never true of the Jews. God gave the Jews the laws on the tables of stone; He did not write them in their minds then, nor in their hearts. But, He says, I am going to make a new covenant with you when I send the Messiah, and this will be the great characteristic of the new covenant: 'I will put my laws into your minds and write them in your hearts' [*Hebrews* 8 : 10]. And yet, you see, the people who misunderstand Paul's argument here tell us that the Apostle is saying in these verses that God had already written the laws in the hearts of the Gentiles long ago – that from the very beginning He had done this thing to them which He only promises to do when the new covenant comes in. Surely, therefore, there can be no question about this – the Apostle is not saying here that the Gentiles have the law of God written in their hearts. There is no teaching in the Scripture about some natural law written in the hearts of men. All Paul claims for them is that they have a certain moral sense and a moral consciousness.

That brings me to the last matter, which comes under this negative heading. The Apostle does not teach in this parenthesis that if we live up to the light that we have, we shall be saved. And I emphasize that because what he is actually saying here, and in the entire passage, is that no one ever does live up to the light that he has, whether he be a Jew or whether he be a Gentile. The light that the Jew has is the light of the law given through Moses – and none of them live up to it. The light that the Gentile has is this moral consciousness – and none of them live up to it, either. That is why they can accuse one another and try to excuse themselves. They have all sinned, even against their own moral consciousness. Nobody does or can live up to the light that he has, so how foolish it is to say that we can save ourselves by doing that! But still more important, if you say that a man can save himself by living up to the light that he has, then, there is no need for the Lord Jesus Christ as Saviour; He need never have left heaven, He need never have come into the world, He need never have died upon the cross on Calvary's hill. How often do we say glibly – sometimes, I am afraid, even those of us who are Christians – 'Ah, the Gentiles never heard the gospel, but they are saved if they live up to the light they have'. No one ever does, no one ever can. And if anybody can, then, I say Christ's death for us would never have been necessary. But the whole teaching of the Bible from beginning to end is that He and He alone is the Saviour. There is no salvation outside Christ. 'For there is one God, and one mediator between God and men, the man Christ Jesus' [1 *Timothy* 2 : 5].

Finally, as a very practical argument, have you ever considered this: if you really believe that a man can save himself by living up to the light he has, then you must stop supporting foreign mission work. Because by sending missionaries from this land to pagan lands and teaching them the Bible, the Ten Commandments – the moral law – and the Sermon on the Mount, and things like that, you are putting before them an altogether higher standard than they had before, and you are therefore making things still more difficult and impossible for them. It would have been much better to leave them where they were with their low standard; they stand a better chance of coming up to that. They do not even come up to that, but it is easier and more hopeful at any rate than this other standard. It is a complete condemnation of the missionary enterprise. In fact, such a false interpretation of these verses is quite monstrous and utterly ridiculous.

The Apostle is teaching none of these things whatsoever in this important and vital parenthesis. We must deal next with what he does teach, which is much simpler, and can be dealt with more briefly. And then, having done that, I will try to take up certain further problems which are so frequently raised on the basis of this parenthesis. What of the pagans? What of those Greek philosophers before Christ ever came? What of people like the father and mother of John the Baptist, who are described as just and righteous and so on – what of them?

These are important problems which, together with the others that we have already considered, have frequently been misunderstood. God grant that we shall be clear in our understanding of what the Bible does teach.

Ten

*

(For not the hearers of the law are just before God, but the doers of the law shall be justified. For when the Gentiles, which have not the law, do by nature the things contained in the law, these, having not the law, are a law unto themselves: which shew the work of the law written in their hearts, their conscience also bearing witness, and their thoughts the mean while accusing or else excusing one another;) In the day when God shall judge the secrets of men by Jesus Christ according to my gospel. Behold, thou art called a Jew, and restest in the law, and makest thy boast of God.

Romans 2 : 13–17

We have spent some time in dealing with what this parenthesis does not say, and we have done that because so often people have tried to prove that it says a number of things which it simply does not say at all. We have seen that it does not teach justification by faith or the way of salvation. It does not say that anybody can keep, or is capable of keeping, or ever has kept the law. It does not say that the Gentiles have the law of God written on their hearts. And it does not say that if we live up to the light we have, we shall be saved.

And so, having understood all that, we come now to what it does say, to its positive teaching, and this need not detain us very long, because in dealing with the actual statement, with the actual words, we were more or less giving a positive exposition. But it may be a good thing for us to have it in the form of principles, and the first is this: It is a statement to the effect – and this is its main purpose – that God's judgment is always fair and is always according to a standard. God always judges us according to a standard of which we are aware, whether, as we have seen, it be the law or this sense of right and wrong that is in the whole of the human race. What Paul is setting out to prove is that God's judgment is always just, and that, as he puts it in the second verse of this chapter, it is always 'according to truth'.

Another principle is that the law which had been given to the Jews, and which was therefore the standard for them, is the very thing that condemns them – that is in verse 13. And in exactly the same way, it is his moral consciousness that condemns the Gentile. And so the law and the moral consciousness, far from saving the Jew and the Gentile, are in both cases the means of their condemnation. The Apostle is anxious to say that, because his whole purpose here is to show that everybody is under the wrath of God, and that there is none just, no, not one.

So, then, my next principle is that the Jews and the Gentiles, from the standpoint of condemnation, and therefore from the standpoint of salvation, are in precisely the same position. As the Apostle will tell us later more than once, there is no difference at all between the Jew and the Gentile. The Jew thought there was a tremendous difference. The Apostle is here establishing that there is none; the Jew is condemned by the law, the Gentile by the moral consciousness. They are both condemned.

You see, to know the law as it was given by Moses is not going to save anybody; it only condemns. To have this moral sense does not save anybody; it, too, only condemns. So any knowledge that we may have in one form or another of this will of God and of right and wrong, far from helping us, simply turns out to be the source of our condemnation.

There, then, we have the positive teaching of this most important parenthesis, and that now leaves us in the position of being able to take up the main problems which have often been raised by expositors and others on the basis of this parenthesis, and which have often stumbled people.

The first problem is that statements are made about certain people, apart from the gospel, to the effect that they were righteous or that they were just. Here were people who lived before the atoning work of our Lord and before His resurrection, and that is how they are described. 'In that case', says someone, 'surely all you have been telling us about the teaching of the parenthesis must be wrong?'

But let me give you examples. In Luke 1 : 6 you will find this statement about the parents of John the Baptist, Zacharias and Elisabeth: 'And they were both righteous before God, walking in all the commandments and ordinances of the Lord blameless'. Now there are many who have tried to argue that this is a categorical statement to the effect that here at any rate were two people who, by keeping the law and observing God's commandments, have made themselves righteous and blameless, and therefore just in the sight of God. The other statement is about the aged Simeon, the old man who held the Lord Jesus in his arms and said, 'Lord, now lettest thou thy servant depart in peace . . .'. We are told about him in Luke 2 : 25, '. . . and the same man was just and devout'. And, indeed, we might as well raise at this point the whole question of all those great saints of the Old Testament who died long before the Lord Jesus Christ ever came into this world.

How then do we reconcile what we are told about them with the teaching of the parenthesis as I have been expounding it? And the answer, of course, is this: we are not told of a single one of them that they had kept the whole of the law perfectly and that on that basis they were justified before God. What we are told about them is that they were the kind of people who are mentioned in Romans 2 : 7: 'who by patient continuance in well doing seek for glory and honour and immortality', and who because of that will receive the gift of 'eternal life'.

In other words, the position of these people was that they were aware of the law and the commandments of God, but that does not mean that they were only aware of the Ten Commandments and the moral law; they were equally aware, as the passage tells us, of the ordinances that had been appointed by God himself. I mean by that the commandments concerning the sin offering and the trespass offering and the various meal offerings, and so on; and these were people who received all these commandments and ordinances from God. They did not understand them perfectly, but they understood this much – they understood that God was teaching them that this was the only way whereby they could approach Him, that they were not good enough as they were, and that every one needed to be covered by these offerings and sacrifices. And so they were people who conformed to God's law in that way. Not that they kept the Ten Commandments perfectly, because we have the word of the Apostle in chapter three and elsewhere, 'There is none righteous, no, not one . . . all have sinned, and come short of the glory of God'. No one has ever been able to keep the commandments of God perfectly, but God had provided a way to cover over their sins, and they believed that, and availed themselves of it and so, putting themselves under this provision, they were righteous. The High Priest went in once a year for the sins of the people and God accepted his offering, the sacrifice and the blood, and when he came out, the people knew that their sins had been covered, that they were forgiven, and that they therefore could regard themselves as righteous in the presence of God.

Now that is what we are told about these people, and it is important that we should grasp it. These were people, in other words, who had believed the teaching which God Himself had revealed, that He was going to make a great provision in some future age for the sins of mankind. These were people who had spiritual minds, they were called 'devout' people. They did not rest on these things alone; they saw that these ordinances were but pictures, but shadows and adumbrations. They were types pointing to some great Anti-type who was going to come, who was going to do this work in a perfect manner. So, you see, you find in the case of Simeon and the prophetess Anna that we are told they were looking and waiting for the salvation of Israel, they were longing for the day when the Messiah, the Deliverer, should come, and it is in that sense that they are righteous people. They have put themselves under all the provision that God has made for mankind to have communion with Him.

And anyone, therefore, who was concerned about keeping the law, and anyone who observed all these ordinances, as Zacharias and Elisabeth did, can very rightly be described as being righteous people, and blameless in the presence of God. But only in that sense. Not on the basis of their own activities; not on the basis of their own good works and their good deeds and their excellent morality. Not at all. Notice what we are told about them by the Scripture itself: they were 'walking in all the commandments and ordinances of the Lord blameless'. Now that is true, of course, of all the Old Testament saints. These people were submitting to God's provision, and they were looking through and beyond these things for the coming of the great salvation that was yet to be revealed.

Then under this same heading we are bound to consider the case of Cornelius, as it is recorded in Acts chapter ten. We read in verses 34 and 35: 'Then Peter opened his mouth, and said, Of a truth I perceive that God is no respecter of persons: but in every nation he that feareth him, and worketh righteousness, is accepted with him'. Now those words have often been used, as this parenthesis has been used, as an argument for saying that surely there is direct scriptural evidence that here is a man who is a Gentile and who, because he was living up to the light he had and was a good man and was living a righteous kind of life, had been accepted by God, though he was not a Jew and not a Christian. Now that may seem to be a plausible argument, but let us examine the evidence. There is nothing so dangerous as just to pick two verses, right out of their context, and say, 'Now, there it is – what have you got to say to that? However dim a man's light may be, if he fears God and does righteousness he is accepted by God'.

But listen to what we are told about Cornelius at the beginning of the chapter: 'There was a certain man in Caesarea called Cornelius, a centurion of the band called the Italian band, [notice this] a devout man, and one that feared God with all his house, which gave much alms to the people, and prayed to God alway. He saw in a vision evidently about the ninth hour of the day an angel of God coming in to him, and saying unto him, Cornelius. And when he had looked on him, he was afraid, and said, What is it, Lord? And he said unto him, Thy prayers and thine alms are come up for a memorial before God . . .'.

Now what is the meaning of that teaching? Surely it is perfectly clear and plain. Here again is a man who is not at all relying on his good works. The important thing about this man is that he is a devout man, praying always, because he realizes his need of prayer, he realizes his own imperfection and his own sinfulness. Here is a very godly man. He is not an idol worshipper – indeed, everything we are told about Cornelius makes it quite clear that he was a Jewish proselyte, and that we must never think of him as a Gentile entirely apart from Judah. We are told that he 'gave much alms to the people', and in the Book of Acts 'the people' always stands for the Jews, while the rest are those who do not belong to them. So, here is a devout man, clearly a Jewish proselyte, so that he, exactly like Simeon, and Anna the prophetess, and like Zacharias and Elisabeth, was one of these godly people who was looking for and waiting for the coming of the Messiah.

There are those who say, and I am very ready to agree with them, that when the vision appeared to Cornelius he was probably offering this prayer: he was saying, in effect, 'How long, O Lord? When is this great thing going to happen?'

And the angel said to him: 'It is going to happen now. Your prayer has been heard, so send your messengers to this man Peter, who is down there at Joppa, and he will come and will tell you all about it – this very thing you have been praying for. I am going to let you know how it has already taken place'.

Looked at thus, in the light of the evidence and context, it is quite clear, I think, that in the case of Cornelius, we are not dealing with a good pagan, a man who has never had the Jewish or the Christian teaching, but who, because he has lived up to the light he has got, is acceptable to God. Acts chapter ten and the accompanying passages teach nothing of the kind. Here is a man who is waiting for the salvation that God is going to send, and who is now informed that it has actually come.

All these people come under the same general category. They are all people who had realized that the business of the law, to use this Apostle's phrase, was to be a schoolmaster to bring us to Christ. Every one of them realized that they could never keep the law, they could never fulfil it. Not a single one of these would have claimed that he had made himself acceptable before God. No, the picture we have of them is that they are humble, devout, godly persons who are relying on God's provision and waiting for the manifestation of this great salvation. They are the very opposite, then, of what certain people have tried to prove from their particular cases.

And, that I may round off this argument, let us come to the whole question of people like Plato and Socrates, and the great Greek philosophers, and others. You know how often it is said of them that they were Christians before Christ, that they come under this category of good people who, living up to the light they had, and holding exalted and idealistic views, and doing good works, were undoubtedly accepted of God. But the simple answer concerning them is just to point out that they were all idolaters and worshipped idols. They were guilty of that thing which is condemned without any qualification in the Bible, in both the Old Testament and the New. They were not even God-fearers. They had a certain general philosophy and by means of that philosophy they had elaborated the teaching of the moral consciousness in a very remarkable manner, but that is useless as far as salvation is concerned.

You remember how the Apostle puts it in Romans 1 : 18: 'The wrath of God is revealed from heaven against [first] all ungodliness and [then] all unrighteousness of men' – but ungodliness comes before unrighteousness. And it does not matter how good a man's moral theories may be, if he is not godly he is guilty of the greatest sin of all. And as the Apostle has proved to us, they are without excuse, for God has already revealed His great and eternal power and divinity in creation. But they were blind and they could not see it. So that the case of all such men is dismissed in that way – because of their wrong relationship to God. They are under condemnation as all others, and their philosophy and their good works avail them nothing. 'The world by wisdom [by philosophy] knew not God . . .' [1 *Corinthians* 1 : 21], and whatever else we may have, if we do not know God, it is of no value to us. So their case is to be seen in that particular light.

Then that brings me to the second question, a question that is very often raised on the basis of this parenthesis. What, then, is the position of pagan people who have never heard the gospel at all? How are they saved? By what are they saved? The simple answer to that question is that it is neither raised nor considered at all in this parenthesis. It is not even hinted at. Let me say it once more. This whole section is not concerned at all about the way of salvation; it is simply concerned about the matter of condemnation. Therefore it is important to realize that there is not a shred of evidence in this parenthesis which bears on the position of these pagans who have never heard the Christian gospel.

'But', people say, 'we are concerned about this. Are they, who have never heard the gospel at all, to be condemned?' Well there is a very definite answer to that question. They are condemned, but they are not condemned for not obeying the gospel. They are condemned for not obeying the moral consciousness that is within them. They have the work of the law written in their heart and they do not obey it, they do not come up to it, so they are condemned by that. But they are no more condemned than anyone else. Not condemned, I repeat, for rejecting the gospel, which they have never heard, but condemned equally and quite as definitely by their failure to conform to the dictates of the moral consciousness that is within them. So, you see, there is nothing unfair about their position either.

'But what of their salvation?' you say. Well, there is only one thing to say about that – salvation is possible only in and through the Lord Jesus Christ. It has always been possible only in and through Him. The saints of the Old Testament were saved by the fact that they believed the message concerning Him in the way that they had it. I have proved that to you by their conformity to the ordinances which were given simply to point to Him. The blood of bulls and goats and the ashes of an heifer cannot save, they cannot make the conscience clean. No, their value is that they cover for the time being, and that they point forward. They stimulate faith. These people believed by faith that God was going to fulfil His promises and therefore they were justified by faith, not by these other things. So in answer to the question about the Gentiles, we must say about them as about everybody else – everybody is saved by the Lord Jesus Christ, and there is no salvation apart from Him.

'But', you ask, 'what about the people who have never heard of the Lord Jesus Christ? Is that fair?' Ah! We are dealing now with the kind of question which should never be asked. That is the kind of question that makes Paul say, in Romans chapter nine, 'O man, who art thou that repliest against God?' [v. 20]. But let me put a question to you. You ask me about these Gentiles who have never heard the gospel, who have never had an opportunity, and who, we have said, are under condemnation. But what about all the Gentiles during the centuries before the Lord Jesus Christ ever came into this world? They had never heard about Him. They did not have the Jewish law. They did not know about these ordinances. God gave the law only to this one nation, He did nothing about the others. How do you answer that? It is exactly the same question. There were all those centuries with millions of pagans outside Israel who had none of this teaching. What of them?

And, you see, there is only one answer – we do not know. We cannot answer the question. All I can say is this: I know that they were all condemned by their moral consciousness, and I can say equally that no one can be saved outside the Lord Jesus Christ. And I know no more. But I will go further: I am not meant to know any more. There would be something about it in the Bible if I were meant to know more, and there is not a word. All I know is that those in the world today who have never heard of the Lord Jesus Christ are under the wrath of God and under condemnation, and that it is my business and your business and the business of all Christians to do all we can to send the good news of salvation to them. It is the mighty argument for the missionary enterprise and for sending men with the good news.

We are not told anywhere in the Scripture how these things are ultimately to be reconciled in the justice of God. But we do know this – that the Judge of all the world will always do that which is right. God never does anything unjust. I do not know the answer, we do not understand it, but, as I have said, the question should never have been raised. The parenthesis does not raise it. You cannot raise it on the basis of Scripture – Scripture does not deal with the question at all, and we cannot go beyond that. The moment you do, you are beginning to speculate, and the moment you begin to speculate you are doing something very dangerous. 'Ah, but', you say, 'my idea of a God of love is this . . .'. Well, it may be, my friend, but you know you are very sinful, you are finite, and God is eternal and absolute; be very careful what you say God ought to do, lest you find yourself blaspheming and guilty of pitting your ideas against the thoughts of this eternal and holy God. There is only one thing to do – we bow our heads before Him. We are content with the absence of clear teaching, with the absence of revelation. We submit to it. And we do all that we can to propagate the gospel and to spread it abroad, with this final assurance that God's ways are always perfect whether I understand them or not at any particular moment. Those, then, are the problems that are generally raised on the basis of the parenthesis.

We move on now to the next section, which goes on to verse 24. Now in these verses, from the beginning of verse 17 to the end of the chapter, the Apostle is going to apply and drive home to these Jews the principles which he has been laying down. What a wonderful preacher this man is! He brings out his points, he sets out his principles, and he establishes them, but he does not pronounce the Benediction when he has done that. Not at all! You have not finished preaching until you have applied your teaching.

Let me once again say this as a parenthesis: I know of nothing more dangerous to the soul than to treat the Bible as if it were just an ordinary text-book, so that you feel quite happy when you have a fresh translation or have divided up your chapter, and you think, 'That is all'. It is not all! You are only beginning. It must now be applied. As you read it alone, apply it to yourself. If you speak to others, apply the message, do not just leave it with the thing stated plainly or with a new translation. A man should never handle the Scripture without preaching. It is a Word to be preached, to be applied. And if we fail to do that, we are not only disobeying Scripture itself, we are departing very far indeed from the example set us here by this great Apostle. He is now going to take all this and bring it right home to the mind and heart and conscience of the Jews whom he is addressing.

And what he is going to apply, in particular, is what he says in verses 1, 3, and 13: 'Therefore thou art inexcusable, O man, whosoever thou art that judgest: for wherein thou judgest another, thou condemnest thyself; for thou that judgest doest the same things' [v. 1]. That is the accusation – you are doing the very same things that you condemn in others! He says it again in verse 3: 'And thinkest thou this, O man, that judgest them which do such things, and doest the same, [notice that!] that thou shalt escape the judgment of God?' And then in verse 13: 'For not the hearers of the law are just before God, but the doers of the law shall be justified'. Now that is what he intends to drive right home; and that, especially, is what he drives home in verses 17 to 24 where he points out their failure to act in terms of their knowledge of the law. In verses 25 to 29 he is going to do the same thing, in a sense, but there he will be showing their failure to act particularly in terms of their reliance upon circumcision.

Let us look, then, at the first section. The essence of the charge Paul brings here against these Jews is that of hypocrisy; and nowhere in the whole range and realm of Scripture is there a more devastating exposure of hypocrisy and its evil ways than in this very section. Therefore, as we look at this castigation and this exposure of the Jews of old, may God give us grace to examine ourselves. Hypocrisy is a sin that besets us all. It is the thing of which we constantly have to beware. You remember our Lord's warning to His own immediate followers: 'Beware ye of the leaven of the Pharisees, which is hypocrisy' [*Luke* 12 : 1]. It is a snare, He says, because you can be an unconscious hypocrite, as these Jews were – and that makes it very terrifying.

So the Apostle brings this matter home to them – and we must watch him as he builds up his case. It is really one of the most cogent arguments, I think, that he ever used. Watch him marshalling his facts. First of all he reminds the Jews of what they claim for themselves: 'Behold' he says: or you can translate it 'If'.

> Behold, thou art called a Jew, and restest in the law, and makest thy boast of God, and knowest his will, and approvest the things that are more excellent, being instructed out of the law; and art confident that thou thyself art a guide of the blind, a light of them which are in darkness, an instructor of the foolish, a teacher of babes, which hast the form of knowledge and of the truth in the law . . .

He seems to be going on for ever, but he suddenly stops and says, 'Thou therefore' – this man, you, whom I am addressing, you, who are called a Jew –

> . . . Thou therefore which teachest another, teachest thou not thyself? thou that preachest a man should not steal, dost thou steal? thou that sayest a man should not commit adultery, dost thou commit adultery? thou that abhorrest idols, dost thou commit sacrilege? thou that makest thy boast of the law, through breaking the law dishonourest thou God? [*then a quotation*] For the name of God is blasphemed among the Gentiles through you, as it is written.

You see the law court? You see the prisoner in the dock and the prosecuting counsel? What a devastating thing it must have been to have been confronted by a man like this. Paul puts the case of the Jew better than any Jew could himself put it; he knew it so well, he had been in it himself. He said, 'I know this is what you are boasting of, that this is what you are relying on'.

These verses can be sub-divided, because there does seem to be a natural division here. First of all Paul reminds the Jews of what they primarily claim for themselves, that is in verses 17 and 18. Then in 19 and 20 he goes on to ask them a series of questions based on their claim. First of all, then, 'Thou art called a Jew'. What does he mean by this? Well, to be called a Jew was one of the greatest things that could happen to anybody, because the Jews, after all, were the people of God. The whole world was divided into Jews and Gentiles. Who are the Jews? They are a people, a special people, chosen and separated from all others for a special possession for God Himself; the opposite of being a Gentile, an outsider, an alien from the commonwealth of Israel. They were members of God's church; members of God's family. What a privilege! Called a Jew! The highest privilege a man could ever have. And the Apostle knew how the Jew boasted about that, and how he rejoiced in it; he remembered how he himself used to boast that he was an 'Hebrew of the Hebrews'. The same thing!

Then the second statement is, '. . . restest in the law'. This means that the Jew was relying on the law, in the sense that he was relying on the fact that the law had been given to him and to his nation and to his people. He was relying on the mere possession of the law, saying to himself, 'We have received the law, those Gentiles have never had it; they are dogs; they are outside. God gave the law only to us because we are His special people, we are His children, we are His favourites. We rest upon the law'. And they were doing that in all respects. They were resting upon the mere possession of the knowledge of the law; they were resting upon all the ritual and the ceremonial and the whole of the Mosaic system. The Jew was, as it were, making a pillow of it and putting his head on it and saying, 'I can go to sleep happily while those other people are in terrible danger'.

The third thing is, '. . . makest thy boast of God'. He was proud of the fact that he worshipped God. He said, 'We are the only people who know that there is only one God. All other people believe that there is a multiplicity of gods; they make gods out of wood and stone and precious metals, and then they bow down and worship them. Idolatry! It is all nonsense! Projections of their own ideas! There is only one true and living God. God is one God. We are worshippers of God'. You

[139]

recognize the modern ring about all this, do you not? They made their boast in the fact that they worshipped God! What a terrible thing is this hypocrisy, this blindness of sin, that can make a man think that he is a worshipper of God when the whole time he is bringing the name of God into disrepute, and causing others to blaspheme it.

The next thing is, he boasts that he knows the will of God; and in a sense he had every reason to boast of that, because he had the law. And, furthermore, he approves of 'the things that are more excellent'; that really means that he tests things that differ. Having been given this revelation, he is able to discriminate between good and evil in a way that the Gentile with his moral consciousness cannot. He is on a higher level. He has a deeper understanding. He is able to discriminate. And then Paul sums it up by saying that the Jew has been 'instructed out of the law'. And it was his great boast that he had received this teaching concerning the law in the synagogues from his teachers, the Pharisees and scribes. And oh how proud of it he was! He said, 'Look at those Gentiles, they have not got such marvellous teachers, they have not got the knowledge, the revelation. We have the oracles of God, we are instructed people, we have been taught out of the law'. And they made their boast of these things.

Then, as the result of that, the Jew said this about himself – and here is the second couplet of verses – 'And art confident that thou thyself art a guide of the blind'. That is to say, he maintains, as a Jew, that he is able to instruct others. And not only is he a guide of the blind, he is also 'a light of them which are in darkness' – people who have never heard these things. The Jew has this enlightenment, and therefore he can teach and guide others, and throw light upon their condition and upon the way in which they can come to God. He is in this marvellous position of enlightenment which enables him to speak down to others and to teach them.

And then the second thing the Jew says about himself is that he is 'an instructor of the foolish, a teacher of babes'. Now this 'teacher of babes' is interesting. The 'babes' are undoubtedly the proselytes; those people from among the Gentiles who, having observed the religion of Israel, and having realized its superiority, said that they would like to become Jews. And so they were instructed, and circumcised, and they became Jews; and the 'teacher of babes' therefore is this Jew, who, being a Jew already, can help these beginners, these neophytes, as it were, who have just come into Judaism. And then Paul says of the Jews that they have 'the form of knowledge and of the truth in the law'. Now what does this expression 'form of knowledge' mean? Does he mean here that it was merely an appearance of knowledge but not real knowledge? No, it cannot mean that, because the Jews had knowledge in a very definite manner as it had been given in the law. It means knowledge of the truth set forth in an orderly manner, and that is, of course, the Ten Commandments and the teaching of the moral law. It possesses 'form'. It was not inchoate and indefinite, as was the teaching of the moral consciousness and other teaching. Here it had been codified, it had been put into a form; so the Jew had a form of knowledge and of the truth as it had come to him through the law.

Now all that is what this Jew – and it was typical of all the Jews that they did this – claimed for himself. These are the things in which they boasted; these are the things on which they rested. But, as the Apostle goes on to show them in detail, it is of no value at all. That is the whole tragedy of the Jew; that is the tragedy of hypocrisy. You notice how Paul goes up from step to step as he outlines this knowledge and this possession. Here is a man whom you would think would be absolutely perfect: he has got all this and he is able to do so much. What more can be desired? But the tragedy is that, because of his terrible failure in the matter of application (as the Apostle says here in verse 23), he is guilty of dishonouring God and causing the Gentiles, the nations, to blaspheme the name of which he as a Jew boasted, and which he thought he honoured and exemplified in his life more than anybody else.

Eleven

*

Behold, thou art called a Jew, and restest in the law, and makest
thy boast of God, and knowest his will, and approvest the things
that are more excellent, being instructed out of the law; and art
confident that thou thyself art a guide of the blind, a light of them
which are in darkness, an instructor of the foolish, a teacher of
babes, which hast the form of knowledge and of the truth in the
law. Thou therefore which teachest another, teachest thou not
thyself? thou that preachest a man should not steal, dost thou
steal? thou that sayest a man should not commit adultery, dost
thou commit adultery? thou that abhorrest idols, dost thou
commit sacrilege? thou that makest thy boast of the law, through
breaking the law dishonourest thou God? For the name of God is
blasphemed among the Gentiles through you, as it is written. For
circumcision verily profiteth, if thou keep the law: but if thou be a
breaker of the law, thy circumcision is made uncircumcision.
Therefore if the uncircumcision keep the righteousness of the law,
shall not his uncircumcision be counted for circumcision? And
shall not uncircumcision which is by nature, if it fulfil the law,
judge thee, who by the letter and circumcision dost transgress the
law? For he is not a Jew, which is one outwardly; neither is that
circumcision, which is outward in the flesh: but he is a Jew, which
is one inwardly; and circumcision is that of the heart, in the spirit,
and not in the letter; whose praise is not of men, but of God.

Romans 2 : 17–29

We are dealing, you remember, with the argument which the
Apostle is employing to press home to the Jews the utter futility
of relying upon their knowledge of the law, and upon the
mere fact that it had been given to them. He has already dealt
with it in detail, showing that there is no difference between
them and the Gentiles, but now he is really pressing his own
principles home upon them. He knew that it was their tendency
to say, 'But after all, the law was given to us, we are the people of

the law, and therefore it is inconceivable that we should be under the wrath of God and under condemnation'. He therefore puts the case as we have seen. He first reminds them of what they claim for themselves and then he asks them that devastating series of questions which simply go to the root and vitals of the matter, and expose the terrible hypocrisy of the Jews of that age, speaking generally – the hypocrisy of all Jews who disputed his proposition that they were all under the wrath of God, and that nothing but the righteousness of God in Jesus Christ could possibly save them. By these questions he simply probes them to the very depths, and shows that they have not a leg to stand on, nor a single plea to offer.

I think you will agree with me that this is one of the most terrible exposures of hypocrisy that is to be found anywhere in the Scriptures. There is a great deal in the Scriptures about hypocrisy, and that is not surprising, because hypocrisy is one of the most subtle and terrible sins that can ever afflict us, and we cannot be warned of it too frequently. We have seen how our Lord Himself warned His own disciples about it: 'Beware ye', He said, 'of the leaven of the Pharisees, which is hypocrisy'. Indeed, it is alarming to notice the attention that is given to it in the Scriptures, and to realize that this is so, because it is such a common condition. And let me add this: it is something to which we are all prone and which threatens every Christian, but it is a temptation to some more than others; and the people who are most exposed to this terrible sin and danger of hypocrisy, are preachers and teachers of the gospel. This is something which, again, we tend to forget; but it is a very serious thing to preach the gospel. There are some people who give the impression that it is one of the simplest things in the world, and that a man can just walk into it, and appoint himself to it without any consideration at all. But James warns us very seriously about this when he says, 'My brethren, be not many masters, knowing that we shall receive the greater condemnation' [*James* 3 : 1]. It is a very serious thing to be a teacher or a preacher of the gospel, because the moment one begins in this work one, in a very peculiar and exceptional manner, becomes a victim of this particular attack of the devil, and that for very obvious reasons, which we must now consider.

Paul takes it up in verse 21 by saying, 'Thou therefore . . .', and the 'Thou' refers to the same man as the one whom he has addressed in verse 17: 'Behold, thou art called a Jew . . .' You who are resting in the law; you who make your boast of God, and who know the will of God, and approve things that are more excellent . . . Come along, then, he says, let us face it – and then we have this description of hypocrisy. It seems to me that we can divide up what the Apostle says under three main headings. First: the general characteristics of hypocrisy.

The first is this: a hypocrite is one who tends to take only a general and theoretical and intellectual interest in truth. That is his first characteristic, and that is the one that explains everything else. That was just the position of these Jews; they were tremendously interested in the law, but Paul's whole case against them was that it was only in a theoretical manner, only in an intellectual and an abstract manner. Nothing gave greater pleasure to the typical Jew than to have an argument about the law. They had been taught in it, trained in it, and they knew parts of it by heart. They had heard the great doctors of the law disputing about it, and enjoyed it all: what could be more wonderful? In exactly the same way today, there are people to whom nothing is more delightful than an argument about religion or theology, so long as it is purely intellectual. That is always the first characteristic of the hypocrite.

And here, you see, comes in the danger for preachers and teachers. Obviously if a man is going to preach at all, or to teach at all, he must use his intellect. A preacher does not merely stand up and read out verses and make a few running commentaries, that is not preaching, whatever else it may be. It is not true teaching even. No! It is the business of a true preacher and teacher to get a message and to present it, and he must use his mind and his intellect. And there the danger slips in, the danger that he becomes interested only in the form of his sermon, or the form of his message, or in the intellectual aspect of the truth itself: interested in ideas, possible explanations, possible expositions. And it can be exciting and very entrancing. But one can be handling the truth as if one were handling Shakespeare, or as if one were teaching some ordinary, secular subject, with a kind of intellectual detachment. And people will say, 'What a wonderful, intellectual treat that was!' It may have been, but the business of a preacher is not to give people intellectual treats; it is to present spiritual truth to them in a spiritual manner. You see, therefore, the danger of hypocrisy coming in at that point, because of this tendency to take a general, theoretical, and purely objective interest in the truth.

The second general characteristic is a kind of complacency that is always characteristic of the hypocrite. He is always self-satisfied, always pleased with himself, and never conscious of any deficiency. There is never any humility about the hypocrite. You notice how Paul brings it out in his terms: 'Behold, thou art called a Jew, and *restest* in the law . . .'. That is typical of the hypocrite; he is always resting on something. He rests in the law in a wrong way, as we have seen, and he also makes his boast of God. He is on wonderful terms with himself. He says, 'I am a godly man, I am a worshipper of God. I do not know about those heathen . . .'. You remember our Lord's picture of it all in His account of the Pharisee and the publican who went up to the temple to pray. The Pharisee went right forward and he said, 'God, I thank thee, that I am not as other men are . . . or even as this publican' [*Luke* 18 : 11]. Typical! On wonderful terms with himself! He is a religious man, a godly man, a good man.

Then there is the other term that Paul uses, this term 'confident' in verse 19 – '. . . and art confident that thou thyself art a guide of the blind, a light of them which are in darkness, an instructor of the foolish, a teacher of babes'. Why, he is absolutely complete! He never knows what nervousness is. He is the antithesis of the Apostle Paul who, when he went to preach in Corinth, says that he did it 'in weakness, and in fear, and in much trembling'. The hypocrite is a man who is full of confidence, self-confidence; a man who bounces into a pulpit or on to a platform – everything is perfect. He does not know anything about the 'fear of the Lord'; he has no queries as to his own capacity or as to his own honesty, or anything else; he is on perfectly good terms with himself. He never has imagined that there is anything wrong with him. That is what Paul is saying about the Jews. And it is always true of hypocrites – this complete absence of humility, a complacency, a confidence, a boastfulness.

Now these are terrifying things to say, are they not? But you notice that they are taught everywhere in the Scripture. These are the marks of the hypocrite. And yet, when you look at the modern situation you can see that something very subtle has come in. Some people are taken up with the idea that we must always give the impression that because we are Christians we are very happy, and they put on a kind of confidence and boastfulness, exposing themselves to the charge of hypocrisy. The truly godly man is never a showman. He knows enough about the plague of his own heart never to be guilty of that. But this other man knows nothing about it. And that is our third general characteristic: the hypocrite is a man who, obviously, for all these reasons, never examines himself, because he has never seen the need for self-examination. What? He is resting in the law, he makes his boast of God. He is confident, he knows all about it, and he can teach everybody. If only everybody were as he is, everything would be much better in this world, and the church, too, would be much better! What need is there for him to examine himself? He is not conscious of sin; he honestly cannot say that he has ever felt he is a sinner. He is doing such wonderful things, he is such a good man, and God is so well pleased with him! That was the condition of the Jews. That is always the general characteristic of the hypocrite.

But let us look at it more in detail and in action. Now here you come to the specific charges. Here is the Apostle's first charge against the hypocrite in action: Paul says that this man teaches and preaches to others but never to himself. 'Thou therefore which teachest another, teachest thou not thyself?' A preacher who does not preach his sermon to himself before he preaches it to anybody else, is exposing himself to hypocrisy; he is in a very dangerous condition. If a man has not preached to himself or taught himself, all his teaching of others is vain and useless. But the hypocrite never does that. He never teaches himself. He never applies the truth to himself. He can apply it to others, never to himself at all. It is always outside him. He needs nothing, he is complete. So he never preaches to or teaches himself.

The second charge is still more serious, of course. He is actually guilty of doing things that he tells other people not to do: 'Thou that preachest a man should not steal, dost thou steal?' Paul puts it in the form of a question in order to make it still more incriminating. What he is really saying is, 'Do you steal?' It is always a good way of emphasizing a thing like that.

Instead of saying to a man, 'I know that you are guilty of theft', you say, 'Look here, you who preach that a man should not steal, do you steal?' And there the conviction comes in. 'Thou that sayest a man should not commit adultery, dost thou commit adultery?' And let us not forget our Lord's exposition of adultery in the Sermon on the Mount in Matthew 5 – how He interprets what the law means by adultery. This man is guilty of that.

'Thou that abhorrest idols, dost thou commit sacrilege?' This is a slightly more difficult point and there has been some dispute as to what it means, but it seems to me that it almost inevitably must mean this: 'Thou that abhorrest idols . . .'. And the Jews did, you see; they had fallen into idolatry before they were taken captive to Babylon, but they never went back to it after coming back from Babylon. They learned their lesson there and they had abhorred idols ever since. And so they were always preaching against idolatry. And yet, says Paul, you are so avaricious that you literally go into those idol temples and commit theft and robbery, and thereby you are committing sacrilege, you are defiling yourselves by thus going into those temples at all. You denounce people who do go there, but you are prepared to go there for your own purpose, and you are guilty of sacrilege whether you worship or not.

Now it is the principle here that is the important thing for us, the principle that these men, in practice, are guilty of doing the very things for which they denounce others. That again is always the characteristic of the hypocrite. He sees it so clearly in the case of others, he sees it so clearly theologically, but he is guilty of the very thing that he condemns. What a terrible thing!

And the third thing is that he dishonours God through breaking the law, though he boasts so much about the law and about his knowledge of the law. 'Thou that makest thy boast of the law, through breaking the law dishonourest thou God?' This man who has boasted in God, is dishonouring God, and he does so by breaking the very law of God which he claims to know so thoroughly and so well that he can even teach others!

Now these are permanent features of hypocrisy. May God give us grace to examine ourselves in the light of them! As you read your Bible day by day, do you apply the truth to yourself? What is your motive when you read the Bible? Is it just to have a knowledge of it so that you can show others how much you know, and argue with them, or are you applying the truth to yourselves? As we face the beginning of each new year, we may make resolutions to do daily Bible reading in a more diligent manner. God grant that we may do so and follow some scheme of Bible reading. Go through the Bible every year if you can, do as much as you can . . . and as you read it, always apply it. As you read about the Pharisees say to yourself, 'That is me! What is it saying about me?' Allow the Scripture to search you, otherwise it can be very dangerous. There is a sense in which the more you know about it, the more dangerous it is to you if you do not apply it to yourself. Again there is another danger here for the preacher and the teacher, whether he be a Sunday School teacher or holding some other position. Let us beware of simply preparing a lesson and dividing it up beautifully, and having sub-divisions and presenting it in an intellectual form – it can be the high road to disaster. We must apply the truth to ourselves and be humbled by it. We must be very careful that we are not talking about things theoretically, without troubling about the application of them to our personal lives, lest thus unconsciously we may be dishonouring the God whom we claim to be worshipping and whom we desire to serve.

All this is important because of the results to which it leads – and that is my third point; that is the third thing that he tells us about hypocrisy. Here is the message of verse 24: 'For the name of God is blasphemed among the Gentiles through you . . .'. You very Jews who claim to be God's people, you are causing others to blaspheme the name of God. Here is something which has an obvious application to us. I wonder whether any of us who are Christians are causing people to blaspheme the name of Christ and of God as the Jews were doing? It works like this: 'We are God's people', the Jews would claim. They boasted about God and about the law. They said, 'God has ignored all the other nations, He has chosen us and He has blessed us so signally in this way'. Now the Gentiles heard all this and they looked on. And they drew certain deductions which were perfectly fair. To begin with, the Gentiles were obviously judging God by what they saw in the Jews. They had no personal or direct knowledge of God, but here was a nation that claimed it was God's own people, that they were the representatives of God. So the Gentiles judged God by what they saw in the Jews, and you cannot blame them.

In the same way, you cannot blame people today for judging Christ and Christianity by what they see in church members. And the blindness of many Christians at this point is something I cannot understand at all. People seem to think that the masses are outside the Christian church because our evangelistic methods are not what they ought to be. That is not the answer. People are outside the church because looking at us they say, 'What is the point of being Christians? – look at them!' They are judging Christ by you and by me. And you cannot stop them and you cannot blame them.

They not only judge God and Christ by this, they judge the truth of God in the same way. The Gentiles said, 'These people are always talking about truth. They say we are in darkness, that they have some marvellous revelation, that God gave the law to their great leader, Moses; they talk about truth. Very well', they said, 'look at the lives that the Jews are living; is that what truth leads to? Is that kind of life and behaviour the result of truth?' And so they judged the truth by what they saw in its representatives. And people are doing that today about Christianity. They say, 'Look at those Christians! Look at them when they are ill, look at them when they think they are going to die, look at them when something goes wrong! They can talk marvellously when the sun is shining and when the business is going well, and when there is no trouble in the family, but the moment anything goes wrong they do not seem to have anything, they are even worse than many who are not Christians. Is that Christianity?' – perfectly logical, perfectly fair deduction.

And then the third way in which it works is this – they judge the salvation of God by what they see in its representatives. The Jews were always talking about deliverances and about God's salvation, and the Gentiles looked on and they said, 'Is this the sort of person that God blesses? Is this the kind of blessing that God gives His own?' So they judged the whole of salvation by what they saw in the Jews. And people are judging Christianity, the glorious message of the Advent season, and the cross and the resurrection, and the Holy Ghost . . . all this is being judged by what people see in you and me. Take those words of our Lord to the woman of Samaria: 'Whosoever drinketh of this water shall thirst again: but whosoever drinketh of the water that I shall give him shall never thirst; but the water that I shall give him shall be in him a well of water springing up into everlasting life' [*John* 4 : 13–14] – and then look at Christians, church members! Do we give the impression that we are enjoying this glorious gospel of the blessed God, that we are holding on to and benefiting by the exceeding great and precious promises? Are we partakers of the 'unsearchable riches of Christ'? Are we living as princes, or do we give the impression that we are paupers? The Gentiles are looking on!

And then the fourth point is this: they judge the power of God by what they see in us. Now this is very important. In verse 24 the Apostle is quoting Isaiah 52 : 5, taking it almost word for word from the Septuagint translation: 'The name of God is blasphemed among the Gentiles through you'. That happened in this way: here were these people who claimed that they were God's own people and that God was concerned about them and loved them, and would never permit any harm to come to them. Suddenly they were carried away into the captivity of Babylon. They were defeated by the Chaldean army and they were quite helpless. Their city was sacked and demolished, and they were taken out of their own land. And the Gentiles looked on and said, 'Where is their God? They always said that their God was the only true God, and that the others were not gods at all . . . but it looks to us', they said, 'as if these other gods are more powerful than the God of Israel. If the God of Israel were the all-mighty God that they have talked about, would He have permitted their enemies to defeat them? Would He ever have permitted them to be humbled and humiliated and carried away?' They said, 'Their God has no power! These other gods, Baal and Ashtaroth, these are the gods that give victory. The God of Israel has no power at all'.

This, again, is important. Not only do you find it in Isaiah, there is a very extended statement of this same principle in the prophet Ezekiel:

'And when they entered unto the heathen, whither they went, they profaned my holy name, when they said to them, These are the people of the Lord, and are gone forth out of his land. But I had pity for mine holy name, which the house of Israel had profaned among the heathen, whither they went. Therefore say unto the house of Israel, Thus saith the Lord God; I do not this for your sakes, O house of Israel, but for mine holy name's sake, which ye have profaned among the heathen, whither ye went. And I will sanctify my great name, which was profaned among the heathen, which ye have profaned in the midst of them; and the heathen shall know that I am the Lord, saith the Lord God, when I shall be sanctified in you before their eyes' [*Ezekiel* 36 : 20–23].

Then follows the prophecy of what God is going to do, and verse 36 concludes: 'Then the heathen that are left round about you shall know that I the Lord build the ruined places, and plant that that was desolate: I the Lord have spoken it, and I will do it'.

You see, you cannot expect the Gentiles to understand this, but this is how it works: the children of Israel were defeated and carried into captivity because of their own sin, and because God, as a part of His chastisement of them, allowed the enemy to come in and defeat them. He could have stopped it, but He allowed it in order to teach them, in order to chastise them. But you cannot expect the enemy to understand that. He does not know, he has not got a spiritual mind. All he saw was the defeat and the captivity of Israel, and so he profaned the name of God, and said that God could have stopped it. And it was the sin of Israel that led to that. As far as these outsiders were concerned, it led to an utterly false impression of the power of God. And it is as true of us as it was true of the Jews of old. 'Whom the Lord loveth he chasteneth' [*Hebrews* 12 : 6]. There are times when He chastens us by just withholding His smile from us, and we are left to ourselves and we become miserable and wretched, and the whole world looks on and says, 'Look at that miserable Christian!' But the worldling does not know that we are like that because God is punishing us and chastising us; he sees nothing but the misery, and he says, 'What sort of God is a God who leaves people like that to be defeated by circumstances and trials?' And so we dishonour the name of God and bring it into disrepute – exactly as these Jews did of old.

There, then, is the Apostle's mighty exposure of hypocrisy. His object in doing it, as I remind you, is to show the final and complete futility of resting upon a mere knowledge of the law and not putting it into practice. 'Not only will it avail you nothing', says Paul in effect, 'it is bringing God into dishonour and into disrepute; it is causing these Gentiles to blaspheme His name'. And this was a very clever quotation, if I may so put it. You see, Paul shows them that it is not only his idea, not only his argument, he quotes the Scriptures which they know so well, and shows them how their own Scriptures condemn them, and they are left without a single argument at this particular point.

But now, let us look at the next section, which starts at verse 25 and goes on to the end of the chapter. Here, you see, Paul comes to the final argument. Here we come to what we may well call the last bastion of the Jew's defence. The Apostle has begun dealing with him at the beginning of this chapter, and he has been following him on. He has been saying things that the Jew cannot answer, and the Jew has been retreating step by step. We have been watching him, and Paul is following with argument upon argument and increasing pressure; and at last the Jew's great argument about the law has suddenly gone.

'All right', he says, 'I fall back upon my final line of defence. Circumcision! Now then', he says, 'this is something that you cannot knock down. The sign of circumcision was given to the Jews and to nobody else. And, still more important, circumcision is older than the law. The law, after all, only goes back to Moses, the great lawgiver. Yes, but you know even greater than Moses, in a sense, was Abraham, to whom the sign of circumcision was given. So then', he continues, 'we will go back beyond Moses and the law, we will go back to the fountain, to the beginning, to Abraham our father – the one man out of whom the whole race has come, to whom God gave this sign and this seal of circumcision, which surely is indissoluble. And as we are Jews who are circumcised, how can you say that we are under the wrath of God? Are you telling us that God can create a nation for Himself and then destroy it? Are you telling us that God can be angry with His own people? The thing is unthinkable! The sign of circumcision is a conclusive argument that you are wrong. We may have sinned, we may have failed, but we are God's people and He will never go back on His own family, on His own people; circumcision proves it'. This was the Jew's final bastion.

So the Apostle takes it up. Here again there is only one word that I can think of to describe his argument – it is devastating! Let us work through it quickly like this: 'For circumcision verily profiteth, if thou keep the law; but if thou be a breaker of the law, thy circumcision is made uncircumcision' [v. 25]. Now what Paul is saying here is that it is true that circumcision is of great value but it has no intrinsic and inherent value in and of itself. Circumcision, he says, proclaims that you are God's people – yes, but only on the condition that you really are one of God's people in a true and in a vital sense – namely, that you are a holy people, for God is a holy God and His people are holy. Circumcision *is* a sign that you belong to Him, but it is not the only one; it is an outward sign of something inward, which is still more important. So you see, 'circumcision verily profiteth, if thou keep the law', but if you do not keep the law you might as well be uncircumcised, your circumcision is made uncircumcision.

Then in verse 26 he puts it like this: 'Therefore if the uncircumcision keep the righteousness of the law, shall not his uncircumcision be counted for circumcision?' Here is one of the Apostle's hypothetical arguments again. '*If* . . .'. Paul is not asserting here that any uncircumcised person can or ever has kept the law. He is putting up a theoretical, hypothetical case. If the uncircumcised should keep the righteousness of the law, well then, says the Apostle, the fact that he happens to be uncircumcised would not make any difference, because what God wants is people who keep the law. He wants a holy people, and if a man is holy, whether he is circumcised or not is immaterial, it does not count at all. That again is a very shrewd thrust, buttressing the first statement.

He goes still further in verse 27: Indeed, he says, if this uncircumcised man thus keeps the law, 'Shall not uncircumcision which is by nature, if it fulfil the law [hypothetically], judge thee, who by the letter and circumcision dost transgress the law?' What does that mean? Just this: If this uncircumcised man did keep the law, though he is uncircumcised by nature, though he is born amongst the race where they do not circumcise, he would absolutely condemn you, the Jew, who have got the letter of the law and circumcision. He condemns you in this way: you are resting on the letter of the law, you are resting on your circumcision, and you have not kept the law, so it is of no value to you. He is not circumcised, he has not got the written law in letters before him, but he has kept the law and therefore he is just; he condemns you who have the written law and are circumcised; he damns you! Again an unanswerable argument.

And that brings Paul to the end, which is the great principle of it all, stated in verses 28 and 29: 'For' – summing up the whole mighty argument of the entire chapter in these two verses – 'he is not a Jew, which is one outwardly; neither is that circumcision, which is outward in the flesh: but he is a Jew, which is one inwardly; and circumcision is that of the heart, in the spirit, and not in the letter; whose praise is not of men, but of God'.

Let me put that in this way: what makes a man a Jew, says the Apostle Paul, is not primarily that he belongs to a particular nation, it is not a matter of national attachment, or some external position. What then? Ah, he says, it is an inward state. It is exactly the same with circumcision. That which is really circumcision is not something external, in the flesh, as the Jews thought; it is something of the heart and of the spirit, of the inner man. It is not something merely in the letter but is an inward process – that is, an external sign of some inward grace, of some inward operation. God gave it externally, merely to help them, but the real thing is within.

And then look at that final phrase: 'whose praise is not of men, but of God'. The Jew, you see, boasted about the externals, and he got a good deal of praise out of that. The Pharisees were greatly admired by the common people; they respected them and praised them. They thought that these Pharisees were perfect men, these great teachers of theirs. But our Lord said to them one day, 'Ye are they which justify yourselves before men; but God knoweth your hearts: for that which is highly esteemed among men is abomination in the sight of God'. That is Luke 16 : 15. Underline it! It is a very simple thing to impress men; you can impress men as a preacher and as a teacher and as a moral person. They see only the outside; they see only the mechanics, the performance; they do not see the heart; they do not see the spirit; they know nothing about the inner man. But God sees the heart, for that which is highly esteemed amongst men is abomination in the sight of God. What makes a man a Jew is not that he is born of the nation of Israel, it is his relationship to God. It is not circumcision, it is the heart. Indeed, I can put it in one word – we have been saying it right through the whole chapter as an argument. Nothing avails before God except holiness. The author of the Epistle to the Hebrews puts it like this in chapter twelve, verse 14: 'Follow peace with all men, and holiness, without which no man shall see the Lord'. There it is! Or again: 'Blessed are the pure in heart: for they shall see God' [*Matthew* 5 : 8]. Nobody else. That is what Paul is saying here. It is not that you belong to the nation of the Jews, it is not that you have got the external sign of circumcision – that does not make a man a Jew. It is not that. It is the inner man of the heart, it is this holiness, it is this truth, it is this relationship to God.

And so, my friends, as we come to the end of the chapter, shall I apply all this to every one of us? Shall I ask a series of questions, as the Apostle asked a series of questions of these people? From beginning to end he has shown that the whole argument of the Jews could not stand up to his examination, to his cross- examination. The case has collapsed, the last bastion has gone, the Jew is condemned: 'There is none righteous, no, not one'. The whole world is guilty before God. There is no difference between the Jew and the Gentile – all are equally lost.

But let us apply this to ourselves. Is any one of us relying upon nationality? There are many people who are doing this. They never go near a place of worship except occasionally – a marriage, a death, a christening service, some special occasion, perhaps Easter Sunday. But, you know, they really believe that they are going to heaven, they say that they want to go there. 'I believe in God', they say. I remember talking to a man in this position once who never went near a place of worship at all. 'But I never miss the morning service on the wireless', he said, 'would not miss that for anything'. He believed he was a godly man, that he was pleasing God. He took the view, that so many take, that everybody in this country is more or less a Christian because it is a Christian country. They are relying on that, and when you talk to them they say, 'Of course I believe in God, of course I want to go to heaven', and they believe they are going there. They do not like you, and they do not believe you, when you tell them they are not going there. But they have nothing to rely on except their nationality.

Or is anyone hearing this who is relying upon his or her baptism? I do not care whether you were baptized as an infant or whether you were grown-up – it makes not the slightest difference, if you are relying upon it. If you think that the act of baptism is the thing that saves you and puts you right, whatever you may be doing with your life, you are in the identical position of the Jews. As they relied on circumcision you are relying upon baptism, whether it is sprinkling or immersion, or anything else you may like – mode, age, it does not matter. Anyone who relies upon it, and upon it alone, is in the position of the Jew who was relying upon circumcision.

Or are you, I wonder, relying upon the fact that you are a church member, that your name is on a church roll? There are many who are relying on that. That is again to rely on circumcision. It is finally useless and worthless if you rely on it alone. Is there anybody relying upon taking the sacrament of the Lord's Supper? Ah, I know many people who rely on this, especially if they have it very early in the morning. If they go to their early morning Mass they are absolutely convinced it puts them right; they have no doubt about it. But that whole sacramental idea, of course, falls under this castigation of the Apostle; it teaches people to rely upon this grace which is transmitted, they are taught, in a material manner and is inevitably in the water, and in the wafer. They receive the grace, they say, and they rely on it to cover everything.

Or to come a little nearer to ourselves: are we relying, any of us, upon our knowledge of the way of salvation as such? Are we relying upon our familiarity with evangelical terms? I am afraid I know numbers of people who are relying on this, who are guilty of this. They can use the terms very glibly, they can state the whole way of salvation to you.

'So what is wrong with them?' you say.

Well, what is wrong with them, it seems to me, is that if a man is a true Christian, he is born again, he has a divine seed in him, he is a partaker of the divine nature, and it must show itself – and the lives of such people sometimes clearly indicate that they have no such divine life. They are worldlings, though they say the right things. There are people who rely upon a knowledge of the terms and the way of stating them, and they think that their mere knowledge of it saves them. It is not in their hearts at all, it is purely in their heads. Or I could put that in another way: is there anyone reading this, at this moment, who is relying upon his or her belief of the gospel? Because if you are, then you are in the position of the Jews. We must rely upon nothing save the Lord Jesus Christ himself. Faith does not save us, it is Jesus Christ who saves; faith is but the instrument. So if we rely on any of these things we are in the position in which these Jews were.

Or is there anybody, I wonder, who is relying upon some theoretical assurance? By that I mean the people who say, 'Well, I go to the Scriptures and find that it says, "Whosoever believeth on him shall not perish . . ."; I do believe on Him, therefore I shall not perish, I am all right!' And they stop at that. That is a ground of assurance, but if you stop at that without looking for the fruits of the Spirit or any of the results of the divine life, I say you are heading straight for this hypocrisy of which the Jews were guilty, in their reliance upon the mere fact of circumcision.

Those, then, are the practical questions that arise from this chapter, one of the most important, one of the most serious chapters in the whole of the Bible. No chapter so searches profession as this second chapter of the Epistle to the Romans. Am I saying, then, that there is no value in these things? No! There is great value in all the things I have mentioned, as there was in circumcision; they are all great privileges, but they do not save, and they are not enough in and of themselves. If I may use the technical term, they none of them work *ex opere operato* – in and of themselves, almost by a mechanical process. Not one of them! They are good signs, but they are not to be relied upon for salvation. They are excellent if the inward reality is there. Nothing really matters, finally, but the new nature, the new life, the divine seed. Believism will not save. A fideism that simply knows the terms may lead men to hell. What is important is not that you and I should say that we believe this or that; though we say we believe the whole gospel, even that is not the ultimate thing of importance. The thing that ultimately matters is this: have we received the new nature? Have we got the life of God in our souls? Are we partakers of the divine nature? You can be highly moral, you can be well versed in Scripture, you can argue about it, you can teach others and preach to others, you can do all these things, even more than the Jews did, and still be condemned. It is the state of the heart that matters. Have we got the new heart, the clean heart, the heart in which the Holy Spirit dwells? That is the thing that proclaims that we are truly Christian.

And therefore my last word is this: if we want to make sure that we are unlike the Jews in this respect, we must examine ourselves. The Jews did not, they never would. They put up this citadel around themselves and said, 'We are the Jews, you must not talk to us. Go and preach to the Gentiles, do not preach to us'. They are like the lady, if I may say so, who once complained of my preaching in Westminster Chapel and said, 'This man preaches to us as if we were sinners!' Unthinkable! You see, if you erect that kind of citadel around yourself you will never know that you are a hypocrite. We are all hypocrites by nature, every one of us. That is the result of sin. And the only way to discover it and to avoid it and to escape from it is to examine ourselves, to pay heed to these exhortations – 'Examine your own selves, prove your own selves, see whether you are in the faith'. That is what the Apostle says to people like this. You remember how he puts it in that passage about the Communion in 1 Corinthians 11: 'Let a man examine himself'. It is, he says, because some are not examining themselves that they are sick. 'For this cause many are weak and sickly among you, and many sleep', he says – 'For if we would judge ourselves, we should not be judged'.

So let every man examine himself. Let us take these searching questions which Paul addresses to these Jews of old and let us turn them upon ourselves. Let us live with them, let us be able to answer them. May I suggest to you humbly that you can only be sure that you have answered them truly and faced them honestly when you look at yourself and say, 'In me, that is to say, in my flesh, dwelleth no good thing', when you abhor yourself and hate yourself, and get down on your knees quietly, in your own room, not on the street corner, not in a public place, but in your own room with the door shut and the blinds drawn and acknowledge it before God and break your heart before Him, reminded again that if we do confess our sins He is faithful and just to forgive us our sins and to cleanse us from all unrighteousness. Oh, may God give us honesty and truth in our inward parts that we may allow the Scriptures to search us. And therefore as we decide to read the Word of God more diligently, let us resolve to allow it to search us to our vitals, to be honest with it, and to be careful, because there are millions outside looking at us and watching us, judging God and His Christ and the glorious gospel of salvation by what they see in us.

Twelve

*

What advantage then hath the Jew? or what profit is there of circumcision? Much every way: chiefly, because that unto them were committed the oracles of God.

Romans 3 : 1–2

We find ourselves now at the beginning of the third chapter and obviously it is vital that we should remind ourselves of the larger context in which this chapter must of necessity be considered. I would remind you, therefore, that we are still considering the statement which the Apostle has given us in the first chapter, verses 16 and 17. He is 'not ashamed of the gospel of Christ' for the reason that 'it is the power of God unto salvation to every one that believeth; to the Jew first, and also to the Greek. For [again still going on with his reasons for not being ashamed] therein is the righteousness of God revealed from faith to faith: as it is written, The just shall live by faith'. Now that is his fundamental proposition; he then, at once, goes on to show why this is such marvellous and wonderful good news. Why does he thus thrill at the very thought of it? He puts it in that form of litotes, you remember, he says, 'I am not ashamed . . .'. What he really means is, 'I am very proud of it, and proud of being a preacher of it'.

What is there, then, about this gospel, about the righteousness of God which causes this Apostle so to rejoice? The answer is that 'The wrath of God is revealed from heaven against all ungodliness and unrighteousness of men, who hold [down] the truth in unrighteousness'. You notice that the statement is 'against *all* ungodliness and unrighteousness of men'. That is a universal statement about the whole of mankind. Then, of course, the Apostle feels that it is necessary for him to demonstrate the truth of that, and so he begins to do so at verse 18 in chapter one. Then from that verse to the end of the chapter he is proving this in the case of the Gentiles – that the wrath of God is against the Gentiles because of their ungodliness and their unrighteousness. And then in chapter two he proves that the same thing is true also of the Jews. This was much more difficult, of course. We saw as we considered that chapter that the Jew felt that because he was a Jew, because he was circumcised, and so on, he was in a very special position, he was not under the wrath of God, and God could surely never regard His own people as being in the same position as these pagans, these Gentiles. So the whole of the second chapter is just given to prove that in reality there is no difference in that respect between the Jew and the Gentile; that the Jew, though he is a Jew and has the sign of circumcision, is as much under the wrath of God and as much under condemnation as is the Gentile. And that is the position at which we arrived at the end of chapter two. The Jew must not rely upon his circumcision, he must not rely upon the fact that he has the law, and has a kind of superficial knowledge of the law. That makes no difference from the standpoint of salvation.

Now we come to this third chapter, and those who first divided up the Scriptures into chapters were right indeed when they put a chapter division at this particular point, because here we are clearly taking up something new, something which is slightly different. What, then, is the theme of chapter three? The answer is that it can be divided up very conveniently into three main sections: the first section is from verse 1 to verse 8, the second section goes from verse 9 to verse 20, and the third section from verse 21 to verse 31. These are the three natural divisions of the chapter, and let me summarize what Paul does in each of them. In this first division, from verses 1 to 8, he takes up a difficulty with regard to what he has just been saying in chapter two. Now there is a good deal of dispute amongst the authorities as to whether an actual objection is put up here – a difficulty raised by a Jew or by somebody else – or whether the Apostle, as a very wise teacher, anticipating difficulties and seeing that it would be almost inevitable that certain Jews would find themselves in difficulty at this point, therefore takes it up and deals with it, and unfolds it and answers it in his customary manner.

Then in the second section, from verses 9 to 20, he does something which is, clearly, important from the standpoint of a Jew. He does nothing but marshal together a great number of quotations from the Old Testament to prove his case, and of course he could do nothing better when dealing with a difficulty or an objection put forward by a Jew. The Jew, obviously, regarded his Scriptures as authoritative, and so Paul says, 'This is not my opinion only; listen to what the Scriptures say'. Then he quotes these specific statements which prove that his argument – that the Jew is under the wrath of God – is something that was said repeatedly in many places in the Old Testament Scriptures. That is a very effective piece of argumentation. He has here a kind of catena, a chain of scriptural quotations, which he carefully chooses in order to make his argument absolutely perfect; then having brought in his Scriptures he winds up his case in verses 19 and 20 by saying in effect, 'So then, there it is'. It is perfectly plain and he draws his deduction again when he says that every mouth has thus been stopped and all the world has become guilty before God, 'Therefore by the deeds of the law there shall no flesh be justified in his sight: for by the law is the knowledge of sin' [3 : 20]. Finally, then, he has proved that the whole world is guilty before God, that the wrath of God is upon all ungodliness and unrighteousness of men, whether they are Gentiles or Jews. It is universal.

And having thus established it and proved it beyond any doubt, he goes back again to the theme that he had indicated in chapter one, verse 17, this method of righteousness which God has brought in. Listen to him in chapter 3 : 21: 'But now the righteousness of God without the law [apart from the law] is manifested, being witnessed by the law and the prophets'. That is an exact repetition of the statement in 1 : 17. Having gone the whole round to prove his case and to deal with objections and with difficulties, back he comes to it; he has not forgotten what he set out to say. And so from verse 21 to the end of the chapter he sets out in perhaps the most glorious and explicit way that even this Apostle himself has ever done, this amazing doctrine of God's righteousness in Jesus Christ – why it was necessary and how exactly he has done it. And this passage includes, as you know, that great *locus classicus* with respect to the doctrine of the atonement, which we have in verses 25 and 26. So we are again facing one of the great chapters of the Bible, one of the greatest of all. And from the standpoint of doctrine, certainly, there is no chapter in the whole Bible which is more vital than this particular one.

That, then, is a general analysis of the whole of chapter three. Now we must go back and look at the first section. I cannot refrain from remarking that it is most instructive to notice the carefulness of this great teacher. He takes nothing for granted. He does not care how much he extends a digression (or what may appear to be a digression) as long as he is giving light and knowledge and information. Of course, these days, people do not like this sort of thing. I am well aware of that! But Paul does it and we can do nothing better than follow in his footsteps and copy his example. 'Let us get on to the doctrine of chapter three', says somebody, 'or to chapters five, six and seven'. Not at all! The Apostle finds it is essential to lay down a firm foundation. There are many people today who are in such a hurry to erect some kind of an evangelical house, that I am afraid it is not going to be very durable. And then you will find that in times of trial and testing, they will not quite know where they stand. They are carried away by every wind of doctrine, they have no discrimination and they cannot see the subtle error in false teachings. The only way to avoid that is to make certain that we are looking at every difficulty and dealing with every conceivable objection.

So let us follow Paul as he does that, and what he does is ask a rhetorical question: 'What advantage then hath the Jew? or what profit is there of circumcision?' – as if someone were saying, 'Wait a minute, Paul, you have gone a little bit too far, have you not? You have been carried away by your own eloquence, and you have finished off by saying that there is no difference between the Jew and the Gentile. Are you really saying and teaching that the Jew literally had no advantage whatsoever over the Gentile, that really there was no point at all in being circumcised? Is that your teaching? Are you really suggesting that when God called Abram and turned him into Abraham and into a nation, that when He gave the promises and introduced the seal of circumcision and formed this nation for Himself and gave them the law and so on . . . are you really saying it was all a waste of time? That seems to be your conclusion because you say that the Jews are as much under the wrath of God as the Gentiles, and that all they have got does not save them. You seem to be saying that there is absolutely no difference at all. Does that therefore mean that there was no purpose and no point in being a Jew and that the Jew has no advantages whatsoever? Has the Jew no overplus (that is the word Paul uses) over the Gentile, and is there no profit at all in circumcision? Furthermore,' the questioner continues, 'are you not virtually saying that there is really no value at all in the Old Testament, so why, therefore, do we have an Old Testament? This argument of yours, Paul, in chapter two, must surely be wrong because it seems to be leading to the inevitable conclusion that you can wipe out the Old Testament because there was no point at all in having it'.

Now those are the questions which the Apostle is taking up and he deals with them at once. 'This', he says in effect, 'is an entirely false deduction. If that is what you are thinking, it means that you have just completely misunderstood what I have been saying. What I have been saying in chapter two', Paul says, 'is not that the Jew had no advantage over the Gentile. I have never said that. All I have been asserting, and all I have been demonstrating, is that the mere fact that a man is a Jew, the mere fact in and of itself that he has been circumcised, does not save him, does not bring him out from under the wrath of God and automatically declare that he is saved. Now', the Apostle continues, 'that is a very different thing from saying that there was no advantage at all in being a Jew'.

Paul might, indeed, have gone on to say, 'I have already agreed that the Jew has an advantage'. Look back to chapter 2:25: 'For circumcision verily profiteth, if thou keep the law . . .'. That is a positive statement that circumcision does profit if one keeps the law. It does not profit in and of itself. It does not act, to use again that technical phrase I used earlier, *ex opere operato*. It is not something magical. The mere fact that a man is circumcised does not save him, any more than the fact that a child is sprinkled at his christening, saves him, or that an adult is immersed at his baptism saves him. There is no transmissible grace in a sacrament. Now the trouble with the Jews was that they had fallen into that particular error, and that is the thing that Paul is countering in chapter two. But to say that a man is not saved by circumcision, or that a man is not saved by being a Jew, alone, does not mean for a moment that there is no advantage in being a Jew, and that there is no profit in being circumcised. In other words, it does not mean that there is no difference at all between the Jew and the Gentile – indeed, says the Apostle, the answer is the exact opposite. 'What advantage then hath the Jew? or what profit is there of circumcision? Much every way . . .'. Much advantage; much profit in every respect.

'Let us be perfectly clear about this,' says the Apostle. Chapter two does not for a moment say that there is no difference between Jew and Gentile; it does say that there is no difference between Jew and Gentile from the standpoint of salvation. Let us underline this, lest anybody should be in trouble about it. Paul has been asserting that the whole world is guilty before God, Jew as well as Gentile. The Jew is not saved by being a Jew or by being circumcised; that does not save. But to say that does not mean that there is no difference at all between Jew and Gentile, or that there is no advantage in being a Jew. There is a tremendous advantage in being a Jew. What is it? It is – and notice that instead of giving us a great list of things, he says, '. . . chiefly, because that unto them were committed the oracles of God'. Now, in passing, here again is an interesting technical point. Paul says, '. . . chiefly . . .', which should really be translated 'first of all'. We saw how he did exactly the same thing in chapter one, verse 8, when he was introducing his letter. He says, 'First, I thank my God through Jesus Christ for you all, that your faith is spoken of throughout the whole world'. You expected him to go on to say, 'Secondly, thirdly, fourthly, fifthly . . .' but he did not, he said, 'First', and then left it. He does exactly the same here: 'First of all . . .'. He does not follow that up with a list; this is the only thing he does say. So that 'First of all' really means first in importance, chiefly. Far from saying, therefore, that there was no advantage in being a Jew, Paul is showing that there was a tremendous advantage. And the greatest advantage of all was '. . . that unto them were committed the oracles of God'.

Now that again is not as good a translation as it might be. A better translation is that they were 'entrusted' with the oracles of God. God gave the oracles into their charge, to look after and to keep. I want to examine this statement with you, because it is so important. This very word 'oracles of God' attracts our attention at once. It is a term that is used four times only in the New Testament, and this is one of the four. Let me remind you of the others. It was used by Stephen, the martyr, in his apologia, his great statement before the Council that condemned him. You will find it in Acts 7 : 38: 'This is he', says Stephen, speaking about Moses, 'that was in the church in the wilderness with the angel which spake to him in the mount Sinai, and with our fathers: who [Moses] received the lively oracles to give unto us'. This, he said, is what happened to Moses; he received from God the living oracles to give to us. That is one use. Then you will find it here in this chapter. The next instance is in Hebrews 5 : 12. The writer is remonstrating with these Hebrew Christians and he says: I do not quite know what to do with you. I have very profound doctrine to give you about the Lord Jesus Christ as a High Priest after the order of Melchisedek, but I am doubtful as to whether you can take it, 'For when for the time ye ought to be teachers, ye have need that one teach you again which be the first principles of the oracles of God . . .'. There it is the third time. And finally you find it in 1 Peter 4 : 11: 'If any man speak, let him speak as the oracles of God'.

What then does this term mean? It means a divine utterance, a divine revelation. We have a term which we sometimes use; we use it sarcastically, when there has been a discussion, and suddenly a man speaks in a somewhat pompous and authoritative manner. He says, 'This is the position . . .' and we say, 'The oracle has spoken!' Now that was the kind of way in which the term came into use in New Testament times. In those old countries with their ancient civilizations, there were men who were famous for their learning and their understanding who were called 'oracles'. They delivered oracles, or oracular statements, they made pronouncements, and that term is taken up in the Scriptures, and so we get 'the oracles of God'. It is a divine statement, God has revealed truth in words. It does not just mean the thought or the idea. An oracle really means the statement itself, not merely the sentiment but the exact words. So what Paul means here – and this is very important – is the Word of God, or words spoken by God.

Did you notice in the other instances of the word 'oracles', what the references are? Stephen is obviously referring to the law that God gave to Moses. 'Who was this Moses?' he asked in effect. Well, he is the man to whom God gave His living oracles, and Moses passed them to us. Here, in our statement in Romans 3 : 2, the oracles of God patently refers to the whole of the Old Testament. The Jews had the whole of our Old Testament, they were very proud of it, and that is the thing to which the Apostle is referring. Now in Hebrews 5 : 12, in a very interesting way, it is clear that the author has in mind the preaching of the gospel, the New Testament gospel, because that is the thing he is dealing with. I must go back, he says, and deal again with the first principles of the oracles of God. And then in the beginning of the sixth chapter, he takes it up saying, 'Therefore leaving the principles of the doctrine of Christ, let us go on unto perfection', so that evidently the term is used with respect to the New Testament gospel. And you see the significance of this, that it is something that has come directly from God. As we saw in discussing the meaning of the term 'Apostle' in chapter one,[1] one of the things that makes a man an Apostle is that he has not only been commissioned, he has been given his authority to speak as from God, so he speaks as the oracle of God.

Peter, too, in 1 Peter 4 : 11 is obviously using the term in a similar if not an identical manner. But the point for us here is that it is clearly a reference to the Old Testament Scriptures, and therefore it is very important that we should pay attention to it. It is one of those proofs which we have in the New Testament of the fact that the Old Testament – and the whole of the Old Testament – is the Word of God: not merely that it contains it but that it *is* it. The whole of the Old Testament is the oracles of God. We know other statements that say the same thing: 2 Timothy 3 : 16; 2 Peter 1 : 19–21, but this is another which is often forgotten. Therefore, as you are discussing and defending the Scriptures never forget this particular argument from Romans 3 : 2, where the Apostle says quite explicitly, with all his apostolic authority, that the Old Testament Scriptures are the oracles of God.

[1] *Romans, Exposition of Chapter 1; The Gospel of God* (The Banner of Truth Trust, 1985).

But what we want to discover now is this: Why does he single this out as being the greatest privilege of all? He says that this is the greatest advantage that the Jew possessed, this is the greatest profit of being circumcised, this is the most marvellous thing of all about belonging to the nation of Israel. It is much more important than the fact that they had crossed through the Red Sea and that the army of Pharaoh was drowned trying to follow them; much more important than that they were fed with manna, and that various miracles were performed, that they walked again through the divided waters of Jordan, or that they took Jericho by just marching round it; infinitely more important than all these things is this – 'that unto them were entrusted the oracles of God'.

Are you surprised at this? Does it come to you with an element of amazement that the Apostle says that this is the supreme thing about being a Jew? I emphasize this because it seems to me, as I hope to show you, that we are all in grave danger of not realizing this truth as we ought to. So let me give you, therefore, some reasons why the Apostle says that this is obviously the supreme thing. Here is one: there is no higher privilege that can come to any human being than to be spoken to directly by God. People boast if some great personage, a king or a queen, or some important person should happen, while walking along, to notice them and to turn aside and speak to them, and they say, 'He actually spoke to me!' It is much more important than if he had just looked; that would be wonderful, but if he actually spoke to them – there is nothing beyond that. Multiply that by infinity: there is nothing greater than this, than that God should speak to man – the oracles of God. In Deuteronomy 8 : 3 Moses says to the children of Israel that God has dealt with them in the way He has, 'That he might make thee know that man doth not live by bread only, but by every word that proceedeth out of the mouth of the Lord doth man live'. That is what gives life and being and everything – 'the word that proceedeth out of the mouth of the Lord'.

But I want to emphasize this by putting it to you negatively. If the greatest privilege that can ever come to a man is to be spoken to directly by God, it is equally true to say that there is no greater loss that a man can suffer than that God should cease to speak to him. 'Behold', says the prophet Amos, threatening a recalcitrant

people, 'Behold, the days come, saith the Lord God, that I will
send a famine in the land, not a famine of bread, nor a thirst for
water, but of hearing the words of the Lord' [*Amos* 8 : 11]. It is a
terrible thing to have a famine of bread; it is a terrible thing to
have a drought; but there is something infinitely worse than
that, said Amos, and it is coming upon you, a famine of hearing
the words of the Lord; God being silent and man being left to
himself and his own inventions and his own thoughts. There is
nothing more appalling than that. And that is something which
is very significant for the Christian. The Christian is a man who
ought to be wretched and miserable if he feels that he does not
hear God speaking to him, if he feels he has lost contact with
God. There is nothing more terrible than to feel you are
abandoned of God. It is the loss, you see, of the oracles, of the
Word of God.

But let me go on and give you some further reasons. Receiving
the oracles of God is the supreme privilege that can come to any
man, and the point is that this was the only nation to whom God
had done this. He did not speak to the other nations, He spoke
only to this one nation that He had made for Himself, as a
peculiar treasure and possession for Himself. He spoke to the
nation of Israel – God spoke to man. There is no higher privilege
than that. And that is why there is this 'much advantage every
way', and every conceivable profit in being a Jew and in
belonging to this circumcised race. But that, in turn, leads to
this, of course: think of the light and the knowledge and the
information that this Word of God has brought to them. There
were the other nations, living in a pagan darkness and in
ignorance and blackness. They were worshipping a multiplicity
of gods, building their temples, living in a state of fear, seeing
gods in trees and in stones and in the very elements – utter
darkness and ignorance. God had spoken to this nation of Israel
and had given them to understand that there was only one true
and living God. God is One. He had given them knowledge
about that and about Himself. He had revealed His character,
His nature and His works, but He had not stopped at that. He
had made a covenant with them. He had entered into a covenant
with their father Abraham. He had said, 'I will bless thee . . . in
thee shall all families of the earth be blessed' [*Genesis* 12 : 2, 3].
Go back and read it all in the book of Genesis – the covenants

and the promises and the purposes of God. Now, later on in chapter nine, the Apostle goes over all this again; he says, '. . . who are Israelites; to whom pertaineth the adoption, and the glory, and the covenants, and the giving of the law, and the service of God, and the promises; whose are the fathers, and of whom as concerning the flesh Christ came . . .'. But here it is all in a nutshell for us.

The greatest thing of all, however, was the fact that through these oracles of God they were given the hope – the hope of the coming of the Messiah. The other nations had no hope at all, but Israel had a hope. There was a great Deliverer to come. God had said to Moses, 'The Lord thy God will raise up unto thee a Prophet from the midst of thee, of thy brethren, like unto me; unto him ye shall hearken' [*Deuteronomy* 18 : 15]. The promise! The Messiah! The Shiloh that was to come! [See *Genesis* 49 : 10.] It was a light in the darkness. They alone had it. What a privilege! But over and above that, God had not only given them these oracles and given them the information contained in them, He had entrusted the oracles to their safe keeping, He had handed them over to them: they were to be the guardians and custodians. They had the knowledge and they were to make it known. What a privilege to be God's spokesmen, God's representatives.

One other thing comes in at this point which is, it seems to me, germane to the Apostle's argument in this section. It was a great privilege to have all this knowledge, because it is this knowledge that leads a man to see and to know that he is a sinner, that he is under the wrath of God, and that leads him, therefore, to go to God seeking mercy and deliverance and salvation. The pagan does not know that. He is ignorant. He does not have this light; he does not have this information. He does not know God and the character of God, therefore he remains under the wrath of God and under condemnation. But the Jew has the advantage of all this knowledge, and this knowledge should lead him to repentance and to seek salvation from God: 'Much every way: chiefly, because that unto them were committed [entrusted] the oracles of God'. That is the Apostle's argument.

But once more I say that I cannot leave it just at that; we must apply all this to ourselves. We do not study the Scriptures simply to have an academic discussion. We do not take an objective view of Scripture; we know that it is speaking to us as we read it. I want to put it to you like this: the highest privilege of the Jew was that he had his Old Testament Scriptures. There is no greater privilege than that. Do we realize, I wonder, what a privilege it is that we have these Scriptures, New Testament as well as Old? Do we realize the advantage of having an open Bible? Do we realize the advantage and the privilege of having these living oracles of God? Let me ask a further question: do we realize that our Bible is the Word of God? That is what the Scripture is saying. The Old Testament is the 'oracles of God', the New Testament, too, is the 'oracles of God'. That is the claim that is made for them.

So the point, therefore, at which you and I start is this: we say, 'This is no ordinary book, this is the Word of God'. Do we show that we realize that and what a privilege it is, by reading it, studying it, delving into it, spending our time praying over it? Do not misunderstand me – you have other things to read which you must read, but I am asking this – do you, when you come to this Book, read it, as a matter of custom or of practice, because you have decided to have a quiet time in the morning and read a few verses before you run off to something else – is that the way you approach it? Or do you say, 'Here God is speaking to me, speaking to man and I am reading because it is God's direct word'. Again, I ask, do we give as much of our leisure time to it as we do to other words, newspapers, for instance? My friends, if we do not give more time to this than to these other things it is simply because we do not realize that it is the oracles of God. We may say so theoretically, but if we really believed it, we would soon show it in practice.

But there is something further: 'Unto them were *committed* the oracles of God', and, you know, the oracles of God have been entrusted to us to guard them, to keep them, to defend them. The Apostle puts it like this to ministers, in 1 Corinthians 4 : 1, 'Let a man so account of us', he says, speaking of Apollos and himself, 'as of the ministers of Christ, and stewards of the mysteries of God'. The same thing exactly. I am a very poor minister if I do not realize that one of my first calls is to be a steward of this mystery, a guardian of this deposit, one to whom God has entrusted His own Word. That is why this so-called higher critical movement of the last century has been such a terrible thing. I tremble to think of the position of men who have been called to be stewards of the mysteries, men to whom God has entrusted His oracles, who themselves have attacked it, and undermined it, and shaken the faith of other people in it! There is nothing more terrible than that.

But the Scriptures have been entrusted not only to ministers but to all. Jude says that he is writing to '. . . exhort you that ye should earnestly contend for the faith which was once delivered unto the saints' [v. 3]. But even that is not as popular today as it once was. We are living in times when evangelical people are increasingly saying, 'Well it does not matter, we must all co-operate together. What if the man is not quite with us on the Scriptures, what does it matter? What if he is not quite with us on the atonement, that does not matter either, he is preaching Christ in a sense. Let us all be together, let us all be one'. But we are specifically commanded to 'earnestly contend for the faith [this message, this Word] which was once [and for ever] delivered to the saints'. You as Christian people, as members of the Christian church, are to defend this truth as the Word of God, and to contend for it. We must therefore know the arguments, we must busy ourselves with these things, because it is the Word of God that God has entrusted to us; and obviously it has been entrusted to us not simply that we should keep it and guard it, but that we should teach others.

And that is the argument, you see, for the missionary enterprise, and it is in particular the argument for seeing to it that men who are converted in other lands should have the Scriptures. It is not enough that they just be converted, they must learn the Scriptures, they must be taught how to read them and to understand them. It is not enough that they have an experience. We must put the Word of God into their hands. It is the greatest argument of all for that particular enterprise. So you see, this Word here makes us examine ourselves. What is the use of getting excited about sending out Bibles and portions of Scripture to pagan lands where people are converted, if we who have got them do not use our own Bibles ourselves in this country? We contradict ourselves thus.

And then, finally, it seems to me that we are entitled to deduce this principle: 'What advantage then hath the Jew? or what profit is there of circumcision?' Sometimes today that is put in this way – people say, 'Do the children of Christian parents have any advantage at all over other children?' They say, 'You evangelical preachers are always saying that the child of Christian parents has got to be converted quite as much as the child of people who are not Christian. Is there any advantage, therefore, in having Christian parents?' It is precisely the same question. And there are people who have said, 'You know, I have almost wished, sometimes, that I had been a terrible drunkard or something like that in my past life in order that I might have some great change-over in my experience'. Now if we say things like that we are uttering the very same fallacy with which the Apostle is dealing here. The advantage that the children of Christian parents have is that they have this teaching, this Word of God, these oracles of God, this learning, this knowledge, this information. They ought to come to repentance long before anybody else, because they are under the sound of it all, they are hearing it, they are familiar with it, and it ought to bring them to conviction. We cannot guarantee that it will, but they have the advantage, they have the opportunity. It is a marvellous thing to be children of Christian parents, if the Christian parents are truly behaving as such. So we can deduce that argument also from these verses.

But we can also put it the other way round. It is the business of Christians to make known to their children these oracles of God, which have been entrusted to them, so that in later life the children shall say, 'I thank God I had a Christian father, a Christian mother. I cannot tell you what I owe to them. I first came into this Christian life because of what my mother taught me when I stood at her knee, or sat upon her lap; or because of something I heard my father say out of the Word of God'. There it is! This is the advantage. And we should not only rejoice in it but we should have a sense of compassion for all little children who are denied such an opportunity, and we should do all that we can to enable them to hear the oracles of God and their wonderful teaching. Oh yes, what an advantage – 'Unto them were committed the oracles of God'!

Thirteen

*

For what if some did not believe? shall their unbelief make the faith of God without effect? God forbid: yea, let God be true, but every man a liar; as it is written, That thou mightest be justified in thy sayings, and mightest overcome when thou art judged. But if our unrighteousness commend the righteousness of God, what shall we say? Is God unrighteous who taketh vengeance? (I speak as a man) God forbid: for then how shall God judge the world? For if the truth of God hath more abounded through my lie unto his glory; why yet am I also judged as a sinner? And not rather, (as we be slanderously reported, and as some affirm that we say,) Let us do evil, that good may come? whose damnation is just.

Romans 3 : 3–8

Now this, it is generally agreed, is one of the most difficult passages not only in the Epistle to the Romans but in the whole of Scripture. You notice that it is a very fine, a very closely woven argument, and some may be inclined to ask, 'Is all this necessary? Why all this subtle argument? Why does the Apostle bother with this kind of thing, which is so difficult to follow and understand?' And the answer is that the fault is not the Apostle Paul's. He had no desire to write like this, I am perfectly certain, and probably dearly wished that it were not necessary for him to do so. But he has to do it because of the questions people ask and because of the arguments which they put up. And as a wise teacher and one who is anxious that these Christians in Rome should be well grounded and established in the faith, he has to meet all possible arguments and every kind of eventuality. Paul as a preacher had the same experiences as every other preacher – he makes a statement which he thinks is perfectly plain and clear, but it seems to arrive at the receiving end in a somewhat different manner and people put an odd twist to it and say, 'But, what about this . . . ?' And they begin to ask their questions. People had been doing things like that with the Apostle – you notice how he complains in verse 8, '(as we be slanderously reported, and as some affirm that we say)'.

Now I am not sure but that those words in brackets are not some of the most comforting words in the whole of Scripture for a preacher. The Apostle Paul's preaching was completely misunderstood by certain people, and they made out that he was saying the exact opposite of what he was saying. That is why, then, he is driven to this bit of argumentation, and we must now consider it. Let me try to put it as clearly as I can, though, again, I say that it is an extremely difficult statement and a very difficult argument to follow.

First of all, we need to remind ourselves of what he is dealing with. Here is the position: in view of what he has been saying in chapter two – that there is no difference between the Jew and the Gentile in the matter of the wrath of God, and the judgment of God – people, especially Jews, were asking what, if that was true, was the advantage of being a Jew? Why was the Old Testament ever necessary? Why did God ever call Abraham and separate him from all others? Because God chose Abraham when he was a pagan, God chose him and called him out. It was not Abraham's choice, it was God's choice, and God, out of that one man, produced a nation for Himself and He said to them, 'You only have I known of all the families of the earth' [*Amos* 3 : 2]. That is the great story of the Old Testament. 'And now', Paul's questioner continued, 'in view of what you have just been saying in this second chapter, you seem to be dismissing the whole of that and saying that there is no point in it'.

Not at all, says the Apostle. There is – 'Much every way . . .'. There is a great advantage and we have seen that what Paul emphasizes as the chief thing is 'that unto them were committed [entrusted] the oracles of God' – God's Word, God's promises, God's teaching, God's Word in the Old Testament in all its fulness.

Then, having laid that down, Paul immediately foresees another difficulty; he foresees people raising a query out of what he has just been saying. He has been telling them that there is a tremendous advantage in being a Jew, because it was to them that these oracles were given, these great promises about the coming of the Messiah, and so on. And then he imagines a man saying, 'But, wait a minute, that does not help at all, that is not an answer, that does not satisfy me'. Why not? 'Well, for this reason: the Jews, speaking generally as a nation, had proved unfaithful to God's Word and had never really understood His promise. This was especially true of the Messiah. When He actually came, the bulk of the nation refused Him and rejected Him'. Now the Apostle was well aware of this, and he deals with it in chapters nine, ten and eleven of this Epistle. So the argument which he envisages here – and no doubt it was an argument that had frequently been brought forward – can be put in this form: it is no use saying that the advantage of the Jew was that to them had been entrusted the oracles of God, because the oracles of God do not seem to have benefited them because of their unbelief. Their lack of faithfulness has surely nullified and negatived all the value of God's promises. That is the statement which he makes in verse 3, where he puts it in the form of a question, 'For what if some did not believe?'

Here we must point out with all the learned commentators what a careful man the Apostle was, what a diplomatic man he was in many senses. And it is a point worth noting. He says, 'What if *some* did not believe?' giving the impression that most Jews had believed but that some had not. Whereas the actual fact was that the vast majority had not believed and there was only a very small remnant that did. But you notice how diplomatic he is, how he is always courteous. You will find examples of that in the Acts of the Apostles. Read, for instance, in chapter twenty-six, about the famous occasion when Paul addresses King Agrippa. Look at the introduction to his address and notice how Paul does everything to make his argument as commendable and as pleasing as he can. He is all things to all men that he might be the means of saving some. And here is another example of that – 'What if some have not believed?' – whereas in reality it was the majority.

Now the translation here is a great cause of debate. It does not seem to me to matter very much. 'What if some did not believe?' says the Authorized Version. Perhaps a better translation would be to say, 'What if some were not faithful?' – not faithful to the promises, nor to the Word that had been delivered to them –

'shall their lack of faith' – their unfaithfulness – 'make the
faithfulness of God of none effect?' That is the position with
which he is dealing. In other words, we shall see, as we work
through this paragraph, that he deals with three possible
arguments which people may raise on the statement which he
makes in the first verse. First: does it not seem, therefore, that
the unfaithfulness of the nation of Israel has really done away
with all the benefit and the value of having the oracles of God? It
does not seem to have led to anything, it did not seem to lead to
anything in the old dispensation, it does not seem to lead to
anything now, with the coming of the Lord and this new
dispensation. His answer to that is in verse 4, and he starts with
a statement which is translated in the Authorized Version as
'God forbid'. Now actually that is a very poor translation
because in the original the word 'God' does not appear at all. It
really means, 'Out upon the suggestion! Impossible suggestion!
Unthinkable!' And then the answer is given in the rest of the
verse: 'Yea, let God be true, but every man a liar; as it is written'
– he quotes some words from Psalm 51 – 'That thou mightest be
justified in thy sayings, and mightest overcome when thou art
judged'.

At this point the important thing for us is to observe the
apostolic method. He states the question, and then his first
answer is that this is an impossible suggestion. Why? Well, on
general principles, as I shall show you. But having laid it down
like that, he then comes and looks at it in a little more detail, he
elaborates it for us. The essence of his answer is that the failure
of the Jews does not, and cannot, in any way affect the purposes
or the faithfulness of God. God gave His promises, He gave them
to the Jews, and to the Jews only at first, and the failure of the
Jews to receive them and to appreciate them makes not the
slightest difference to those promises. That is what Paul is
really saying, 'Shall their unbelief make the faith of God
without effect?' or, 'Shall their unfaithfulness nullify the
faithfulness of God?' By no means, it is unthinkable.

And here, of course, is one of those tremendous principles
which we must grasp firmly. God's unconditional promises do
not depend upon the faithfulness of man – indeed, were that to
be so, there would never have been a salvation at all! That, in a
sense, is the great message of the Old Testament. God has

chosen this people. He has made them for Himself. He gives them all the promises. He treats them in grace, and yet look at their constant and repeated failure! If it had been left to them, the nation might very well have been exterminated, and none of the promises of God would have been brought to pass or would have had any effect. But it is in spite of His people that God goes on with His great purposes and fulfils His wonderful covenant. Let me emphasize again that this is a most important principle for us to lay hold of. What God has purposed, God will most surely bring to pass. 'He which hath begun a good work in you will perform it until the day of Jesus Christ' [*Philippians* 1 : 6].

What a comforting doctrine this is! Take the Christian church herself: if she had been a human institution only, it is perfectly certain that she would have ceased to exist centuries ago. The reason why she is still in existence, in spite of man's failure, is that she is in the purpose of God. The Apostle puts it very strongly: 'Let God be true, but every man a liar'. God's faithfulness and God's justice are absolutes. Paul just lays it down as a principle that if all men were to fail completely, God's veracity, God's truth, God's righteousness and God's purposes would still be right. That is his declaration. He tells us that there are certain questions which should never be raised. In other words, we should never ask whether, because so and so has happened, or because people have not done this or that, it therefore means that God's great purpose is nullified. If you ask a question like that, says the Apostle, it means that your whole thinking about God is wrong. God is never wrong. God cannot be wrong. Let the whole world be wrong but not God. 'Let God be true, but every man a liar'.

Indeed, Paul goes on and adds that quotation from Psalm 51 : 4. David, let me remind you, had committed that terrible sin in the matter of Bathsheba and in the murder of her husband, and then he went on imagining that all was well. But God visited him through the prophet Nathan and at first David did not like it. God dealt with him very severely, and at last David came to see it all and so he wrote Psalm 51, and this is what he said in verse 4: 'Against thee, thee only, have I sinned, and done this evil in thy sight: that thou mightest be justified when thou speakest, and be clear when thou judgest'. You notice the Apostle does not put it exactly like that, because this quotation is taken – as are most of the Old Testament quotations in his Epistles – from the Septuagint, which was so commonly used at that particular time. It was the Greek translation of the Old Testament that had been done (according to the tradition) by the Seventy, and what we have here is a direct quotation of Psalm 51 : 4 from that particular version.

But, of course, the message really comes to much the same thing in both versions. David is saying to God, in effect, 'There was a moment when I thought that you were wrong and that I did not deserve this punishment, I felt this was not right and that it was not fair. I am your servant and you have called me, and honoured me, and I began to feel that it was wrong that I should be treated in this way'. The Jews often argued like that. But David has now been enlightened, he has come to himself, and in this verse he puts it quite simply and plainly. He says, 'I have sinned and I have not a single plea, and what you have done and what you are doing to me is perfectly right. I want it to be made known and clear', says David, 'that you are absolutely just in all you are doing'. The Apostle here takes up this quotation, and you notice how very apposite it is. He says, whatever man may do, God always does that which is right; yes, though the whole world were wrong, God is still right: 'Let God be true, but every man a liar'. Indeed, he says, God is always right and history will justify God – as David has put it: 'That thou mightest overcome when thou art judged'. It is a very bold picture. It is a picture, as it were, of God on trial, with mankind querying and questioning Him. No, says David, when the ultimate facts are revealed, God will be justified, and the world will have to admit, as I am having to admit now, that God is right and I alone was wrong.

Now that is exactly the Apostle's point in these verses and we can say that his argument here is working up to this climax – that not only does the failure of the Jews not nullify the purpose of God, the failure of the Jews, indeed, seems to put into greater relief, and into greater prominence, the justice and the right-eousness and the truth of God's way. Go back through your Old Testament, says the Apostle, and if you read it properly this is the conclusion you will come to – not that the failure of the Jews has brought God's purpose to nothing, but that in spite of that failure God's purpose still goes on. There, then, Paul has dealt with the first argument and shown the right way to look at this failure on the part of the Jews.

But that leads to yet another, a second, argument, and oh, how subtle is the sinner! How clever he thinks he is! He now raises an argument based on that statement, and this is it: 'Well then', says this imaginary opponent, 'if you are saying that our unrighteousness commends the righteousness of God and makes it stand out still more gloriously, what shall we say? Is God unrighteous who takes vengeance?' Do you follow the argument? Let me put it like this: their contention is that if the failure of the Jews puts God's justice into greater relief, if that very failure has, in a way, contributed to His majesty and His glory and His greatness, on what grounds is He punishing them? Paul, they say, has been trying to prove that the Jews are going to be punished as the Gentiles are going to be punished. But how can God punish people who are magnifying His righteousness and His grace and His glory? Is that not unfair? Now that is their question, and you notice that the Apostle is very careful in the way he puts it. He slips in the sentence in brackets at the end of that verse – '(I speak as a man)'. What he means by that is that this is the way in which the natural man argues. There is a very modern ring about these arguments, is there not? Have you not heard people doing the very same thing when they have been given the gospel? They try to catch you on every word you say – if this, then why that . . . ? And that is exactly the kind of arguing which the Apostle is dealing with here.

That is, indeed, a typical argument from the side of the unbeliever. He says, 'You know, you cannot have it both ways. If you say that my sin and my failure brings out in a wonderful way the mercy and the compassion of God, well surely, then, that very mercy and compassion of God must forgive that sin'. Now let me put that in modern language. Evangelical preaching of the gospel says that we are saved without money and without price. I stand in the pulpit and I say, 'If there is somebody listening to me who has come from the very jaws of hell and has spent a lifetime in sin it does not matter at all, you are forgiven freely by the grace of God. How wonderful is that grace', I say. 'The more sin abounded, the more did grace superabound, as it were'.

'Ah', says the sinner, 'if that is so, and if this grace of God is as great and as marvellous as that, how does it become possible that God should punish at all?'

Now that is the question which Paul puts here in verse 5 and the answer, which is given in verse 6, is exactly the same again – 'God forbid'. It is an impossible suggestion, it must never even be put up as a supposition. You should never have used such language, says the Apostle.

But then he does not stop at that, he goes on again to give a further reason, and he regards this as being sufficient. If that is so, he says, how, then, shall God judge the world? Now this is a brilliant piece of argumentation. The Apostle knew that the Jews did believe in the final judgment, they all believed that. They believed that God was going to judge the world in righteousness. Of course, what they believed was that *they* would be all right. They would not be judged, but the Gentiles would, the world would, and it would be judged because of its sin. Very well, says the Apostle, don't you see where you have landed yourself? If you are now going to argue that because the unrighteousness of man brings into greater relief the righteousness of God, God cannot judge sin and punish it, why do you at the same time teach that God is going to judge the sin of the Gentiles at the end of the world? Surely the unrighteousness of these Gentiles makes the righteousness of God stand out in relief, in exactly the same way as does that of the Jews? In other words, he is proving to them that they have gone too far, and have proved too much. If what they are trying to argue is true, then even the Gentiles cannot be judged, and the Jews believed the Gentiles certainly would be judged. That is a final and a conclusive argument. If that is right, says the Apostle, then God will not be able to judge anybody at the end of the world.

But he goes still further, and here we come to verse 7, where he now puts it in a more personal form: 'For if the truth of God hath more abounded through my lie unto his glory; why yet am I also judged as a sinner?' Now this is a sub-division of the second question. In verse 5 Paul put it in general terms and now in verse 7 he expresses it personally and says in effect, 'Here am I as a sinner and if my sin has made the truth of God stand out more abundantly, well, why then am I also at the same time judged as a sinner?' Paul does not give an immediate answer. Of course, the fact is that he has already dealt with it in verse 6, in his answer to the general argument. He has pointed out that the conclusion of that argument is that nobody can ever be judged, and that at the end of the world nobody will be condemned at all, everybody will be saved and God will smile indiscriminately upon all kinds and conditions of men. However, instead of repeating his own argument, he goes on and puts it in a slightly different way in verse 8: 'And not rather' – you see, he is developing the point – '(as we be slanderously reported, and as some affirm that we say,) Let us do evil, that good may come?'

What Paul is saying here, in effect, is this: 'You are saying to me that if this sin of mine makes the righteousness and the truth and the glory of God stand out still more gloriously, why should I be punished? But wait a minute', says the Apostle, 'you ought to go further than that and you ought to say, "Would it not be a good thing, therefore, if I sinned still more, because according to what you are saying, the more I sin, the more the grace and righteousness and mercy of God shine out?"' You will find that the Apostle repeats this kind of argument many times in the body of this Epistle. He puts it very explicitly in chapter five, where he says, 'Where sin abounded, grace did much more abound'. People were misunderstanding that, and they were saying slanderously that the Apostle was teaching that the more we sin, the more God's grace will shine out; therefore there is no need for us to live a good life, there is no need for us to bother about the law. The worse we are, the greater will be God's mercy to us, therefore let us plunge into sin that the grace of God may abound towards us. 'Why don't you say that?' says the Apostle here, and then he says in parenthesis, 'You know some people are actually saying that I and the other evangelists are preaching that'.

Now that is what makes this argument a little bit difficult, the fact that the Apostle should put the two things together in this rather strange and difficult construction. But that is the argument, and it is a perfectly fair one. If the contention is that because our sin produces the grace of God more marvellously than ever, therefore God will not punish sin, then it is quite logical to say that the more you sin the greater will be the righteousness of God. That is the point, says the Apostle, at which you land yourselves. And what is his comment upon it? It is this: '. . . whose damnation is just'. Any man who can say, 'Let us do evil that good may come', has no defence, his damnation is just. He is violating every moral principle, he is committing moral and intellectual suicide. There is nothing that is too bad for such a person, his condemnation is just.

Very well, there we have dealt with the three arguments. Let me summarize them again because we must make sure that we understand them. The first says, 'All right; you say that the giving of the oracles of God to these people was a great privilege, it was a wonderful thing for them. But how can you say that in view of their failure? Does not their failure prove that the oracles were of no value at all?' The answer is, no, because in spite of their failure, what God has promised will be carried out. Later in chapters nine, ten and eleven Paul will deal with this in much greater detail; here we have the essence of it. Actually, there was at that very time a 'remnant according to the election of grace', and in the later chapters the Apostle proves that 'they are not all Israel, which are of Israel'. There is a division in this big classification of Israel; there is a true Israel and a false Israel. Paul himself is one of the Israelites who have realized the privilege and have got the benefit. There is a remnant according to the election of grace, and there are yet other things to happen. So the false argument falls to the ground even to the extent of our being able to say that this failure of Israel, far from making it of no effect, has really brought it out in a still more wonderful way.

The second argument says, 'Does not that mean, therefore, that God is wrong when he punishes sin, if you say that the effect of sin is to make his grace shine out more gloriously?' Again, it is the kind of thing that should never be said, says the Apostle. If that were so, how can God judge the world? Indeed, he says, you had better be careful what you are saying. If you were going to say that because God's love and mercy shine out in contrast to sin, God therefore cannot punish sin, why not go to the logical conclusion and say, 'Let us sin as much as we can because our sinning seems to be recommending God's grace and drawing it out and making it still greater?' You realize what you are saying, says the Apostle in answer to this third argument. It is unthinkable, and a man who says a thing like that is a man whose damnation is just.

In this way, he has dealt with the arguments which have been put forward, and now, at the beginning of verse 9, we shall see how, having disposed of all these arguments, Paul comes right back and says, 'What then? are we better than they?' – Are we better than the Gentiles? – 'No, in no wise: for we have before proved both Jews and Gentiles, that they are all under sin'. He is back again with what he was saying at the end of chapter two, and he is now going to prove it by his great demonstrations from the Scriptures themselves.

But what I want to do now, is to draw certain lessons for ourselves from these verses which we have just been considering, and it is important that we should do this. Here is the first lesson: sometimes, I am afraid, we modern Christians tend to think that it is we alone who have these struggles against unbelievers, that the early church lived a lyrical, delightful kind of life, with no opposition and no difficulties at all. In fact, it was quite the reverse. This great Apostle was having to argue constantly; his preaching was misunderstood; the Jews with their subtle arguments were always trying to trip him. They did exactly the same with our Lord. You remember how they came with the tribute money and asked, 'Are we to pay tribute to Caesar or not?' They tried to trip Him and catch Him on words – they were constantly trying to do it. The early church had to fight for her life, for her faith; she was surrounded by all kinds of subtle argumentations, and they had to be met. Thank God that Paul and others were thus led to meet them! You notice that in those days men tried to be clever, even as they try to be clever now. Have you not noticed, when you have been putting the faith, putting the position to somebody, how they do not seem to be really listening to the truth that you are explaining to them? But they try to catch you and to trip you on words. They are chopping logic with you, and trying to show that you are contradicting yourself somewhere. That is the very thing they did with the Apostle Paul. Take courage and do not be stumbled by that, do not be discouraged. The world has always behaved like that; it is a characteristic of unbelief.

My next general principle is this. How careful we must be when we speak and express our opinions about things that we do not fully understand, and especially about God and His ways. Now this applies to us all, because, alas, when perhaps we are chastised, or when we are passing through a difficult time we, like these Jews and others, are a little bit prone to ask our questions. We say, 'I don't quite see why . . .'. That is the very thing of which the Apostle says, 'God forbid!' You do not see? Very well, if you do not see, be very careful not to speak in such a way as to blaspheme the name of God. Be careful! Put your hand on your mouth, as Job did. Be very careful in expressing your opinion about God's way. You may not see it all at a glance, but – 'Swift to hear, slow to speak, slow to wrath'. That is always the rule.

But then – and here is a valuable and practical point – how are we to deal with these people who put up their subtle, clever arguments against us? Here, you must have noticed the apostolic method; it is a wonderful and very safe one. In each instance Paul does not start with details, but falls back on some great fundamental principle. You notice his three principles: with regard to the first question his answer is – God forbid. Why? Because, he says, you are querying the faithfulness of God and that is something which must never be done. Can I put it like this: when you are tackling or trying to solve a difficult problem, it is always a good and a wise thing to start with something about which you are absolutely certain. When you have to explain the unknown, start with the known. If you are involved in some difficult argumentation and details, the wise thing always is to ask yourself, 'Now is there some big principle about which I am absolutely certain, which is related to these details?' If there is, go for it and lay it down. In effect the Apostle is saying this, 'Whatever the detailed reply may be about all this, I am absolutely certain that nothing can affect or change the faithfulness of God'.

Then his second great principle is this: God is ever righteous. When they bring up the question, 'Is God righteous in judging?' he has his answer. He says, whatever the detailed answer may be, of this I am certain, everything God does is righteous. Everything. You must never query the faithfulness of God, you must never query the righteousness of God. So if you ever catch yourself putting a question or making a statement that seems to bring these two great things into doubt, you will at once know that you are wrong. And if you are dealing with somebody else who is doing that, you must say, 'Now wait a minute; cannot you see that what you are implying is that God's eternal purpose can somehow be deflected? That is impossible. God would no longer be God'. Or, with regard to the second difficulty, 'Cannot you see that what you are querying is the absolute righteousness of God and the justice of God? You must never do that. These are absolutes. These are not for discussion. God is not God unless these things are always true'.

And finally, you see, if ever you seem to be saying something which leads to the conclusion, 'Let us do evil that good may come', you know already that you are wrong. That is morally impossible. It is unthinkable.

And so that is the apostolic way, and I commend this great method of argumentation to you. Seek for the principle involved in the argument that is put to you, then fall back upon one of these fundamental postulates. Stand there, and then explain the difficulty in terms of that. That is exactly what the Apostle does.

One other word: a very good way of testing any view that you may hold is to ask, 'Is this view humbling to me and glorifying to God?' If it is, it is probably right. You will not go far wrong if whatever view you are holding is glorifying God and humbling man. But if your view seems to glorify you and to query God, there is no need to argue or to go into details – it is wrong. That is a very good universal rule.

And my last word of all is again primarily to preachers – though, indeed, it is a word to everybody in the sense that if ever you are putting the gospel to another person you have got a very good test as to whether you are preaching the gospel in the right way. I can put it like this: if your presentation of the gospel does not expose it to the charge of antinomianism you are probably not putting it correctly. Let me explain that. The gospel comes as a free gift of God irrespective of what man does. Now the moment you say a thing like that you are liable to provoke somebody into saying, 'Well if that is so, it does not matter what I do'. The Apostle, as we have seen, takes up that argument more than once in this great Epistle. In chapter six, verse 1, he writes, 'Shall we continue in sin [do evil], that grace may abound?' He has just been saying, 'Where sin abounded, grace did much more abound'.

'Very well', says somebody, 'this is marvellous, let us go and get drunk. Do what you like, the grace of God will put you right!'

Antinomianism! Now this doctrine of the Scriptures, this justification by faith only, this free grace of God in salvation, is always exposed to that charge of antinomianism. Because he taught that the law could not save them, Paul was charged with encouraging lawlessness and saying that the more they sinned the more God's grace would fall down upon them.

So I say that it is a very good test of preaching. You see, what is not evangelical preaching is the kind of preaching which says to people, 'Now if you live a good life, if you do not commit certain sins and if you do good to others, if you become a church member and attend regularly and are busy and active, you will be a fine Christian and you will go to heaven'. That is the opposite of evangelical preaching, and it is not exposed, there-fore, to the charge of antinomianism because it is encouraging good works, it is telling men to save themselves by their good works, and it is not the gospel. So let all of us test our preaching, our conversation, our talk to others about the gospel, by that particular test – does it make a certain clever type of man say, 'I see now the whole position – it does not matter what I do, all is well!'? And if you do not make people say things like that sometimes, if you are not misunderstood and slanderously reported from the standpoint of antinomianism, it is because you do not believe the gospel truly and you do not preach it truly.

What a wonderful gospel this is, and how we ought to thank God even for a difficult passage like this. But I have drawn great comfort and consolation from it, as I have been trying to show you. We have got the apostolic method of dealing with difficulties and we see here this essential message, and we see that it is of such a character that evil men will always, in their cleverness, as they think, be able to shortcut it entirely and side-track it, and even turn it into saying the exact opposite of what it says. Because we preach that a man is saved in spite of his works it does not mean for a second that therefore we say, 'Do evil that good may come'. Not at all! 'Do we make void the law?' Paul is going to say at the end of this chapter. 'No, we establish the law'.

Fourteen

*

What then! are we better than they! No, in no wise: for we have before proved both Jews and Gentiles, that they are all under sin; As it is written, There is none righteous, no, not one: there is none that understandeth, there is none that seeketh after God. They are all gone out of the way, they are together become unprofitable; there is none that doeth good, no, not one. Their throat is an open sepulchre; with their tongues they have used deceit; the poison of asps is under their lips: whose mouth is full of cursing and bitterness: their feet are swift to shed blood: destruction and misery are in their ways: and the way of peace have they not known: there is no fear of God before their eyes. Now we know that what things soever the law saith, it saith to them who are under the law: that every mouth may be stopped, and all the world may become guilty before God. Therefore by the deeds of the law there shall no flesh be justified in his sight: for by the law is the knowledge of sin.

Romans 3 : 9–20

We come now to this second section in Romans chapter three. Paul has been proving in the first eight verses that there was an advantage in being a Jew and in having the oracles of God. There was an advantage in being the people of God, but that does not mean that they were in a favoured position with respect to the whole subject of the wrath of God or of salvation. They should have been, but they were not. It is an advantage to be a Jew, it is an advantage to have the Scriptures, as it is an advantage to be the child of Christian parents, but you are no more saved than a child who is not born into a Christian family. And that is exactly what Paul is saying here in verse 9. He says, Surely I have already proved that to you – 'We have before proved both Jews and Gentiles, that they are all under sin'. In a sense, then, we really are coming back to the great theme of this entire section which started in verse 18 of chapter one. He has been dealing since then with the objections and the difficulties and the arguments, but now he is right back on to his theme and he is going to give his final proof of it from the Scriptures. We are now engaged in looking into that.

We start by considering this most interesting term that he uses straight away about them all: 'We have before proved both Jews and Gentiles, that they are all *under sin*'. First of all you notice that it is indicative of a state or a condition, and that is the way in which the Bible looks at man as the result of the Fall. According to the Bible every human being is in one of two positions, either under sin or else under grace. That is the only division which is recognized in Scripture. You will find alternative terms for it: 'Under sin' is sometimes equated with being 'under the law', but it is the same thing. The fundamental state is to be 'under sin'.

Now this really cannot be emphasized too much. The Bible, you see, unlike much of our thinking, does not think at all except in these two big categories. The Bible does not say, 'Is he a good man?' The Bible does not ask how much good he does or whether he is respectable; it does not ask any of those questions at all. It says, 'Every man is either under sin or else under grace'. In other words, we must always think of ourselves not primarily in terms of actions or of any particular things that are true about us; it is our whole condition that matters. The teaching of the New Testament is put in terms of 'belonging' to a kingdom – the kingdom of God, or the kingdom of this world.

Let me use an analogy. If you visited a foreign country, the thing which would be of primary interest to the people of that country, the first thing they would want to know about you, is not the colour of your hair or your eyes, not your bank balance, or whether you are a nice person – the first thing they would want to know is what country you belong to. Are you a citizen of this country or are you a foreigner? They would want to know the realm to which you belong. And that is something which is absolutely basic to a true understanding of the Christian faith, the Christian gospel. It does not start with details.

And that is where many people go wrong about this gospel – the people who think that if you are living a good life you are a Christian. You may live a very good life and not be a Christian at all, because you are not in that realm. There are good people under sin, in the realm and dominion of Satan. It is the realm to which you belong that really matters and really counts. Now then, Paul says – and this is the staggering statement – *all*, both Jews and Gentiles, are under sin, under the dominion of sin, and belong to the realm of sin. That statement, of course, includes such things as this: that all mankind by nature is under the guilt of sin, under the power of sin, and under the pollution of sin. It is his fundamental statement, and everything else follows from this.

And you notice that he says that all are in that condition. Jews and Gentiles, every single individual among them. It is not a kind of general statement about Jews in general or Gentiles in general. As I am going to show you later, the Apostle's case is that this is true of every single individual. Indeed, we can go further and put it like this. The case of the Bible is that this is the truth about everybody who has ever been born into this world, since the Fall. We are all born under sin. Now that is simply a biblical postulate; it is something the Bible says about every-body. Children are not born innocent. They are born under sin, with sin in them; they are born with the guilt of Adam's guilt upon them; they have the pollution of his nature. We are born sinners, 'all under sin'. And that term 'under', I think, gives us the impression that we are under authority, that is the whole realm to which we belong. Therefore the Apostle here is just laying it down as his fundamental postulate that as the result of sin and the Fall that is the condition of every single human individual until he or she is born again and becomes regenerate.

Now it is important for us to grasp this because unless we have some conception of what really did happen when man fell, we shall never have a true conception of the gospel itself. There is a sense in which we shall never understand why the Son of God had to come into this world, and especially why He had to die upon the cross, unless we realize what happened when man fell. In the beginning God made man and He made him the representative of the whole of humanity, and his action there-fore had its consequences upon the whole of his progeny: every one of us is born in Adam. You will find that taught later in the fifth chapter of this Epistle, and you will find it, too, in 1 Corinthians 15 in Paul's argument – 'as in Adam, so in

Christ . . .' and so on. But here we are dealing with 'as in Adam', and because we are all descendants of Adam, we are all born under sin. It is the most cataclysmic and devastating thing that has ever happened in this world, and that is the characteristic biblical way of describing and looking at it.

So, then, having made his statement, having laid down this fundamental postulate, the Apostle is going on to prove it: 'We have before proved both Jews and Gentiles, that they are all under sin; as it is written . . .' and then comes this great catena of scriptural quotations, this chain of evidence. Paul marshals together his wonderful proofs from verse 10 to verse 18, and having done that, he makes his own comments in verses 19 and 20. But for the moment we are looking at verses 10 to 18 in which he culls, or deliberately chooses, these particular statements out of the Psalms and from the prophets, in order to substantiate his great contention, that all, universally, without a single exception, the good people, the very best and nicest people, as well as the worst and the most vile – all are under sin.

Now it has been proved quite accurately and beyond any doubt that what the Apostle does here is something that was done very frequently by the early church and particularly by the teachers and preachers of the early church. They knew that certain arguments were particularly valuable, and when they were dealing with Jews they knew that nothing so helped their case as to be able to prove and substantiate it from the Old Testament itself. The Jews believed in the Old Testament Scriptures. They were the oracles of God that had been given to them. 'Very well', says the Apostle in effect, 'this is what your own Scriptures say'. He has a list here and it is interesting to speculate about this. The first Christians had a number of lists which had been compiled by the teachers and which people probably committed to heart, so that when they were involved in a discussion on a particular aspect of the Christian faith they could then remember them and produce their arguments. They called this the testimonium; it was a kind of testimonial to the truth. I call your attention to this because it is something that you and I can do in the same way. When you are arguing, for instance, with a kind of formal, nominal Christian who really has never read the Bible very much, but who thinks that he or she is a Christian; when you are putting the Christian faith to them truly and they are trying to counter it, on such an occasion it is a very effective thing to say, 'But look here, do you realize what the Scripture says?' Take them back to the Scriptures. That is why, as believers, we should be well versed in the Scriptures, and we should either commit them to memory or, if we do not do that, we should at any rate know where to find them. We should have our Bible in our pocket so that we can produce it and say, 'This is what it says'. It was a very valuable form of argument, and it was one that was frequently used by the early church – these proofs to establish certain positions. Let us learn from them and realize that this is still a very good way of bringing people to a knowledge of the truth.

So we are going to look at this chain of evidence that the Apostle brings forward and puts before us, but before we look at the details I want to emphasize the importance of what he was doing, and of what we are doing at this point. This is an unusually important passage. It is full of certain profound and essential lessons for us, and it would be a very foolish thing, it seems to me, to go straight to the quotations without realizing what Paul was doing. Let me therefore show you certain things in general about this list of quotations before we come to look at them.

The first thing that strikes one is the tragic blindness of the Jews with regard to their own Scriptures. There they were, boasting about the fact that they had the oracles of God and that none of the other nations had them – they were very proud of that fact – and yet the whole tragedy of the Jews was that they did not know their own Scriptures; they were reading them but they could not see the significance of what they were reading. Paul puts this in a very striking manner in 2 Corinthians 3 where he says that the trouble with the Jews was that there was a veil over their faces. Then he goes on to say, 'But their minds were blinded: for until this day remaineth the same vail untaken away in the reading of the old testament; which vail is done away in Christ. But even unto this day, when Moses is read, the vail is upon their heart'. There they were, reading their Scriptures, proud of them, boasting about them, and yet they were missing the whole point of those Scriptures. So the Apostle is going to show them that, by quoting their own Scriptures to them, the Scriptures they knew so well but with no real understanding of their meaning and their significance.

You remember how our Lord said the same thing about them in John 5 : 39 – 'Search the scriptures'; or if you prefer it, 'You *do* search the scriptures'. 'Search the scriptures; for in them ye think ye have eternal life: and they are they which testify of me'. What a tragedy! With an open Bible, as it were, with the Old Testament in front of them, with all these prophecies about the Lord, they read the words but they missed the message. There are still many people like that, are there not? They regularly read their New Testament as well as their Old Testament and yet they have never seen the message and the doctrine of salvation. You can be an expert on the words of Scripture and be a complete ignoramus with regard to its truth. It is the terrifying lesson which we get from these Jews. These experts in the Scriptures were ignorant of the very argument, the message, and the teaching of the Scriptures. These quotations remind us of that.

But in the second place – and this is the big thing that the Apostle had in his mind, of course – this passage proves the universality of sin. There is no other passage, perhaps, that does it so well. So if you are ever in a discussion with somebody about the fact that everyone is born a sinner, 'shapen in iniquity', that we are not born in a neutral state, but are already under the wrath of God – as Paul says in Ephesians chapter two, 'we all . . . were by nature the children of wrath, even as others' – then here is the passage to turn to in order to prove that. And notice the way in which Paul brings it out: 'As it is written', he says, 'There is none righteous . . .'. But, it is not enough for him to say 'none', he has to repeat it: 'There is none righteous, no, not one'. What a good preacher this man was. The test of a good preacher is repetition, because a preacher who does not repeat himself is a very poor one, he does not know his congregation.

But let us go on. 'There is none that understandeth, there is none that seeketh after God. They are all gone out of the way, they are together become unprofitable; there is none that doeth good, no, not one'. Do you see it now, the universality of sin? Let us never again be so foolish as to talk about a 'nice' or a 'good' person, or the amount of good they do, as if that makes a difference when you are face to face with the question of salvation. Here is the fundamental statement – 'not one'. Sin is universal, without a single exception. There never has been one exception to this rule since the Fall of man at the very dawn of history. This is the classic passage which proves that.

The third thing I would notice is that we are shown here again, perhaps even more clearly than we were in the second half of chapter one, the terrible character of sin. This is because, after all, in the first chapter he was dealing mainly with the Gentiles, the pagans of those ages; here, he is dealing with everybody at all times. And here we see a picture of what man is really like in and of himself, by his natural birth, apart from the grace of God in our Lord and Saviour Jesus Christ, and it is a terrible picture, but, alas, it is a true picture.

My fourth comment is that it is essential to understand this fact before we can truly understand the gospel. Now the Apostle has announced his gospel in chapter one, verses 16 to 17. He is 'not ashamed' of it. Why not? Because 'it is the power of God unto salvation to every one that believeth; to the Jew first, and also to the Greek. For therein is the righteousness of God revealed from faith to faith: as it is written, The just shall live by faith'. But why is it necessary that God should do something? Why do we need the power of God before we can be saved? Why is a righteousness from God essential? Those are the questions. And the only answer to them is what you have here in these quotations.

This, you see, is the preparation for the gospel. This is the way to evangelize, because evangelism means that we do not simply make a positive statement as to what the gospel does; we show people their need of it. In other words, there must be a conviction of sin as well as a display of salvation, and there are not many passages of Scripture in which the terrible nature and character of sin are brought out more strongly than they are in this particular section. And you notice the apostolic method. Having just made a general statement in chapter 1 : 16–17 about the gospel, its character and its contents, he at once goes on to say, 'For . . .': 'For the wrath of God is [has already been] revealed from heaven against all ungodliness and unrighteousness of men, who hold the truth in unrighteousness', and what he is really doing here is taking us back to that. You could say that verses 10 to 18 of this third chapter are but an exposition of verse 18 of the first chapter – this wrath of God that has been revealed upon all ungodliness and unrighteousness of men.

That is why the gospel is essential, says Paul, that is why God has had to do something, that is why God has sent forth His own Son – because this is the state of mankind.

So when the Apostle evangelizes, you see, he does it in this way. He does not come to people and say in his first approach, 'How would you like to be a bit happier, or would you like to have a Friend, or are you seeking guidance?' He does not say something like that. He does not start with that; he cannot possibly start with it. What is the use of asking questions like that if a man is in the wrong realm, if a man is under sin? The primary thing is not whether I am happy or miserable, or anything else; the question is, what is my relationship to God in the Judgment, what is my realm? If I am under sin, the first thing I want to know is how I can get out of that and be under grace. So we must not hesitate to say that an evangelism which does not start by a call to repentance and conviction of sin is unscriptural. It is wrong to say to people that they can come to Christ as they are and later on repent and learn something about sin. The Apostle does not do that, and it seems to me that no-one else should do so either, for this reason: what is the meaning of the term 'Saviour'? I say I come to Christ, I fly to Christ as my Saviour, what do I mean by it? What does He save me from? What is the content? There must be some meaning. And the moment you stop and ask that kind of question, you see it at once. The business of preaching is to show men where they are under sin, and to show them the only way of getting out of it and of being 'under grace'. Now this section, therefore, is of supreme importance in that respect.

And my last comment is that by showing us the terrible character of sin and the appalling position of man as he is by nature, it therefore shows us by contrast the glory of the grace of God. It is in spite of the fact that all of us are by nature as we are described here, that God 'sent forth his Son, made of a woman, made under the law, to redeem them that were under the law' [*Galatians* 4 : 4–5]. As you look at the blackness and the darkness of sin, by contrast you see the shining glory of this amazing grace of God. I do not know how you feel, but every time I read this list, as it goes on from bad to worse, I begin to say again, 'Is there any hope?' And, you know, there is, and it is nothing but the grace of God. It is the blackness and the

darkness that by contrast display the glory and the splendour of
the Light. In other words, it has always been the case, throughout the centuries in the long history of the church, that the men
who have had the highest conception of grace and of the gospel
and who have the greatest gratitude in their hearts to the Lord
Jesus Christ, have always been those who have been most
conscious of sin. It follows quite inevitably. As our Lord
Himself put it in that incident at the end of Luke 7 – 'Her sins,
which are many, are forgiven; for she loved much: but to whom
little is forgiven, the same loveth little'. That is just another way
of saying that the greater your understanding of the sinfulness of
your condition, the greater will be your understanding of the
love and the grace and the compassion and the mercy of God.

There, then, are my general comments. Now let us move on
and look at the quotations. From the strict standpoint of
classification you may be interested to know that verses 10, 11
and 12 are quotations from Psalm 14 and Psalm 53. Then,
verse 13 is taken from Psalm 5 : 9; verse 14 is a quotation from
Psalm 10 : 7 and verses 15, 16 and 17 are taken from
Isaiah 59 : 7–8. Of course, the Apostle could have chosen many
other passages; he was familiar with them. But he selects these
particular ones in order to bring out the point he is anxious to
make. So, then, is there any rhyme or reason about these
quotations? Did he think it out, or did he just quote verses at
random? Surely, it is perfectly clear that he had a definite
system in his mind. The Apostle Paul was essentially logical; he
thought very clearly and he goes on from point to point. So that
you can, if you like, divide it up in this way. The texts quoted,
the passages which he adduces, can be classified under three
main headings; the first, which comprises verses 10, 11 and 12,
is a general description and account of man in sin. The second
section, verses 14 to 17, is a particular account of sin in action,
the kind of sins that men are guilty of because of their sinful
state. You see how logical he is! First of all, general description,
then particular manifestations. That is the way to put them.
And then in verse 18, to sum it all up again, he gives the cause of
it all, which is that 'there is no fear of God before their eyes'.

That, then, is the general classification in the three sections,
but he sub-divides these three sections, and the sub-division
again is perfectly plain and clear. Let us take the first and

consider this general definition or description of man in sin found in verses 10, 11, and 12: 'As it is written, There is none righteous, no, not one: there is none that understandeth, there is none that seeketh after God. They are all gone out of the way, they are together become unprofitable; there is none that doeth good, no, not one'. Now there is an obvious division of that into two sub-sections: first of all the actual state of man in sin, and then the general result of being in that state. Here is the general state – 'There is none righteous . . . there is none that under-standeth; there is none that seeketh after God . . .'. And, because they are like that, the result is that 'They are all gone out of the way, they are together become unprofitable; there is none that doeth good, no, not one'. Now one of the most fascinating studies that I know of is just to watch the working of Paul's mind, because there is never anything accidental here. He always puts the cause before its effect; he does not just rush to the details; he is always concerned about the principles. And if we are to have a true understanding of Christian doctrine, and of the message of the Christian faith, we have really got to do that. We must start with a man's state before we consider the manifestations of that state.

So, then, let us look at man's state as the result of sin and at this general description of his condition. And the first thing which Paul tells us is that there 'is none righteous, no, not one'. Now to be 'righteous' means to be upright in thought and in life, and this is a very important term. To be righteous means that you are blameless with respect to God and with respect to your fellow men. To be righteous does not just mean being good, or moral, or respectable. 'Righteous', as the term is used in the Scriptures, means that you are blameless as regards God and as regards your fellow men. Indeed, our Lord Himself has given the perfect description and definition of righteousness in His reply to the lawyer who asked Him, 'Which is the great commandment in the law?' And our Lord replied, saying, 'Thou shalt love the Lord thy God with all thy heart, and with all thy soul, and with all thy mind. This is the first and great commandment. And the second is like unto it, Thou shalt love thy neighbour as thyself' [*Matthew* 22 : 36–39]. You notice the order: He starts with man's relationship to God, and then He goes on to consider his relationship to his fellow men and women. And Paul always puts them in the same order. In chapter 1:18 he talks about 'all ungodliness and unrighteousness of men' – God first, man second. And it is the same here. So that we can define righteousness in this way: it means living a life in perfect conformity to the law of God; it is living as God desires man to live.

Now it is absolutely vital that we should be clear about this, because if we do not define it accurately we shall find that some people will say, 'Ah, well, certain men are very righteous. Other people are not and they will do you down if they can, but the righteous man will not do that'. But 'righteous' does not mean that. It is not a classification among men. It is man defined in his relationship to God and God's law, and to be righteous means to be in absolute conformity to that law, without any blemish or without any lack. And you notice the Apostle's assertion. He simply says that ever since the Fall of man there has not been a single righteous person. Not one! Not Enoch. Not Abraham. Not a single one. Ever since man fell from his state of innocency he has never been upright, he has never been righteous. He has always failed either in his relationship to God or in his relationship to man – indeed, in both respects. The best man, the noblest, the most learned, the most philanthropic, the greatest idealist, the greatest thinker, say what you like about him – there has never been a man who can stand up to the test of the law. Drop your plumb-line, and he is not true to it, he is not straight, he is not upright, he is not pure, he is not blameless: 'There is none righteous, no, not one'.

Now that, therefore, is the way to preach the gospel. I am quite sure that we have all met people who come to us and say, 'Do you know, I cannot honestly say that I have ever felt that I am a sinner', and they are quite genuine, they are quite sincere about it. You see, they have always thought of sin in terms of drunkenness and things like that, and as they have never done such things, they say, 'I would be a real hypocrite if I said I felt I was a sinner!' – people have actually said that to me! The way, then, to deal with such a person is just to say this: 'The Scripture says there is none righteous, no, not one; that there never has been. Are you the solitary exception?' In other words, you say to them, 'There is something wrong with your understanding of righteousness, and with your whole conception of sin. You have never yet realized that what makes a man a sinner is that he is not as God made him. God made him perfect. He gave him His law; He said, Keep that; I have made you to live like that and to be like that – are you like that? If you are not, then you are not righteous, and if you are not righteous you are a sinner, you are under sin and under the wrath of God'.

Do you see how tragic it is that though we have got our open Bibles, we still have our own private opinion as to what sin is and as to what righteousness is, and as to what satisfies God's demands? The Scripture is perfectly plain, and if you have ever read this chapter before without knowing what it is to feel that you are a sinner, I say it is because you are blinded, as the Jews were; you are looking at the words but you are not seeing the meaning; you are looking at the letters but you are not getting the words; you are looking at the mere mechanics and you have never got the spirit. There is *none* righteous. And who would like to claim that he or she is righteous in this sense? The moment you realize the meaning of this word, you see at a glance that the statement of Scripture is perfectly right. When you really look at the standard of righteousness, being good or bad or a little bit better or a little bit worse is a complete irrelevance. There is your plumb-line and you are either straight or you are not, and the fact that you are a little bit nearer than another man does not help you; you are meant to be straight, dead straight, absolutely upright. And not to be upright is to be sinful, to offend against God, to mar His perfect creation. And, alas, as I have been saying, the result of the Fall, and the result of sin, is that this is the state of every human being that has come into the world since that appalling calamity took place. Here is very profound doctrine; here is the reason, you see, why some of us still say that you must hold on to the early chapters of Genesis and that we cannot co-operate, even in evangelism, with people who do not hold on to them, because we do not quite know what sort of a Christ they are offering, and we do not quite know what they are offering Him for. This is the biblical and the scriptural position; you start with this fundamental fact, that everybody is unrighteous.

May I sum up by putting it like this: the preacher never needs to know the individual facts about his congregation. That is a wonderful thing about preaching. It does not make any difference to the preacher who may be sitting before him; he does not need to know, he should not be interested. Why? Well, because he knows that every single human being is not righteous, and it really does not matter from the standpoint of the preacher whether they have just emerged out of a gutter or whether they have come out of the best appointed drawing room in London; it does not matter whether they have come from the West End or the East End, the North Pole or the South. What does it matter? It does not matter how they are dressed, what they look like, how respectable or disreputable. Nothing like that matters. They are souls; they are people; and therefore they are not righteous and they need this gospel because it is the only thing that can save them. And when they come to see the preacher at the end, and they begin to give a catalogue of their sins, the preacher who really knows his Scriptures should say, 'Stop! I do not mind what you have done or what you have been. You are just a sinner like everybody else and you need the same Saviour'.

So we are not interested in people giving us testimonies as to what they once were; it does not matter. There is nothing more marvellous about one person being saved than another; there is nothing more marvellous about a man who has been a terrible drunkard being saved, than a man who has never had a drop of drink in his life; there is no difference at all, none whatsoever. But, you see, people are interested – 'Oh, was it not a wonderful testimony?' they say. 'Did you hear it?' My dear friend, I could easily prove, if you pressed me, that it is much more difficult to save the person who has not been a drunkard, because he does not know that he is not righteous. The drunkard does know it, he is terribly aware of it, poor fellow. You see how we pervert the whole gospel through being unscriptural and by pandering to the flesh and the carnal excitement of meetings. We deny the plain teaching of the Scripture. How important it is that we should go quietly, slowly and carefully through these Scriptures and observe these profound statements. It is absence of righteousness that puts every human being under sin, under the law, under the wrath of God.

Fifteen

*

As it is written, There is none righteous, no, not one: there is none that understandeth, there is none that seeketh after God. They are all gone out of the way, they are together become unprofitable; there is none that doeth good, no, not one. Their throat is an open sepulchre; with their tongues they have used deceit; the poison of asps is under their lips: whose mouth is full of cursing and bitterness: their feet are swift to shed blood: destruction and misery are in their ways: and the way of peace have they not known: there is no fear of God before their eyes.

Romans 3 : 10–18

We are dealing with this list of quotations which the Apostle here gives us, and we are in the process of looking at the first group in verses 10 to 12, where, I have suggested, the Apostle gives us a general description and account of man under sin. We have already dealt with this first statement: 'There is none righteous, no, not one', and we have seen that as the result of the Fall every man is lacking in that original righteousness which man had, and which God demands of all of us because He made man in His own image and He made him righteous.

Next, we take up this second statement, which gives us an account of the actual state and condition of man as the result of sin, and here it is: 'there is none that understandeth . . .' You notice the universality of the statement. There are no exceptions. What does Paul mean here by 'understandeth'? Well, there is an alternative word, which can be used, and we can say, 'There is none that is wise'; 'There is none that has the possession of wisdom'. Now this is a really great theme throughout the Bible. Indeed, in many places it is clearly the essence of the biblical teaching with respect to sin. What is sin? Sin is folly. It is the fool who has said in his heart, 'There is no

God'. It is an absence of wisdom. In Ephesians 4 : 18 Paul puts it like this: 'Having the understanding darkened . . .'. That is the same thing. To have the understanding darkened is the same as not to have understanding, because obviously the understanding is meant to be enlightened. If it is darkened, therefore, it means there is no understanding. Or it may be put like this: when Paul says, 'There is none that understandeth', what he is saying is that there is nobody who comes up to this description in Psalm 111: 'The fear of the Lord is the beginning of wisdom' – it is an absence of that.

So, then, when Paul says, 'There is none that understandeth', he means that they are lacking in apprehension of spiritual truth, they are lacking in an understanding of divine things. They have, perhaps, a kind of secular, earthly, carnal understanding; some of them may be very proficient in art or in science or in various other branches of knowledge and of culture. They have got an understanding there – expert in politics, expert in business, full of understanding and insight. But, says the Apostle, as the result of sin every single man who has ever been born into the world since the Fall, does not have a spiritual understanding; in other words, he is dead in trespasses and sins. As far as these things are concerned, he might as well be dead, they mean nothing at all to him, he has no insight, he has no understanding at all. You can put them before him, but to him they are quite irrelevant.

Now this, you notice, is a perfect description of the average person today, who really just dismisses Christianity; it is a bad joke so far as he is concerned. With his sophistication and his learning he feels that all this is utterly remote from life and from his problems, and thereby, of course, he is betraying his complete lack of understanding. Understanding of what? Primarily, of course, an understanding of the truth about God. God is not in his thoughts at all. He may say, as I have quoted to you, 'There is no God'. He completely lacks an understanding apprehension of God. The Apostle is going to elaborate that, so we do not stay with it here. Another thing it means is that man in sin, man under sin, lacks an understanding of himself, of his own nature, and of his spiritual character. He is content to regard himself as an animal, and he even boasts of that. He dislikes this biblical account of himself as a living soul. He puts himself among the animals. He says that he has evolved from them, that he belongs to them, and that that is his state. He has no conception of the biblical teaching of man, which is that man is essentially a spiritual being meant for God, and meant to live a spiritual kind of life in relationship with God.

In the same way he has no understanding of sin, no understanding of his own sinful nature, no understanding of the precarious position in which he finds himself, no understanding of the wrath of God, and no understanding of God's way of salvation. He has never seen the need of it. It means nothing to him and he ridicules it and pours his scorn upon it. Neither has he an understanding of his own true happiness. He thinks he is an expert on happiness, but he has no conception of true happiness. He has no understanding of the real way of having joy, a heavenly joy, a spiritual joy; he does not understand it at all. What is offered to him in that respect he regards as boring and dull, something which is insulting to him.

Above all, as I have said, he has no conception of his eternal destiny; he does not think about it; he does not like to think about it; he does not like to be invited to think about it; he regards that as being morbid. He does everything he can to postpone thoughts of death and of the end of his life and of the unknown eternity to which he is going. He hates it. He does not want to be reminded, and that is because he has no real understanding of it. Indeed, the case of the Bible from beginning to end is that this fatal lack of understanding is, in a sense, the cause of all our troubles.

That brings us to the next thing which the Apostle tells us under this particular sub-section, and it is the third and last thing which he tells us about our actual state as the result of sin: 'There is none that seeketh after God . . .'. Again I must emphasize the universality; it is still 'none' – not a single exception. The Apostle's assertion is that there is no individual who seeks after God. Again, we cannot but notice the marvellous sequence and order and logical arrangement of these thoughts. You notice how Paul puts it. Man, he says, is unrighteous and he is unrighteous because he has not got understanding; and it is because he has not got understanding, that he does not seek after God.

Now it is very important that we should be clear as to what this means. What Paul means by 'seeking after God' is a desire for God, a desire to know God, and a desire to enjoy Him. Paul also means a desire to worship God and to seek Him in prayer, like Job, for instance, who cried out, 'Oh that I knew where I might find him!' [*Job* 23 : 3]. Or like the psalmist, who said in Psalm 42: 'As the hart panteth after the water brooks, so panteth my soul after thee, O God'. That is it. He longs for the living God, he pants after Him. He is seeking God. That is the content of this term 'seeketh after God', and, of course, it includes also a seeking to know the will of God in obedience, because he is anxious to do the will of God. Now the Apostle says that man, as the result of the Fall, and because he is under sin, does not seek God like this. He says the same thing in chapter eight in these words: 'The carnal [natural] mind is enmity against God: for it is not subject to the law of God, neither indeed can be'. The natural mind is at enmity, and because it is at enmity against God it does not seek Him, it does its best to avoid God, to get away from Him; and because it does not seek God it does not seek His law.

I have gone into this in such detail because it may well be that there is someone who says, 'Surely the Apostle is going too far? Surely he has no right to say that every person who has been born since the fall of Adam has been guilty of not seeking God?' This person says, 'I know many people in this world today who are not Christians at all and who never go to a place of worship, but I would not like to say that they do not seek God, because I do know that they say their prayers; I do know that when they are in trouble they offer up a prayer to God. Is not that seeking God? They are good people'.

The answer of the Apostle to that is: No! If you put its full content into this word 'seek', you see that they do not seek God at all. To have some kind of intellectual interest in the possibility of God, or the being of God, is not to seek God. To seek God does not just mean that you mechanically say your prayers, because you have not really thought enough about it, perhaps, to stop saying the prayers you were taught when you were a child. That is not seeking God. Seeking God means that you are really looking for something. You remember the sequence used by our Lord, 'Ask, and it shall be given you; seek, and ye shall find; knock, and it shall be opened unto you' [*Matthew* 7 : 7]. Seeking is much more active than asking. The moment you realize this content of the word 'seek' you begin to see that the Apostle's statement is quite right. Mechanical prayers do not mean that we are seeking God. Seeking God means that you are trying to find God, and to get into His presence, and to realize His presence. That is seeking. And what the Apostle says is that there is none who seeks God in that way. To seek God means to desire God above everything and everybody, to seek His glory, to be anxious to promote His glory. To seek God in the biblical sense means that God is the centre of our thinking, and it is the supreme object of our lives to know Him and to love Him, and to live to His glory. Let me quote again the first question in the Shorter Catechism of the Westminster Assembly: 'What is the chief end of man?' The answer is, 'Man's chief end is to glorify God and to enjoy Him for ever', and a man of whom that is true is a man who is seeking God. And what the Apostle says is that no man by nature and left to himself has ever sought God.

Now this is an important statement. It is one of the most valuable Scriptures by means of which you can convict the so-called good person who has never committed any big, open, flagrant sins, who always does a lot of good and has been philanthropic, and who has always said his prayers, and so on. Here is the way to convict such a person. The Apostle lays it down categorically that there has never been a single person who has sought God – and you will find that these people have never really sought God at all. Like the Pharisee that our Lord Himself depicted in His picture of the publican and the Pharisee who went into the temple to pray, these people have very often told God what wonderful people they are, but like that Pharisee they have never sought for anything. On that occasion, you remember, the Pharisee just gave God a list of his excellencies – that is not seeking God, it is almost patronizing God.

It is important, therefore, for us to realize something of the implications of this statement, this doctrine. For it means that if you and I can claim as Christian people that we are seeking God, there is only one explanation for it, and that is that God has first sought us. Man in sin, under sin, does not seek God: 'There is none that seeketh after God'. There is nothing so unscriptural as to say that the natural man is seeking for God, and that his trouble is that nobody has ever given him the gospel that he has been waiting for and expecting to hear. This is a blank contradiction of the scriptural declaration that there is 'none that seeketh after God'. Man by nature is a God hater; he is at enmity with God; he is 'dead in trespasses and sins'. Show me a man who can say honestly that he is seeking after God, and I will show you a man who has been quickened by God's Spirit, whom God has sought. 'We love him' – Why? – 'Because he first loved us'. Left to ourselves we would never seek Him, we would remain permanently at enmity with Him. You can see, now, that these quotations which the Apostle brings together here in this great catena of evidence are all of tremendous significance and importance. Never rush over them. Look at them, examine them, give them their full content, and see the inevitable deductions that must be drawn from them.

That, then, is the end of his general description and account of man as he is by nature. That is the description of his actual state, and because of that, something inevitably follows: these things cannot be true of a man without their having an immediate effect upon his general conduct and behaviour. (Notice the word *general*. We still have to come to the particular effect on conduct.) And here it is for us in verse 12: 'They are all gone out of the way, they are together become unprofitable; there is none that doeth good, no, not one'. Once again I must emphasize the extraordinary logical sequence which we are dealing with. The Apostle did not choose these verses at random; he obviously has a scheme in his mind, and he is working it out with us.

If that is man's state, then, because of that, this must be true, and this is the first thing, 'They are all gone out of the way'. Here again we must remember that it is every one, and that there is no exception to it. What does 'gone out of the way' mean? What 'way'? God's way, obviously, the true path, the path which God had marked out for man, the highway on which God had set man and on which He intended him to travel. They have all turned their backs and have gone in the other direction. Or, as our Lord puts it, instead of walking on the narrow way they are walking on the broad way, they are on the wrong road. I need not remind you that this, again, is something that is stated very frequently in Scripture. For example, in Isaiah 53 : 6 we read: 'All we like sheep have gone astray; we have turned every one to his own way . . .'. And there are many other quotations which say the same thing.

Now let us not lose sight of the universality of the pronouncement. This is the devastating effect of the Fall, that every person born into this world since that fall of Adam, has deliberately gone his own way, and it is the wrong way. Like a sheep he has gone astray, he is not walking in God's way, not on the highway that leads to God and to heaven – all have gone out of the way. What a terrible thing sin is! How important it is that we should look like this at humanity in sin – they are on the road to hell, they are on the road to the devil. They have their backs turned to God and they are going in entirely the wrong direction. That is how we are to look at them.

But come to the second point which he gives, '. . . they are together become unprofitable'. This also means wholly, and without exception, and simultaneously – together they have become unprofitable. And the word 'unprofitable' means, of course, that they are worthless. The actual word that the Apostle used is a very interesting one, it is very graphic and descriptive. The word that he used here, to bring out this idea of unprofitable, is the word that was used for milk when it had gone sour. You suddenly want your milk for a cup of tea or something and when you find it, you at once see that it has gone sour and that it is worthless. You do not like sour milk in your tea so you throw it down the drain. The milk that was meant to be food and meant to give satisfaction has turned sour, and is useless. That is the condition of mankind as the result of all that has become true of it. It has become unprofitable, of no value, it is useless; it is like the salt that has lost its savour and is henceforward good for nothing but to be thrown on to the rubbish heap. And that is a result which has followed in the case of mankind because of the sin of Adam.

It is important that we should understand this again quite clearly. Unprofitable! 'Ah', says someone, 'surely, this is once more too sweeping a statement. I know of many people who are not Christian but who are doing a great deal of good. They are very good citizens and they give large sums of money to good causes and things like that, surely you cannot say that they are unprofitable?' But the Bible says that they are unprofitable. In what way? Well, they are unprofitable from the standpoint of God, not from the standpoint of secular morality. It is important that we should keep these distinctions clear. The Bible does not say that a man is as bad or as rotten as a man can ever be or ever become. But, from the standpoint of salvation, it does say that every single one of us, apart from the grace of God in Jesus Christ, is entirely without goodness and completely unprofitable.

Let me give you some other quotations that say the same thing. The Scripture says that 'all our righteousnesses are as filthy rags' [*Isaiah* 64 : 6]. That is another way of putting it. Or take the way in which the Apostle Paul puts it after his conversion. In the autobiography in Philippians chapter three, he describes how, before his conversion, he was very proud of his proficiency in the law and very proud of his own righteousness as he judged the law, excelling over others, a wonderfully good, godly, righteous man. And you remember what he says about it afterwards? After he came to see himself, after he saw the law in a new light and was convicted of sin, what does he say about his righteousness then? He says, 'I have suffered the loss of all things, and do count them but dung, that I may win Christ' [*Philippians* 3 : 8].

Now that is very strong language, is it not? But it is perfectly accurate. This selfsame man, when he saw that righteousness, that religious righteousness, that morality of his – and he had lived it very thoroughly – when he saw it in the sight of God said, This is refuse, it is vile, it is foul, it is putrefaction. Paul does not throw around words like that without considering what he is saying. He did not just say that it was not quite good enough, he said it is all wrong, filthy rags and complete loss. Now this is what we may call the prolegomena, if you like, to the gospel. It is a realization of such a truth that makes the gospel of Christ so glorious. It is this fact that necessitated the incarnation and the death upon the cross. Man does not need simply to be improved a little, or to be helped, he is as vile and as hopeless as this – nothing less. We should take time with these descriptions, terrible and awful though they are, and hateful though they are. They are true, and true of every one of us by nature.

That brings me to the last thing under this particular heading: 'There is none that doeth good'. And then, for the sake of the self-righteous, the repetition, 'no, not one'. Again you see that it is goodness in God's sight that is meant here, and it is at this point that so many good people go astray because they never see the need of the death of Christ – indeed, they have never seen the need of forgiveness at all, they are doing so much good! But the Apostle says, 'There is none that doeth good, no, not one'. Once more let me, therefore, interpret it like this: why is this true about all the natural man's goodness? It is because all the natural man's goodness is invariably self-centred. 'But', you say, 'he does not do everything for himself, he may be very kind to others'. Yes, but while he is being kind to others he is really being very kind to himself also, he is doing it to please himself more than he is to please them. Man's actions, every one of them, are polluted at the source. Sin is in control, it vitiates everything. All our actions are self-centred. There is no such thing as disinterested action in the natural, sinful man.

What, then, is goodness? Well goodness really means to do things for the glory of God, and your naturally good man does not do things for the glory of God. He does not think of God. He is doing it entirely for his own glory and satisfaction. That is why it is useless. The test of doing good is this element of God's glory, and, of course, you can very easily prove that. You may have to be just a little bit brutal, but you may have to do it at times to convict people of sin. The next time you meet one of these good people of the world, put some questions to them, or query their goodness, and they will very soon show you, by their reaction of annoyance and perhaps temper, that after all it was entirely self-centred and self-interested. There is no such thing as a disinterested action in a sinful man; it does not come up to God's standard.

Now in case anybody may think that I am going too far, or that the Apostle Paul went too far, listen to the Son of God saying it: 'Ye are they which justify yourselves before men; but God knoweth your hearts: for that which is highly esteemed among men is abomination in the sight of God' [*Luke* 16 : 15]. Do you know, that is worse than dung and refuse; it is worse than this curdled milk – it is 'abomination in the sight of God'. He hates it – all this natural goodness that gets such prominence in the newspapers, and that people talk so much about, and praise one another so much for: all that, in the sight of God, is 'abomination'. He hates it all because He sees the heart, and He sees that it is all polluted at the very source. There, then, is our first section. But the Apostle does not leave it at that, and he does not leave us at that. That is only the general description.

So we move on to the second section, in which we have the particular description, or, if you prefer it, the manifestations of all this. Because man under sin is like this, then, how does he behave? What is it like in operation? The section runs from verse 13 to verse 17, but again we can sub-divide it quite simply. The first sub-section, verses 13 and 14, might be called 'Sin in words'.

Are you ready for me to hold before you now the most terrifying mirror that you have ever looked into in your life? I warn you now, if you want to be on good terms with yourself you had better read no further. Here is the mirror – sin, first of all, as it shows itself in words. How terrible, how graphic is this description! 'Their throat', he starts, 'is an open sepulchre'; that is his quotation at this point from the Old Testament. What does this mean? It means this – and it is almost too offensive a description to mention, but here we have got to expound Scripture – it is as if you opened a grave in which a body had been buried two or three weeks ago and the process of putrefaction is at its height, the stench is beyond description, foul and offensive. That is the condition of the throat of man under sin, the natural man without the grace of the Lord Jesus Christ! 'Out of the abundance of the heart the mouth speaketh' [*Matthew* 12 : 34], and because the heart is as we have seen it to be, that is the sort of thing that emanates!

But let me go on. 'With their tongues they have used deceit'. In the original, this means that their tongues are very smooth – speaking falsehoods and flatteries and lies, pretending that which is not true, pretending to be delighted to meet people when they wish they had not seen them, pretending they think the world of them, when they are always criticizing them. Tongues that use deceit! These people seemed so wonderful, their words were so full of honey, as it were, but it was all done for a purpose. Now I know I have often said this before, but I must say it again, what really baffles me is how any man reading the Scriptures does not see, of necessity, that it is the Word of God. Can you give me a more perfect description of society and the life of society today than this sort of thing? Look at them in the ballroom, or on their State occasions, and at their dinners.

How friendly and affable they all seem with one another, and yet they are muttering things to one another the moment someone turns his back. Is it not true? Is it not the reason why the gossip columns of the newspapers are flourishing and are so interesting, with the secrets that are let out, and all the rivalries and the shocks about the very people you have seen smiling at one another as if they were really fond of one another! That is life. That is society in its evening dress as well as in its rags in the gutter. How true it is!

But there is worse to follow. Their tongues are so smooth and 'with their tongues they have used deceit; the poison of asps is under their lips'. The Apostle here shows that the Old Testament writers had an amazing and detailed knowledge of the asp, the adder, the serpent, full of venom. How does it work? Well, this is a very fine description in a zoological sense. The adder, or viper, which is so harmful and so poisonous, has the poison concealed in a little bag at the root of the lips. This little bag is under the upper jaw of the adder close to some fangs which lie in a horizontal position. When the adder is about to pounce upon a victim he puts back his head and as he does so, these teeth or fangs drop down and he bites the victim. As he is biting with the fangs one of them presses the bag that is full of poison and into the wound is injected this venom, this poison that is going to kill the victim! So the Bible gives an exact scientific description of how the adder kills by means of his poison.

And according to the Scriptures that is the truth about man, who speaks with such a smooth tongue but under his lips is this venom, this poison, this rancour; honey on the lips, poison under them. This comes out, of course, in conversation, and the poison comes out, too, in entertainment which seems so wonderful, but poisons the minds and the imagination of the young people, and leads them eventually to hell. Look at the advertisements – how wonderful! But there is poison there. The lip, the tongue is smooth. Come, they say, come and enjoy this, how marvellous! And the innocent victim does not see the bag with the poison which is suddenly injected when they are bitten, and leads to destruction.

It is the same with wrong teaching. People regard this sort of evangelical preaching as unpleasant. Many often say that about my preaching. 'Too hard', they say, 'too harsh. It is unpleasant.

Let me listen to somebody who is always talking about love and about the love of God'. Ah, how smooth his tongue is! If you believe that other, which is no gospel – which is always praising you and praising your world, calling it a beautiful world and saying that man is wonderful, and that all is well and there is no need of the blood of Christ – if you believe that, it will inject into you this poison that will damn your soul and send you to hell! Their tongues are smooth, but under their lips is the poison of adders. False teaching that sends people to sleep, and gives them that false exhilaration, finally ruins and destroys the soul.

But there is one other word I must add because it is here in my text: 'Whose mouth is full of cursing and bitterness'. Now we must be clear about these things. It does not mean that every individual curses and swears as much as he can. No, but it does say that cursing and bitterness are there in us all, and we have all been guilty of them. You have simply to listen to the things people say when they are off guard, and to what they say about one another. You can hear them curse and you can hear the bitterness. Do you remember Job's wife? When things went wrong she said, look here, you are a fool, 'Curse God and die!' There are people who, when things go wrong, put it like this: 'Why should this happen to me, or to my child?' And they have cursed God as they have said it. That is the way they curse God. When you have a bitter feeling against Him and want to ask your rebellious questions, it is cursing God. And the whole of humanity in sin is guilty of cursing God, cursing others in this bitterness, with oaths and cursing and swearing, and unkind, revengeful and reproachful language. This Scripture, you see, says that all this is true about us, and is the result of sin and the Fall; that is why it devotes so much attention to these things.

If you go through your New Testament Epistles, you will find that Paul, having handled his mighty doctrine in the Epistle to the Ephesians for example, says at the end of that Epistle, '. . . let it not once be named among you . . . neither filthiness, nor foolish talking, nor jesting' [*Ephesians* 5 : 3–4]. He comes down to particulars, because sin expresses itself in this way. The Apostle James writes a whole chapter on the tongue and on the use of the tongue. Read the third chapter of his Epistle, it is all about this terrible thing, this little organ that we have been talking about that has got the fire of hell in it. He says it is like the rudder that turns the whole ship. He talks about this fountain which emits horrible bitterness and terrible things: the same teaching.

Then, having shown us sin in words, Paul next describes for us sin in deeds: 'Their feet are swift to shed blood'. I need not point out that does not mean that every human being is a murderer. No! But the possibility is there and mankind, humanity, is ever shedding blood in wars and strife. What else? The next thing we are told is this: 'Destruction and misery are in their ways'. Now I know of no more perfect description of the world as it is today than just that. It is a summary of history. Desolation and misery! Destruction leading to misery and wretchedness. Cause and effect. Is not that a perfect description of history? What fools men are to boast of wars and conquests as if wars make a nation great! There you see the perversion of sin, gloating in the number of the enemy that have been killed. How horrible it is! Destruction and misery. All that leads, invariably, to unhappiness and wretchedness. Sin is essentially destructive. It always destroys. It destroys character, our own characters, other people's characters, and it always leads to misery. Look at the destructiveness of drunkenness and the sorrow to which it leads. Look at the destructiveness of vice and the misery and wretchedness to which it leads. Greed, avarice, all these things, they are all destructive and they bring with them in their train wretchedness and desolation – ruins, the bomb sites, the ruination of souls. What a description of sin! How true it is! History is really summarized, for me, in these few words: 'destruction and misery are in all their ways'.

And finally, 'The way of peace have they not known'. Here he puts the same thing the other way. Because they have known destruction and misery, they have not known peace. And they have not known peace because of that fact with which we began this chapter. It is because they have not got wisdom, of which we read in Proverbs 3 : 17 that: 'Her ways are ways of pleasantness, and all her paths are peace'. But if you have not got this wisdom, you will not have the peace, for God has said, 'There is no peace, saith my God, to the wicked' [*Isaiah* 57 : 21].

There, then, we have ended the second section, which leaves us with verse 18, the third section, in which Paul gives us the explanation of all the rest! 'There is no fear of God before their eyes'. But before we go on to consider this, I do trust that we have all seen more clearly than we have ever seen in our lives before, the absolute necessity of God's way of salvation before a single individual can ever be saved. What we have been going through in detail is nothing but the simple, literal, stark truth of every single one of us by nature. No, you are not an exception, my friend! There is no exception to this. You are not a 'nice' person, there is no such thing. These horrors are in every one of us. We are all quite lost. We are dead in trespasses and sins, and the grave is putrefying and foul. As the Apostle puts it in writing to Titus: 'We ourselves also were . . . hateful, and hating one another' [*Titus* 3 : 3]. Let me put it plainly. If you do not accept this, and if you do not accept this description of yourself apart from the cross of the Lord Jesus Christ, then there is no need to argue about it, you are just not a Christian. If you resent all this you are not a Christian, you are not yet convinced and convicted of sin, and you are not a believer in Christ, though you may have thought you were. If you in any way object to this, you are automatically putting yourself outside the kingdom of God and the Christian faith. This description of man in sin is the simple truth, the horrible truth. That is what sin has brought us to. Thank God there is a way out of it, it is the way the Apostle is going on to expound and to unfold, but no man will look at it or clutch at it except the man who has seen his terrifying need. May God convict us by the Holy Spirit if we have never been convicted before to see what we are by nature – the children of wrath, even as others.

'Oh wretched man that I am! who shall deliver me . . . ? I thank God through Jesus Christ our Lord'.

Sixteen

*

There is no fear of God before their eyes. Now we know that what
things soever the law saith, it saith to them who are under the
law: that every mouth may be stopped, and all the world may
become guilty before God. Therefore by the deeds of the law there
shall no flesh be justified in his sight: for by the law is the
knowledge of sin.

Romans 3 : 18–20

As we come to the end of our study of this section of Romans
chapter three, we must first look in particular at the words,
'There is no fear of God before their eyes'. This verse really
belongs to the section that started at verse 10, where the
Apostle began giving us a series of quotations to prove his
contention that the whole world is under sin. That is his point
here, too, for he wants to establish and to prove that the Jew is as
much under the wrath of God as is the Gentile. And as we have
seen, he has been working out a great argument since the
eighteenth verse of the first chapter. He has worked out the
detailed arguments, and now he is clinching the matter by
bringing forward a number of proofs from the Scriptures. It was a
wise and effective method to use with the Jews, who boasted of
their Scriptures and their knowledge of them. That is why the
Apostle tells them that their own Scriptures are proving the
very thing that he is saying.

And so we have been following his argument by looking at
this list of scriptural quotations, and we have divided them into
three groups. The first group, in which he describes the actual
state and condition of men in sin, we find in verses 10, 11 and
12. Then in the second group, from verse 13 to verse 17, he
describes their conduct and behaviour which result from that

state of sin. Finally, there is a third division of the quotations, which consists only of this eighteenth verse. And in this verse the Apostle gives us the cause of it all, the real explanation, both of the state of man in sin, and of the actions of which he is guilty because he is in that state.

Here, then, is his statement: 'There is no fear of God before their eyes'. Now that is perhaps the commonest thing which the Bible has to say about man in sin. Actually, the Apostle here is quoting from Psalm 36 : 1, which reads: 'The transgression of the wicked saith within my heart, that there is no fear of God before his eyes'. We need to look briefly at that verse, because people generally find it extremely difficult to understand. It is, indeed, rather an odd construction, but what he means is this: 'His depravity reveals to my heart that there is no fear of God before his eyes'.

Now while that is rather an odd form of speech, yet it is in a sense a very effective one. David says, I look at those wicked people and I see their depravity, I see the sort of thing they do. And their very way of living, that very depravity, is speaking to me, and what it tells me about them is that there is no fear of God before their eyes. That is really the meaning, the exposition of Psalm 36 : 1. He is, as it were, personalizing the depravity of the wicked. He says that their depravity is speaking, it is revealing something, it is telling him something, and that is the message which it gives him. So the Apostle takes up that quotation, and says that this is ultimately the explanation of why man is as he is in sin, and why, as a consequence, the world is as it is. The real trouble with mankind is that there is no fear of God before their eyes.

This is undoubtedly the big statement which the Bible makes everywhere about sin, and about man in sin. Sometimes, when it is dealing with the true basis of religion, it puts it the other way round. It asks: What is the first and greatest characteristic of a godly man? And how often, in reply, is this statement made in the Old Testament: 'The fear of the Lord is the beginning of wisdom'. You will find it in the Psalms, you will find it in the book of Proverbs, and you will find it stated in different ways in many other places. That is the essence of wisdom. That is really the foundation of all knowledge. If you do not have that as the foundation, as the beginning, then you will certainly go wrong everywhere else. And, of course, that is the thing that is so patently wrong in the world today – the fear of the Lord does not come into so-called human wisdom at all. There is no fear of God before their eyes.

Listen to the psalmist saying the same thing in a striking phrase in Psalm 16 : 8. Here is a wise man, and this is what he says: 'I have set the Lord always before me . . .'. That is the exact opposite of what we have here. The secret of my life, says this man in the sixteenth Psalm, is just this. I always set God before my eyes. I keep God, as it were, in front of me. Now that is, I think, a very good way of putting it. He does not mean that he literally sees God with his physical eyes, but that he always recollects the being of God. It is as if he drew a picture of God, and always put it in front of him.

Many people today do this same sort of thing, though not as much as they used to. People used to hang texts on their walls and, you know, there is something to be said for it, because as you are seated at your table, or as you wake up in the morning, you look at the wall opposite and there is that statement: 'The fear of the Lord is the beginning of wisdom'. There is value in these things. It is God's word and it reminds us. So you set that kind of word before you to remind yourself and you are, as it were, setting God before you. But the wicked man does not do this: 'There is no fear of God before his eyes'.

What, then, does it mean in practice? Well, we can put it in this way. This fear that the text speaks about does not mean that all unbelievers are entirely devoid of any fear of God. Sometimes they are very afraid of God, but still, though they may fear God in that sense, and are afraid of what He may do to them, and are afraid of judgment and so on, the fear that we are talking about here is somewhat different. It is what the author of the Epistle to the Hebrews means when he says in Hebrews 12 : 28–29, 'Let us have grace, whereby we may serve God acceptably with reverence and godly fear: for our God is a consuming fire'. That is what he means. It is reverence; it is godly fear. It is not a fear that has torment, but it is what you may describe as awe, or a reverential awe.

And that, of course, is something that should always characterize our approach to God. That is the way in which Christians should approach God. I emphasize this because I find so often that today they do not do this. They think that the way to show that you have assurance of faith is to be glib, and to rush into the presence of God. But it is utterly unscriptural. In the Epistle to the Hebrews it is *Christians* who are exhorted to approach God 'with reverence, and with godly fear: for our God is a consuming fire'. So setting the Lord always before us means that we should always have a sense of God's greatness, of God's glory and of God's majesty. The unbeliever does not have this, there is no fear of God before his eyes. But a believer is to be the exact opposite. He is to have this fear of God, this 'reverence and godly fear'. So that the more we know God and the more truly pious we are, the less inclined shall we probably be to use in prayer such phrases as: 'Dear God'. Rather we shall be more inclined to say, with the Lord Jesus Christ, 'Holy Father'. The more we realize something of the being of God, the more we realize the importance of treading carefully. You remember what God said to Moses, when He appeared in the burning bush, and Moses was approaching to investigate: 'Put off thy shoes from off thy feet, for the place whereon thou standest is holy ground'. That is it – reverence and godly fear because of His majesty.

The next element in this fear is the desire to worship God, and the desire to praise His name with awe. It is the desire to glory in God, and to commune with Him. 'This is life eternal, that they might know thee the only true God, and Jesus Christ, whom thou hast sent' (*John* 17 : 3). 'Our fellowship is with the Father, and with his Son Jesus Christ' (*1 John* 1 : 3). The man who has the fear of God in his heart is a man who desires God, and wants to be in His presence, and to draw near to Him.

The next element is, of course, a consciousness that God is the Judge of all the earth and that we are all in His hands. I wonder how often these thoughts dominate in our thinking about God. Again, let me quote the Epistle to the Hebrews: 'It is a fearful thing to fall into the hands of the living God'. Why is it, I wonder, that these great declarations of Scripture seem to have dropped out of our modern evangelical vocabulary? It was the great characteristic of the prayer life and the worship of our fathers, and it seems to have gone. But it is scriptural, and you see it supremely in the prayer life of our blessed Lord Himself. We must never forget that God is the Judge of all the earth and that judgment must begin at the house of God. These are scriptural statements, made to believing people in the New Testament. So we must never lose that element. However confident we are, and whatever boldness we may have as we go to the throne of grace, it should never be at the expense of these tremendous truths about the being and the character of God.

Lastly, of course, there is this element of the fear of punishment. The problem with the man of the world, before whose eyes there is no fear of God, is that he is bold and arrogant. He dismisses the Bible. He blasphemes the name of God. He sins without any fear. He says, 'I fear neither God nor man'. How often have we heard people saying this! It is all due to his ignorance, of course. He does not realize what he is saying. If he but knew something about God he would be silenced immediately. He has no sense of God's greatness, he does not desire God and he does not realize that God is his Judge. He does not realize that when he dies, and at the end of time, there will be a last and a final judgment, and that God has power, as our Lord said, not only to destroy the body but to cast both soul and body into hell. What a terrible thought! But that is the position of men and women who have never been convicted of sin, who are not Christians. And that is the reason why their hearts are as they are, and why they do the things they do. It is the cause of war; it is the cause of all the horrible things that we have seen as we have been working through this list. It is the cause of lust and passion, and lawlessness. It is the cause of the muddle in this country and in the life of every other country at this present hour. There is no fear of God before their eyes. That is the ultimate explanation of it all.

So we come to the end of our consideration of this great chain, this great list of quotations from the Old Testament. And that brings us to a consideration of verses 19 and 20, which stand on their own. These are two very important verses, because in them the Apostle does quite a number of things. First, he sums up what he has just been quoting; he makes a statement on the basis of his own quotation. But they are not only that. They are at the same time a summing up of the entire subject which began in chapter one, verse 18. And we must never lose sight of that fact. Paul's great argument starts at that verse and goes right the way through to chapter three, verse 20. There is but one theme in it, and that is the wrath of God, which is upon all 'ungodliness and unrighteousness of men, who hold [down] the truth in unrighteousness'. And the Apostle, let me remind you, has been setting out to prove that it is a statement which can be demonstrated, and that it is as true of Jews as it is of Gentiles. Now then, he says, I have given you all my arguments, I have worked out my evidence, and this is what I say. 'Now, we know' – there is no need to argue about this – 'that what things soever the law saith, it saith to them who are under the law: that every mouth may be stopped, and all the world may become guilty before God. Therefore by the deeds of the law there shall no flesh be justified in his sight: for by the law is the knowledge of sin'.

So, let me emphasize again, these two verses really are of crucial importance. They are essential to an understanding of the mighty doctrine which the Apostle is going to begin to unfold in verse 21 – the central doctrine of justification by faith only, and the great doctrine of the atonement that is included in the paragraph. If we do not understand the argument of these two verses, we shall never understand that, and so we must take time with them.

First, then, verse 19: 'Now we know that what things soever the law saith, it saith to them who are under the law'. There is really no great difficulty about that, though there has been some argument as to what the term law means – whether it just means the law of Moses, or whether it means the whole of the Old Testament Scriptures. There is a good deal to be said for both points of view. Personally, because of the context, I tend to agree with those who say that it means the whole of the Old Testament. The Apostle in the second verse said that one of the Jews' great advantages was that they had had committed unto them, entrusted to them, 'the oracles of God', which we agreed probably meant the whole of the Old Testament.

In any case, in this list of quotations that the Apostle has been giving us, we have noticed that he takes his quotations from the book of Psalms and from the Prophets, not, strictly speaking from the five books of Moses, which are so often referred to as the law. So that as he has been quoting from Psalms and Prophets, and then immediately says 'the law', surely he is referring to the same thing. Furthermore, sometimes in Scripture the whole of the Old Testament is referred to as the law, because in the Old Testament, the law, after all, is central.

It is very frequently referred to; the Prophets deal with it, and show its place and its importance, and the failure of the nation in the light of the law, and so on. So that there is a great deal to be said for regarding it as the whole of the Old Testament.

But in the end, of course, it does not really matter very much whether you take it to mean the whole of the Old Testament or simply the law of Moses. What the Apostle is asserting is that the law speaks particularly to those who are under the law. The Old Testament, of course, is primarily addressed to the Jews. It was given to them. Other people did not have it, so it could not speak to them, but it was given to the Jews and therefore it speaks to the Jews. So whether 'the Law' refers here to the Old Testament as a whole, or whether it is just the law of Moses, the contention is that this speaks particularly to those to whom it was given. What he is saying, therefore, is that the very oracles of God, of which the Jews boasted, prove in and of themselves that the Jews are under condemnation and are as much under the wrath of God as are the Gentiles. That is the thing, you remember, that he wants to prove. The Jew believed that though the Gentile was under the wrath of God, he himself was not, because he was a member of the chosen race.

'Now', says Paul, 'in effect, I have given you the list of quotations. They are from your own law, and from your own oracles, and they are the very things that prove that you are under condemnation. Therefore, these same oracles of which you are so proud, are the very word of God that proves that you have nothing at all of which to boast in the matter of salvation. In other words, what he is saying is this: I have proved to you that you Jews all come short of the glory of God. I have demonstrated to you from the Scriptures that you are all sinners, and if I have demonstrated that you are sinners, how much more is that true of the Gentiles.' That is the real meaning of the argument at that point.

Why, then, has he done this? Why has he been at such great pains to prove that the Jews are under the wrath of God in exactly the same way as the Gentiles? Paul tells us here that he has had two objects in view and he claims that he has done what he set out to do. The first object is: 'that every mouth may be stopped'. Now that is a striking and important phrase. In effect, the Apostle is saying, 'I have gone through all this argumentation, and I have ended by giving these quotations, so that I shall put an end to all talking and disputation about the subject once and for ever. I want to silence every mouth, I want to put a hand over every mouth that is anxious to defend itself. My object', he says, 'has been to render the whole world speechless'.

Perhaps the best way for us to look at it is this: the point of this entire argument and of these scriptural quotations is to silence the kind of Pharisee that our Lord depicted in Luke 18 : 9–14, in His parable of the Pharisee and the publican who went up into the temple to pray. Let me remind you of the story. The Pharisee goes to the temple and he walks right up to the front, as it were, and begins to speak. 'God, I thank thee . . .', and he pours out his eloquence in describing himself and telling God what a good man he is, how unlike this publican he is, how unlike other people, what he does and what he does not do. He talks constantly. He is voluble and eloquent. My object, says the Apostle, is just to silence people like that – 'that every mouth may be stopped'. That is not the way to approach God. The right way to approach God is the way of the publican, who 'would not lift up so much as his eyes to heaven', but stood there smiting his breast and saying, 'God be merciful to me a sinner'.

Another example is the so-called 'rich young ruler'. Here is another man who is very ready to speak. 'All these have I kept from my youth up'. I know all about it, he says. He is ready to talk and to justify himself, and again you notice our Lord's way of dealing with him is just to speak to him in such a way that He silences him. Here is a man who says, 'I have done it all'. Ah, says our Lord, 'Yet lackest thou one thing: sell all that thou hast, and distribute unto the poor, and thou shalt have treasure in heaven: and come, follow me'. And he has nothing to say, but he just goes away sorrowful. What has happened? His mouth has been stopped. He is full of argument, full of self-defence and self-justification. He asks what he must do. He is full of pride and our Lord speaks in such a way that He silences him. And the whole value of this great section of Scripture, that we have been working our way through, is really to do just that – to render us speechless; to take away every desire to assert ourselves, or to say, 'I've done this', and, 'I've done that'.

Wait a minute, say these verses, have you forgotten this? Every mouth has been stopped. There is no argument left. All the arguments have been answered. The ground has been taken from beneath our feet and we have nothing to say.

How, then, have these Scriptures done this? I suggest to you that they have done it like this. In our summing up of this entire great section, the Scriptures have shown us what God is like, because the trouble with all of us is that we do not know God. What a tremendous talker Job was and how much he cried out. 'Oh, that I knew, oh, that I knew where I might find Him!' 'That is my trouble', said Job, in effect, 'if only I could get at God, and tell him, and put up my case. But I cannot find Him. Surely there is somebody, surely there is a daysman somewhere, who can bring me into His presence. Can I not have a fair hearing? I am suffering here. Oh, that I might state my case! I am having a hard time'. And then the time came when Job found himself in the presence of God. God began to speak to him, and you remember the marvellous thing that happened? Job put his hand upon his mouth – he stopped his own mouth. He said, 'I have heard of thee by the hearing of the ear: but now . . .' (*Job* 42 : 5), and having come into the presence of God, and having realized the glory and the greatness, the majesty and the holiness of God, poor Job did not want to say a word. He put his hand on his mouth, he had been speaking foolishly and thoughtlessly. He had had a theoretical knowledge of God, but now he was in the presence of God, and he stopped his own mouth.

If you and I have really understood all these verses that we have been considering, from chapter one, verse 18 to this point, it should have brought us to that. We also, in our lives, know what God demands. These verses show us the standard, and the standard of God is not a negative one. It is not merely that we should be better than the people who are outside the church, or better than the modernists and others in the church. No, it is a positive standard: 'Thou shalt love the Lord thy God with all thy heart, and with all thy soul, and with all thy strength, and with all thy mind; and thy neighbour as thyself' (*Luke* 10 : 27). And the moment we realize that that is the demand, there is nothing to be said. Every mouth is stopped. It is so much easier to be better than other people, but that is not the test. It is this totalitarian demand of God.

And then, you notice, the Scriptures have been searching us and have been analysing our hearts. We have been looking at these quotations and we have seen the real state of the natural, unregenerate heart. What have we found? 'None righteous, no, not one: there is none that understandeth . . . all gone out of the way'. We have found an 'open sepulchre', tongues 'that have used deceit', the 'poison of asps under their lips', mouths 'full of cursing and bitterness', and feet 'swift to shed blood'. Destruction and misery in all our ways. No peace, no fear of God. We have seen ourselves and the whole of mankind. And when you have seen these things, you do not want to speak, do you? In the presence of God we are silenced. And in the presence of the blackness of our own heart we are silenced. What help is it to be a little bit better than somebody else if we ourselves are so black and so vile, so wretched and so hopeless? There, then, are the effects of the Scripture, and that is my first motive, says Paul – 'that every mouth may be stopped'.

Have you stopped speaking? Have you been silenced in the presence of God? Have you given up self-justification? Have you given up arguing against this verdict of the great Apostle? Or are you saying, 'But surely, after all I have done – this good and that, I am not as bad as that?' If you are saying that, you have missed the Scripture, because the effect of this Scripture is to silence, to stop every mouth. If you are still wanting to say, 'Yes, but . . .', you have not understood the Scripture. The effect of an understanding of these Scriptures is to silence us. We have just got to say, 'It is true. I have nothing to say. I give up, I give in'.

We can, perhaps, put it all in terms of a verse in Psalm 46: 'Be still, and know that I am God'. And when we know that He is God, we will be still. There is nothing to say in His presence. And that is why I say once more that if we are not silenced, it is because we have not understood the Scripture, and it is because we have not really known God.

The second object that Paul has in view is that 'all the world may become guilty before God'. Now you notice that he again says 'all the world'. In other words, he is anxious to prove the universality of the condemnation: Jews, as well as Gentiles, every mouth, the whole world. Every man born into this world since Adam and Eve fell is in this condition. There are no exceptions, none at all.

What, then, is the meaning of this word which is here translated 'guilty'? It is an important word in the understanding of the Apostle's doctrine and it is a very odd word that is only used on this one occasion in the whole of the New Testament. There are other Greek words that are translated 'guilty', but this particular word is only found in this one place. Now there is no doubt that the Apostle chose it quite deliberately because it is a legal, or, if you prefer it, a forensic term. It is a term that must always be associated with the law courts and with legal performances, and the Apostle deliberately brings it in here because he is anxious to say that it means being answerable to God; it means being liable before God; it means being liable to and exposed to the punishment of God, on account of sin.

So you can see the importance of this argument with respect to the whole question of justification. The whole world has thus been proved to be liable in the presence of God. Liable to the court. There is a prosecution. In law, if you have done something, you are liable. You are called to appear on a charge and you must give an answer. That is the connotation of the word. And what the Apostle says is that the whole world is guilty before God. Now this is where we must be careful. It is essential to the understanding of the doctrine of justification, to which he is going to bring us, that we should understand that being guilty means just that. It is purely a legal and forensic concept. In other words, what he is saying here is that his object, in all that he has been arguing, is not so much to prove that we are in a rotten state inside ourselves and that we are polluted as the result of sin – we are that, it is all perfectly true – but what he is really trying to prove is that we are answerable and we are under the condemnation and the wrath of God. And what the Apostle says is that this is the state and condition of the whole of mankind, that the whole world may become guilty before God. Not before men, because we are not being tried by men, but by God. And he says that what he has been proving is that the whole world is liable, under the charge, and without an answer.

Now that is what the law proves. I must emphasize this, because it is essential to an understanding of this doctrine of justification. It is not enough just to know that there is something wrong inside you, it is not enough just to know and to admit that you are not everything that you might be, and everything that you ought to be. It is not that. Quite apart from our inward state, which is vile, the great thing which Paul set out to prove in chapter one, verse 18 is that 'the wrath of God is revealed from heaven against *all* ungodliness and unrighteousness of men'. The problem is – guilt. Not so much pollution at this point, that will come later. It is our standing before God rather than our own internal condition.

Now let me say again, if we do not grasp this we will not grasp the meaning of justification. Not only that, we will not be able to evangelize truly if we do not realize this. What is the first need of man? What does any man in the world today, who is not a Christian, need first and foremost? What is the business, the first message, of the gospel? Is it to make men better? And my answer would be that it is not.

'Well', says somebody, 'I wonder whether the first need of man is not the need of help? Here he is, battling against temptations and problems and difficulties, so surely his first need is to be helped. By himself he is too weak. Is not the first message of the gospel, therefore, to present Christ to him as someone who can help him to live life and its battles, and to conquer; Christ as the helper?' No, again, that is not the first thing.

'It seems to me', says someone else, 'that the first trouble facing man is how to get rid of himself. Is not self the first and greatest problem, and should not the gospel, in the first instance, therefore, tell men how to get rid of this self that mars and ruins everything?' Again, I say, No. All these things are not the first business of the gospel, according to the Apostle. The first trouble with man is that he is guilty. He does need to be better. He does need help. He does need to get rid of self. I know he does, but before any one of those things, he needs to be put right with God.

Let me prove this to you. Thank God, the gospel does offer to make us better. It promises to do so. It promises us endless help through the power of Christ. It shows us a way of getting rid of this horrible self that is in all of us. Yes, but my dear friends, all that applies to the future. What if you died in another minute? There would be no time for you to get better. There would be no time for you to experience this help from Christ. There would be no time to get rid of self. What if you are in the position of the thief dying upon the cross, who was going to be dead in such a short time? What then? Ah, you see, you must start with your relationship with God, that is man's first trouble and his first problem. It is the fact that he is a sinner, a guilty sinner in the presence of God. It is his guilt that must be dealt with first. He is answerable, he is a soul, and he goes out of this life into the next. He stands before God. It may happen at any moment. Therefore that must come first.

How, then, can I be right with God? How can I stand in His presence? That is the first problem. So you see why the Apostle puts such great emphasis upon this? What I have been setting out to prove in all this argument, and in all the quotations, says Paul, is that as you stand before God, you are silenced. You realize that you are guilty. There is a demand and you cannot answer it. You can do nothing about it, you are liable and it is no use saying that you are not aware of the law, for either you have the law given through Moses, or else you have this moral sense in your heart, and you are answerable. Can you answer? You cannot. In other words, you are guilty. 'That every mouth may be stopped, and all the world may become guilty before God'.

Ah, my friends, let us never forget this! The first problem is how to escape condemnation, so that when you are speaking to a highly moral, good, philanthropic person, one who never seems to have done any harm to anybody, and is always doing good, but who does not believe on the Lord Jesus Christ, what you say to him is this, 'Is there this fear of God before your eyes? How do you stand before God?' You do not talk about their lives, you talk about their status, their standing, their position face to face with God in the judgment. And there they, like everybody else, are guilty, they cannot answer. 'All have sinned, and come short of the glory of God'; 'all the world' is guilty before God. And the first thing that the gospel of Christ does is to enable us to escape from the wrath to come.

As we understand, therefore, these mighty doctrines, which we have been considering together, let us come humbly before God and admit to Him that we do not know what to say in His holy presence. We confess that we have all been guilty of this much speaking. We have been like that Pharisee. We have tried to defend ourselves and to justify ourselves. Let us thank Him again that He has brought us to the end of that, and to see that we can do nothing, that we are guilty with all others before Him and in His sight, and that we have no answer that we can give in and of ourselves. Let us thank God, as we come before His holy presence, that we can say from our hearts,

> *On Christ the solid rock I stand,*
> *All other ground is sinking sand.*

We thank God for Him, who is our only plea and our only answer. We thank God for the blood of Christ whereby He reconciled us unto Himself while we were yet sinners, and ask Him from the depths of our heart to receive our humble praise.